Civil Society
in Syria and Iran

Civil Society

in Syria

and Iran

Activism in
Authoritarian Contexts

edited by
Paul Aarts and
Francesco Cavatorta

LYNNE
RIENNER
PUBLISHERS

BOULDER
LONDON

Published in the United States of America in 2013 by
Lynne Rienner Publishers, Inc.
1800 30th Street, Boulder, Colorado 80301
www.rienner.com

and in the United Kingdom by
Lynne Rienner Publishers, Inc.
3 Henrietta Street, Covent Garden, London WC2E 8LU

Library of Congress Cataloging-in-Publication Data
Civil society in Syria and Iran : activism in authoritarian contexts /
  edited by Paul Aarts and Francesco Cavatorta.
    p. cm.
  Includes bibliographical references and index.
  ISBN 978-1-58826-881-5 (alk. paper)
  ISBN 978-1-58826-857-0 (pbk. : alk. paper)
    1. Civil society—Syria. 2. Syria—Politics and government. 3. Syria—
Social conditions. 4. Civil society—Iran. 5. Iran—Politics and government. 6. Iran—
Social conditions. 7. Authoritarianism. 8. Regime change. 9. Comparative government.
I. Aarts, Paul, 1949–   II. Cavatorta, Francesco.
  JQ1826.A91C58 2012
  322.40955—dc23

          2012022251

British Cataloguing in Publication Data
A Cataloguing in Publication record for this book
is available from the British Library.

Printed and bound in the United States of America

∞   The paper used in this publication meets the requirements
   of the American National Standard for Permanence of
   Paper for Printed Library Materials Z39.48-1992.

5 4 3 2 1

Contents

Acknowledgments

This book is one of the outcomes of the research project "Civil Society in West Asia," supported by the Dutch nongovernmental organization Hivos (Humanist Institute for Development Cooperation) through its cooperation with the Department of Political Science at the University of Amsterdam in the Netherlands.

We owe a debt of gratitude to Juliette Verhoeven at the University of Amsterdam and Kawa Hassan at Hivos. We also would like to warmly acknowledge the invaluable help of all those activists and scholars who gave their time to the project and enabled us to have a better understanding of the dynamics of civil activism in Syria and Iran.

Preliminary findings from the research project have been presented at a number of professional conferences and meetings with activists across the Arab world, but this book is very important to us because it brings it all together. We are very grateful to all those who participated in the conferences and meetings and commented on our work to help us put the research into sharper focus. We benefited considerably from the input of Steven Heydemann at Georgetown University; Gerd Junnc, Marlies Glasius, Reinoud Leenders, Stephan de Vries, and Maaike Warnaar, all at the University of Amsterdam; Wael Sawah in Syria; Mohammad Mojahedi at Cambridge University; and Katerina Dalacoura at the London School of Economics.

The book is dedicated to all of those activists in both Syria and Iran who have struggled and continue to struggle in the name of freedom and dignity against unaccountable and repressive regimes. *Hasta la victoria, siempre!*

—*The Editors*

1

Civil Society in Syria and Iran

Paul Aarts and Francesco Cavatorta

The Middle East has been at the center of scholarly and policymaking attention for more than a decade, and the Iranian antiregime demonstrations during the summer of 2009 and later during the "Arab Spring" have further intensified interest in the politics of the region. While the Middle East had always featured prominently in international affairs, it is fair to say that the events of September 11, 2001, truly put the focus of the international community on the political, social, and economic dynamics of the region, and the recent wave of mass protests have heightened that focus. Much of the debate on the Middle East centers almost entirely on questions of democracy and democratization, with every issue—from the rise of Islamism to political violence and from women's rights to economic liberalization—crucially connected to democratic governance or absence thereof. The literature on democratization, with its assumption about the inevitable linear development of societies from authoritarianism to democracy, dominated analyses of the region during the 1980s and 1990s. When it became apparent that democracy was not making progress in the region, a significant number of studies were published questioning the mainstream approach of examining the region only through the lenses of democracy and democratization. The emergence of the "authoritarian resilience" paradigm seemed to be better suited to explain the mechanisms through which authoritarianism survived in the region, and this literature supplanted the one on democratization by providing a thorough critique of the main assumptions of transitology.

The popular uprisings of 2009 in Iran and 2011 across the Arab world have contributed to swing the pendulum back toward democratization studies, with enthusiasm for transition processes and regime change prominent once again. The interparadigm debate has been an important contribution to studies of Middle East politics because it has highlighted problems with both paradigms, while providing a number of theoretical assumptions that can potentially be shared by proponents of the two approaches. For one, despite the momentous Arab Spring, it is becoming increasingly accepted in both camps that the belief in a linear path toward democracy no longer permits, if it ever did, a clear analysis and understanding of regional, and even global, dynamics.[1] In many ways, the days of viewing political, social, and economic developments in the region as steps that would move countries either forward or backward on the imaginary linear path between authoritarianism and democracy are gone. This remains also the case in light of the Iranian protests and the Arab Spring for two reasons. First, as highlighted by Marina Ottaway, "presidents have left, but regimes remain in place,"[2] indicating that the changes taking place might be more cosmetic than real, with potential transitions facing significant obstacles. Second, even in the case of successful transitions to democracy, the scholarship on democratization would not be able to explain such processes, given that they seem to constitute a novelty in terms of the protagonists and the dynamics of change, as noted for instance by Hicham Ben Abdallah El Alaoui.[3]

As mentioned, a significant section of the academic literature on the Middle East is now sufficiently developed to offer a different perspective on regional dynamics. The authoritarian resilience paradigm has produced a number of assumptions that allow scholars to examine the broad spectrum of Arab and Iranian politics in a less normative manner, investigating the mechanisms of the reconfiguration of power that still allows authoritarianism to be successful in many countries of the Middle East and North Africa. This literature is certainly on the retreat in the face of events that were not foreseen and that do not seem to make sense in the context of what was assumed to be extremely solid authoritarian rule. Criticism of this approach is well deserved to a certain extent, but some of its theoretical assumptions still provide a useful guide for understanding how authoritarian politics works. In addition, examining authoritarian reconfigurations of power, even in a context where this might be collapsing, is interesting insofar as what follows through path dependency owes much to earlier political, social, and economic interactions.[4]

The issue of civil society activism, with which this edited volume is concerned, highlights some terms of the interparadigm debate. On the one hand, democratization studies postulate that a strong civil society is conducive to democracy and a necessary ingredient for political transformations. This literature places a lot of faith in the capacity of civil society to make democratic demands, but the unexpected revolts in Iran and across the Arab world surprised almost the whole spectrum of activists and associations that one would have associated with the struggle for democracy. The protagonists of the Arab Spring are not to be found in mainstream civil society. On the other hand, the literature on authoritarian resilience focused almost exclusively on the mechanisms of state domination and co-optation of civil society, ignoring informal and unofficial loci of dissent and activism, presenting therefore a picture of stability that did not exist.

Whether it stimulates democracy or reinforces authoritarianism, civil society activism is examined through studies dealing with traditional loci and actors of activism. This has led to neglect potential actors and milieus of dissent production that might marginally exist under the "official" surface. This book addresses specifically the issue of civil activism and builds on previous findings and assumptions linked to the interparadigm debate, to provide a much clearer understanding of civil activism in Iran and Syria. The objective is to examine how societies where authoritarianism has been "upgraded" respond and operate. From a theoretical point of view, the contributors in this project depart from a normative definition of civil society and concentrate on marginal realities of activism. From an empirical point of view, contributors highlight different aspects of civil society activism that characterize Syria and Iran, with specific attention to the dynamics that occur outside formal groups. It is precisely the nature of protests and the reaction to them by the regimes that make Syria and Iran crucial cases to examine, given the nature of such regimes and their status as international pariahs.

Leaving the Mainstream Behind

In an influential article dating back to 2002, Thomas Carothers convincingly argued that the transition paradigm had ended.[5] After two decades of academic and policymaking enthusiasm for the political developments taking place across the globe, theories of democratization seemed no longer useful to explain and predict them. Both the theoretical assumptions of transitology and the empirical evidence quite clearly demonstrated that the transition paradigm had lost its explanatory power largely because a significant number of countries that moved away from authoritarian rule "got stuck" on the way to democracy and developed political systems where elements of democracy and authoritarianism coexisted to create new political systems that deserved to be studied in their own right.[6] This had a profound impact on the study of the Middle East and North Africa, where, more than anywhere else, authoritarian rule still prevails despite the global reach of the third wave of democratization and the Arab Spring. While countries across the globe left authoritarian rule behind to embrace some form of democratic governance, the phenomenon to be explained in the Middle East was the survival of authoritarian rule. The focus on the reasons behind the persistence of authoritarian rule did not simply hold academic interest but had profound political implications because it meant that if one were able to find the explanation for authoritarian survival (the disease), it could then identify the solution as well and proceed to implement the cure. In any case, developments in Middle East countries were predictably analyzed according to the mainstream understanding that changes and reforms were either making these countries move toward democracy or back toward more traditional forms of authoritarianism. The idea of a linear path remained strong.

Carothers's article questioned the assumption of a linear path from a general point of view and did not necessarily address the Middle East specifically. Examples of failed transitions or of countries "stuck" in the middle between authoritarian rule and democracy, in fact, abound outside the region as well. In addition, authoritarian rule has survived the global democratic trend in countries as different as Cuba and North Korea or China and Zimbabwe. Thus, the marginalization of the transition paradigm meant that an intellectual shift could be made that would imply moving away from studying the reasons why democracy was absent in the region toward examining the features of authoritarian rule and politics.[7] In some ways Daniel Brumberg had already indicated in his study of Arab regimes that scholars were probably dealing with political systems that had indeed become "something else" in respect to the traditional forms of authoritarianism they previously displayed, although they had not turned democratic. Brumberg coined the term "liberalized autocracies" to define such political systems that, he argued, should be studied in their own right.[8]

The end of transitology and the necessity to study current forms of authoritarian rule in order to explore how they operate are increasingly accepted in the literature on the Middle East and elsewhere.[9] This remains the case even in the context of the Iranian antiregime protests of 2009 and the Arab Spring for three reasons. First, some countries, particularly in the Gulf, will likely remain authoritarian for the foreseeable future, and therefore authoritarianism will remain a regional feature.[10] Second, the direction of the political changes taking place in Egypt and Libya, for example, is not yet clear, although Tunisia might be moving more smoothly toward the establishment of a more or less democratic system.[11] Finally, even if some sort of democratic procedures and institutions were put in place, "transiting" countries might actually not finish their march toward democracy and might remain stuck in a semiauthoritarian limbo, as many others before them. What the interparadigm debate has shown is that both approaches have shortcomings, and this is true for the question of civil society activism as well.

Transitology and the democratization paradigm gave significant importance to the role of civil activism in regime change. Within democratic political theory and democratization studies, as Michaelle Browers highlights, "Civil society forms the bedrock of good democratic governance."[12] In transitology, the crucial assumption is that the presence of an active civil society is a positive development for stimulating democratization. Policymakers also share this belief. In terms of regional dynamics, Laith Kubba proclaimed that the "awakening of civil society" in the Arab world would be the decisive factor in challenging the authoritarian regimes in the region and eventually lead the Arabs to the "promised land" of democratization.[13] This optimism was largely based on the genuine awakening of activism across the region, with numerous civil society organizations dealing with all sorts of issues, including human rights and democracy, popping up across the Middle East to generate much needed social capital that would be turned into democratic potential.

The problem is that from both a theoretical and empirical point of view, civil society activism is much more problematic as a concept and as a reality than generally accepted, and the literature on authoritarian resilience has built its theoretical assumptions on this recognition of the role of civil society. However, a number of recent studies on civil activism in authoritarian countries run counter to the liberal assumptions that transitology espouses. According to this strand of research, rather than fostering democratization, civil activism seems, in fact, to strengthen, or at least not have any effect on, authoritarian rule.[14] It follows that, first, there is a growing consensus that civil society should no longer be defined through normative lenses.[15] Civil society has carried strong normative connotations that made it almost unquestionably linked to the liberal-democratic form of government. This meant that if civil society activism was growing in authoritarian contexts, the possibility of democratization would increase. Although this view of civil society is still prevalent in the policymaking community, in many academic circles it is now argued that a more neutral definition, stripped of its liberal normative content, can be a more useful tool to analyze what the reality of activism is on the ground in authoritarian systems rather than what liberal democrats would like it to be. Crucially, dropping the normative definition of civil society offers the possibility that within this enlarged field of activism, a number of nontraditional actors not usually thought to be part of civil society, such as individual blogger-activists or organizations more organically linked to the state, could be included.

Abandoning the normative definition of civil society poses two significant problems, however. First is the risk of depoliticizing activism and the "normative" drive toward the establishment of a more responsive system of government, which does an injustice to activists who struggled and still struggle in pursuit of democracy. Second, such a loose definition of the concept might end up encompassing all sorts of activities that are generated within society and that bear no relation whatsoever with political engagement. With respect to the first problem, the analytical choice of a more neutral definition does not equate with an abandonment of a democratic ideal but permits scholars to be more attentive to the reality on the ground rather than looking for an expected outcome. With respect to the second issue, a neutral definition of civil society is the space between the state and the family, where citizens on a voluntary basis engage with issues of societal relevance. However, this definition permits all sorts of issues and groups and individuals to be included without a priori determining their democratic or liberal credentials. This does not preclude that civil society might still play a role in democratization, but the intent of civil society actors to bring about democracy should not be the basis for inclusion or exclusion from the sphere of activism.

The second assumption we abandon is that activism is equated with formal organizations, which has been a shortcoming of both the democratization and the authoritarian resilience paradigms. Indeed, much of the literature on civil activism focuses on formal organizations and associations and more specifically on human rights and prodemocracy groups. Once the normative content of the definition is removed, it is possible to examine not only other types of associations that self-define as apolitical, but, crucially, to look at nonformal processes of activism such as the ones that take place online, which involve individuals who might be physically disconnected with one another but are activated as citizens. To a great extent, much of the liberal and secular prodemocracy and pro–human rights activism in the Middle East has not only failed to bring about democracy but in a number of instances has actually strengthened authoritarian regimes, particularly if one examines how many of these prodemocracy activists acted when called to support a democratic process that would favor political Islam. According to Steven Cook, self-defined democratic associations, parties, and personalities tend to side with authoritarian regimes when Islamist parties make electoral inroads or demonstrate their popularity.[16] Thus, focusing on groups that do not have human rights or democracy as central tenets of their activism and extending the study to processes that do not involve formal organizations contribute to a more realistic picture of what is occurring in society.

It is again worth mentioning how traditional civil society groups contributed little to the departure, for instance, of Zine El Abidine Ben Ali from Tunisia and Hosni Mubarak from Egypt (and even less in the case of Muammar Qaddafi from Libya one might add). In fact, traditional civil society actors have had their role confiscated by a loosely organized youth that has been able to unite the nation beyond class and religion in the struggle for change. As Benoit Challand recently wrote

> I choose the phrase "counter-power of civil society" to describe the ongoing developments . . . because I believe that there is more to civil society than its organized form. There is more to civil society than NGOs [nongovernmental organizations] and the developmental approach which imagines that the key to progress is when donors, the UN or rich countries, give aid to boost non-state actors, in particular NGOs, in the developing south.[17]

The same point is made by Béchir Ben Yahmed, who wrote in an editorial for *La Jeune Afrique* that "no party, no union, no politician gave the impetus for this popular uprising nor were they in any way involved."[18] This might be an exaggeration, and one should not forget the role of political associations in the uprising in Bahrain, of the trade union movement in the Tunisian revolt, and of Egyptian associations and workers' movements in ousting Mubarak, but their role was by no means a predominant one.[19] The majority of the activism that led to the uprisings occurred outside formal and traditional groups.

Finally, and more controversially, opposition parties and civil society organizations that dissent from current authoritarian practices do not seem able and do not have the necessary ideological and material resources to challenge the incumbent authoritarian regimes in the Middle East, which are perceived to be "here to stay." For example, the way in which the Iranian regime dealt with the "Green Movement" protest in the summer of 2009 (after the allegedly fraudulent presidential elections) is indicative of the power and resources still available to authoritarian regimes in the region. This leads many activists to accept the regime's framework, to which they adapt by attempting to maximize their results in the knowledge that an antisystemic approach will not work.[20] It is for this reason that both in Tunisia and Egypt most opposition parties and civil society groups were only tangentially involved in the demonstrations and sought to benefit from the events after they took place. As Sarah Ben Nefissa convincingly argued in her analysis of the Egyptian uprising, "political movements within the opposition lag behind the social protests" occurring in the country."[21] Through a combination of repression and co-optation, incumbent regimes have been able to guarantee their stability, suggesting that the appeal of liberal democracy, on the wane even in established democracies,[22] does not materialize into political change. In his analysis, Samir Aita argued that the social and economic inequalities created by the liberalization of the economy according to the neoliberal doctrine in the Arab world over the last two decades are the root causes of the uprisings and the desire for change, emphasizing that this factor has been and still is more important than political and democratic demands.[23] This means that mass protests due to worsening economic conditions were the force behind the uprisings, with political demands entering the scene later on. It was at that stage that more organized actors within the opposition attempted to take advantage of the breach made by unstructured mass movements.[24]

The almost unquestioned acceptance of authoritarian frameworks on the part of large sectors of organized civil society has profound repercussions on how society itself operates and interacts with the regime because the expectation of change from civil society is no longer as strong as it was in the past, although the aftershocks of the Arab Spring have the potential to change that. This is verified as well by the failure of the most powerful opposition, political Islam, to gain power in any country of the region despite decades of opposition. Whether employing the gun or the ballot box, Islamists have not been able to subvert any of the ruling regimes in the region,[25] although they have profited from the changes that others mainly provoked in Tunisia and Egypt.

The enthusiasm generated by events across the Arab world in the spring and summer of 2011 might yet change the picture, but the analytical validity of looking beyond traditional actors remains intact. The type of activism that nontraditional actors are developing creates new dynamics of interaction between society and the regimes, leading to a reconfiguration of the role and objectives of activism. These new actors have emerged as civil society actors, but their interests and work do not conform to a traditional understanding of activism linked to notions of liberalization and democratization. This does not mean that democracy is the inevitable conclusion, but it should also be acknowledged that while some of the "battles" these new activists undertake might be considered civil in a traditional liberal normative way, other civil struggles might not be liberal or democratic at all. The arrival on the scene of these actors, such as new forms of business associations or individual bloggers, is partly the product of wider political, social, and economic changes taking place in the region and partly the outcome of states' policies in their attempts to reshape and adapt authoritarianism to the modern globalized context. It is therefore in wider society, where less formal and looser ties are formed, that one would potentially find democratizing potential, highlighting an interesting paradox whereby those actors seeking democracy only found authoritarianism and the ones working within authoritarian constraints might be leading the way to democratic change. The Iranian protests and the Arab Spring demonstrate that societies are much more alive than previously believed in both academic and policymaking circles. This is all the more surprising in Iran and Syria where the power of the state to dominate society seemed strongest. While the outcome of the Arab Spring is still in the balance, it is still necessary to analyze the sources and actors behind the recent protests. Examining Iranian and Syrian activism in marginal loci might provide a partial but important answer.

Civil Activism in Syria and Iran

As mentioned, this book challenges traditional understandings and assumptions surrounding the nature and role of civil society activism and provides a more complex account of how civil society actors operate in Syria and Iran, where authoritarian rule has gone through a process of transformation over the last decade. Steven Heydemann analyzed in some detail the way in which Arab regimes upgraded authoritarian rule (for instance, by appropriating and containing civil societies, capturing the benefits of selective economic reforms, controlling new communications technologies, and diversifying international linkages), and this book aims to examine how society deals with and, at the same time, is partly responsible for such an upgrading.[26] In some ways, we intend to look beyond the state and analyze in detail how social groups and actors have reacted to such authoritarian upgrading and, at the same time, how part of the upgrading is the outcome of new social pressures and demands.[27] This leads us to move away from the traditional issues of human rights and democratization that characterized civil society activism in the past. The volume does not intend to argue that such issues are irrelevant, but it simply aims to explore novel forms of activism on issues that are not so overtly political, at least superficially.

The theoretical starting point of our analysis is the assumption that regimes in the region are quite different from each other and rely on diverse tools for ensuring survival. From this, it follows that such regimes generate different types of opposition, implement different policies in order to strengthen their rules, and utilize tools that vary from country to country to manage civil society activism. All this influences the ways in which civil society operates and has an impact on the type of dynamics that are created among civil society actors, particularly if a feedback loop is considered, whereby governmental policies have effects in society that then translate to social actors signaling to the regime to make further changes and meet new demands.

The innovative contribution of the volume does not rest only on the acceptance of assumptions that are controversial and permit an examination of activism through new theoretical lenses but also on the choice of countries studied. It provides, in fact, an examination of the development of civil activism in two Middle East societies that have not committed, even rhetorically, to Western-style political liberalization and that are outside the bounds of what the international community deems to be respectable states, responding instead to popular pressures for change with repressive measures. In addition, these two societies seem to display different degrees of politicized mobilization, with a more politicized society in Iran and a less mobilized one in Syria, even in light of the protests taking place in Syria, because organized dissent is a much stronger tradition in Iran. A number of reasons underpin the choice of examining these civil society dynamics in Iran and Syria.

First, Syrian and Iranian civil societies are underexplored compared with a large number of studies focusing on other countries in the region, and this book fills this empirical void. What becomes apparent almost immediately upon looking at social dynamics in the two countries is that despite the culture of fear, there is an unexpected level of civil engagement on the part of both organized groups and individuals.

Second, Syria and Iran are "confrontational" states (that is, they are often antagonistic toward Israel and the United States) leading the so-called resistance camp and they therefore deal with the added problem of operating in an unfavorable international environment when intensifying their authoritarianism; their respective societies can benefit or suffer from this. The contributions by Line Khatib in Chapter 2 and Ali Fathollah-Nejad in Chapter 3 provide a sophisticated analysis of how the international dimension and domestic factors interact to not only shape the power structures of the regimes and their legitimizing ideologies but also reveal how such a dynamic interaction partly explains how civil society actors respond and operate. Khatib's chapter on Syria examines how the economic liberalization undertaken by Bashar al-Assad has led to significant changes in state-society relations, throwing up different challenges for new civil actors in an environment that has remained, from a strictly institutional point of view, a closed and repressive one. Crucially, the chapter analyzes how the Syrian state has managed and has been influenced by the rise of these new social actors. Fathollah-Nejad's chapter on Iran focuses on the role of the international community in shaping activism. Iran traditionally had a rather lively civil society, and the revolutionary spirit has always called for greater mobilization on the part of citizens. Over the last decade, however, Iran has become the focus of international attention as the country became a much more prominent regional actor. The nuclear issue and the support of Islamist organizations such as Hamas and Hizbullah have heightened significantly the tensions with the West. These international dynamics have considerable domestic repercussions, and Fathollah-Nejad argues that they are crucial in structuring activism in Iran.

The neoliberal doctrine underpinning the globalization of the economy has left its mark on both countries, although to different degrees. Even though this has been tempered by the heavy intervention of the state, both the Syrian and Iranian economies have changed over the last decade, allowing for a reconfiguration of social groups and their relations with the regime. In the case of Syria, we have seen the emergence of a new class of global businessmen, with workers, once pillars of the regime, losing out in terms of political clout and forced to create new networks of social linkages to articulate their demands. In Chapter 4 by Bassam Haddad, the role of business associations, a new phenomenon in Syria, is examined in the context of economic liberalization. Business groups see themselves as civil actors and lobby groups and therefore operate accordingly. This is not particularly surprising, but the main argument in Haddad's analysis is that the political elites are developing an interest in such associations because they detect that the associations have the potential to be autonomous, which they want to prevent. Through a process of interaction, the growth of civil society activism and, in particular, the activism linked to new economic actors legitimize the creation of a new order and set of social relationships, which are as authoritarian as the past ones but take different forms.

In the case of Iran, the progressive marginalization of the *bazaaris* (entrepeneurs in the traditional marketplaces) in favor of economic actors closely linked to the Islamic Revolutionary Guard Corps (IRGC) and sections of the clergy has modified the social dynamics underpinning the regime. Market ideas have now strongly entered the public debate, as the country attempts to mobilize its considerable resources to become a stronger international player and a more efficient provider of goods and services for its citizens. In Chapter 5, Peyman Jafari addresses some of the issues that Haddad's study focuses on but adopts a broader definition of civil society. This becomes a forum for ideas within which market ideology enters the debate and negotiates with the regime the terms of new commercial arrangements. The case of the Chamber of Commerce is used to illustrate how fine the line is between activism and lobbying in the context of the dominance of the state in economic relations.

Economic globalization has brought with it both the technological revolution and by extension a much closer cultural contact with traditions from other societies, be they Western or from the Gulf. Together with the ever-present security issues in a hostile regional environment, both regimes in Syria and Iran have had to deal with the arrival of satellite TV and the Internet. The Web, in particular, has proven to be both a challenge and an opportunity for the Syrian and Iranian states, with attempts to both control it and increase its usage. Activists in the region have also taken to the Web with great enthusiasm, and the novelty of online activism deserves to be analyzed in some detail because it generates dynamics of interaction that affect state-society relations. Thus, that the governments attempt to control activism, while trying at the same time to stimulate it in order to better understand the demands society is making, is a conflicting strategy in a new terrain of cooperation and confrontation between the authorities and activated citizens: the Internet.[28] The analysis of activated citizens is crucial, as it is important to examine the response of the regime to the growth of citizens becoming more active and having the means to do so. Their activism surpasses traditional forms of organizations such as NGOs and, through the use of new technologies, can be a catalyst for and witness to social trends and struggles. There is a growing literature on the role of new media and social activism, and it is interesting to examine how these play out in Iran and Syria.

Roschanack Shaery-Eisenlohr and Francesco Cavatorta analyze in Chapter 6 the "cat and mouse game" that activists and authorities play when it comes to the Internet, but too strong an emphasis on this aspect would neglect what are probably more interesting findings. First, the Syrian civil experience with the Internet and social media demonstrates that the Internet remains an effective tool for expressing political, cultural, and social protest. A number of successful civil campaigns have occurred online—a testament to both the degree of activism present in society and the positive impact of new technologies. The importance of cyberspace certainly increased during the antiregime rebellion that began in 2011. Second, the virtual life and real life of Syrians have had for a long time one characteristic in common: isolation. Despite the ongoing rebellion, many Syrians continue to live under the law of silence. Off-line mobilization took place in the early stages of the antiregime protests, but the inherent weakness of this peaceful mobilization is illustrated by the very rapid descent into armed struggle. While the findings might be contradictory at a superficial level, a closer analysis reveals that weak ties and weak trust among protesters can engender considerable activism in relatively minor civil battles, while they prevent mass mobilization for more engaging and problematic issues. When such mass mobilization occurs, it is repressed and countered with mass mobilization in favor of the regime. In such a polarized environment, resorting to the gun rather than sustained peaceful activism became the strategy of both the regime and sectors of the population.

In Chapter 7, Ali Honari is also preoccupied with the nexus between online and off-line mobilization. He provides rich empirical material to illustrate the complex web of activism in Iran following the 2009 presidential elections and offers a new perspective on such events by arguing that off-line mobilization is crucial to trigger the online one. What Chapters 6 and 7 have in common is the unsurprising finding that regimes pay a lot of attention to what is happening online, at times interfering heavily. This is partly justified with the argument of protecting national security, and in confrontational states this might be both a compelling and plausible argument.

A final aspect of the implications for both society and political rule of the triple challenge of economic globalization, protection in the name of national security, and the necessity to modernize the state bureaucracy's operation is the appearance of new forms of practice of authoritarian rule. These include increased engagement with society in a spirit of "technocratization" of political issues[29] with the objective of depoliticizing them. Thus, authoritarian elites engage with society through technical issues and problems that can be solved by resorting to better management rather than challenging the politics behind decisionmaking. In this respect, the growth of government-organized nongovernmental organizations (GONGOs) is quite telling. It follows that the type of civil activism that regimes wish to deal with shifts partly from purely political demands to focus on activating citizens around more technocratic issues. This does not necessarily mean that technocratic issues, such as the provision of health care to the rural population or Internet petitions to protest the absence of recycling facilities, are apolitical, but they are not overtly political either. This raises the issue of how to account for authoritarian resilience and for authorities' tolerance and even encouragement of this type of activism. It follows that examining GONGOs is crucial, because they are becoming relevant social actors, replacing at times the traditional organizations that managed consensus in society, such as political parties or trade unions, and overshadowing traditional human-rights and prodemocracy associations. At the same time, such GONGOs can acquire a life of their own and offer opportunities for engagement to sectors of society that might not have had those opportunities before because GONGOs were set up precisely to deal with issues that had been ignored before and, therefore, involve social groups that had little voice in the past. By attracting the youth and technocrats outside the formality of state structures, GONGOs might not only defuse political opposition but also significantly change an individual's perception of state involvement in his or her life.

Chapters 8 and 9 by Salam Kawakibi and Paola Rivetti, respectively, deal with this phenomenon. Rivetti's argument is both compelling and controversial insofar as she argues that the rise of associations and groups loyal to the state, used to implement state policy delegated to them in a spirit of cooperation, is not a phenomenon unique to Mahmoud Ahmadinejad's presidency. While there is no doubt that the degree of authoritarianism under Ahmadinejad has intensified, Rivetti contends that the reformist regime of Mohammad Khatami also drew support from civil society organizations that effectively became GONGOs during his presidency. This, according to Rivetti, speaks to the problematic nature of examining civil society through normative lenses. Instead, civil activism in Iran should be understood in terms of power struggles within the regime that subsequently mobilized sectors of society to which it delegated the implementation of key state policies. The picture that Kawakibi paints in Syria is different. For one, the phenomenon of GONGOs is more recent and is aimed at weakening traditional channels of support for the regime such as the Baath Party. Second, GONGOs attract motivated and well-trained officials who take their roles seriously. This might have a profound impact on how they operate and the objectives they wish to achieve in the context of a national development strategy, although the uprising of 2011–2012 will invalidate the process for some time, even if the al-Assad regime survives.

In Chapter 10, Mustapha Kamel Al-Sayyid draws some general conclusions about civil society activism in the region. He returns to the definitional debate, arguing that, despite the potential validity of a neutral characterization of civil society, in practice this is quite difficult to achieve, given the loaded meaning the term carries and the expectations surrounding it. From a more practical point of view, Kamel Al-Sayyid convincingly states that the ability of authoritarian regimes to manage civil society is a short-term strategy, because without popular legitimacy spaces of activism inevitably will be opened and potentially challenge the ruling elites.

This renders the present analysis of new forms of activism necessary in order to understand what kind of different realities exist on the ground in the two authoritarian states that, aside from their standing in the international community, have much in common with the rest of the countries in the region.

Notes

1. Anderson, "Searching Where the Light Shines"; and Valbjørn and Bank, "Examining the 'Post' in Post-Democratization."
2. Ottaway, "The Presidents Left." Also see Friedman, "Egypt: The Distance Between Enthusiasm and Reality" and "Re-Examining the Arab Spring"; Tignor, "Can a New Generation Bring About Regime Change?"; Agha and Malley, "The Arab Counterrevolution"; Carothers, "Think Again: Arab Democracy"; Owen, "Military Presidents in Arab States"; and Paciello, "Egypt: Changes and Challenges." In his recent *The Origins of Political Order,* Francis Fukuyama extensively goes into path dependency phenomena, which look to be highly relevant to understand the Arab Spring's perspectives. "Ultimately, societies are not trapped by their historical past . . . and yet societies are not simply free to remake themselves in any given generation" (p. 478).
3. El Alaoui, "Tunisie, les éclaireurs."
4. Heydemann and Leenders, "Authoritarian Learning"; and Bellin, "Reconsidering the Robustness of Authoritarianism."
5. Carothers, "The End of the Transition Paradigm."
6. Doorenspleet, *Democratic Transitions.*
7. Anderson, "Where the Light Shines."
8. Brumberg, "The Trap of Liberalized Autocracy," p. 56.
9. Schlumberger, *Debating Arab Authoritarianism;* Schedler, "Authoritarianism's Last Line of Defense"; and Levitsky and Way, *Competitive Authoritarianism.*
10. Tétreault, "The Winter of the Arab Spring"; Lacroix, "Is Saudi Arabia Immune?"; and Gause, "Saudi Arabia in the New Middle East."
11. Anderson, "Demystifying the Arab Spring."
12. Browers, *Democracy and Civil Society,* p. 5.
13. Kubba, "The Awakening of Civil Society."

14. Wiktorowicz, "Civil Society as Social Control"; Jamal, *Barriers to Democracy;* Sater, *Civil Society and Political Change;* Liverani, *Civil Society in Algeria;* Cavatorta and Durac, *Civil Society and Democratisation;* and Gengler et al., "Civil Society and Democratization in the Arab Gulf."

15. Berman, "Islamism, Revolution and Civil Society"; Encarnacion, "Civil Society Reconsidered"; and Jamal, *Barriers to Democracy.*

16. Cook, "The Right Way."

17. Challand, "The Counter-power."

18. "Jours de Victoire"; also Chomiak and Entelis, "The Making of North Africa's Intifadas"; and Leenders, "Rethinking the Promotion of Democracy."

19. Also see Lust, "Why Now? Micro Transitions and the Arab Uprisings."

20. This is most clearly exemplified in the case of Saudi Arabia. See Gause, "Saudi Arabia in the New Middle East."

21. Ben Nefissa, "L'Egypte saisie par la fièvre."

22. Cavatorta, "The Convergence of Governance."

23. Aita, "Abattre le pouvoir"; also Samad and Mohamadieh, "The Revolutions of the Arab Region"; Zurayk, "Feeding the Arab Uprisings"; Dahi, "Understanding the Political Economy of the Arab Revolts"; and Springborg, "The Political Economy of the Arab Spring." For a contrary view, arguing against the false dichotomy between politics and economics, see Kinninmont, "Bread and Dignity."

24. Haugbølle and Cavatorta, "Will the Real Tunisian Opposition Please Stand Up?"

25. Brown and Hamzawy, *Between Religion and Politics;* an insightful perspective is given by Hamid, "Arab Islamist Parties: Losing on Purpose?"

26. Heydemann, "Upgrading Authoritarianism."

27. In the context of the HIVOS Knowledge Programme, the book edited by Steven Heydemann and Reinoud Leenders (*Middle East Authoritarianisms. Governance, Contestation, and Regime Resilience in Syria and Iran,* Stanford University Press, forthcoming) will deal more specifically with the issue of state-society relations.

28. On the use (and misuse) of the Internet, see Morozov's iconoclastic study, *The Net Delusion: How Not to Liberate the World.*

29. Seeberg, "Union for the Mediterranean."

2

Syria's Civil Society as a Tool for Regime Legitimacy

Line Khatib

A growing body of scholarship focuses on Arab countries going through the processes of economic and political liberalization, questioning the linkages that were once posited with great certainty as existing between an active civil society and democratization.[1] Such theoretical questioning is particularly salient when one considers Syria, which is a secular authoritarian state experiencing economic liberalization and some political liberalization that are only tangentially connected to the many demands made by prodemocracy forces within its civil society. Such a disconnect underlines the need to reexamine the latest economic and political developments in the country, with a view to both better understanding these phenomena in and of themselves and simultaneously how the country's authoritarian political context is affecting them.

I argue in this chapter that political and economic liberalization have empowered civil society groups that would otherwise have been less influential within the Syrian context. I examine how Syria's economic and political liberalization are the result of a complex regime-survival strategy undertaken by the country's political elites to maintain their ruling coalition in the face of a variety of domestic and regional challenges that developed over the course of 2011 into a low-intensity military conflict within the country. I will also show that this liberalization is, in fact, intended to contain, control, and shape civic activism and civil society more generally, rather than to nourish its free development, which has led to a backlash against the regime at a time of widespread upheaval across the region. This has, in turn, contributed to the empowerment of those groups that would otherwise have been less important.

The process began in the 1960s, when according to some observers the newly installed authoritarian Baath regime sought to eradicate Syrian civil society. But a more nuanced analysis shows that the Baath simply sought to influence and control the country's secular civil society groups, and that these efforts had a generalized dampening effect on them.[2] Based upon this analysis, it is possible to explain the apparent reemergence of these groups after Bashar al-Assad became president in July 2000, with many of them demanding political change and seeking to shape public policy. Yet, this explanation cannot account for the fact that a variety of secular civil society groups and individuals remained active under the Baath prior to 2000, for instance, by becoming members of the National Assembly and thereby influencing social policy. Other examples of actors who remained active include figures critical of the regime who chose to remain in Syria and struggle against authoritarianism, and whose work and writings are highly critical of the prevailing socioeconomic and political situation in the country.

Today, it is possible to discern two main groupings in Syrian civil society. The first is a descendant of the country's traditional secular, leftist, and socially liberal civil society, which was weakened but not eradicated by the regime. This grouping seeks political liberalization followed by a democratization of the political process, though not economic privatization, because it is felt that this would only satisfy a small class of corrupt political *arrivistes* and would prove detrimental to a majority of Syrians.

The second grouping—an interesting mix of businessmen and a number of prominent religious leaders who are in alliance with the political elites—is based on rents, particularistic privileges, and exemptions.[3] Those in this grouping have not expressed discontent with the Assad regime, and are pushing for a move away from *étatisme,* or state capitalism, toward private capitalism, and appear to have largely remained content with and loyal to the regime throughout the upheaval of 2011–2012.[4] In terms of their foreign policy outlooks, both groupings agree that the Western powers are amoral and mainly driven by their own geopolitical and economic interests. They thus dismiss any forms of Western political intervention in the region as unacceptable, although some cracks in this consensus have appeared in the face of the violent repression of 2011 and 2012.

Paradoxically, the religiously oriented and economically liberal grouping has grown considerably more influential than its leftist counterpart despite the fact that pre-Baath civil society was largely leftist and socially liberal in nature and that the Baath aggressively sought to weaken society's cohesiveness and livelihood in the 1960s, 1970s, and early 1980s.[5] Indeed, these Islamic groups and businessmen (there are only a few women in the coalition of traditional businesspeople and newly bourgeois elites) are today more influential and have proven better prepared than the other grouping to take advantage of the openings in Syria's economic and political environment.

This gives rise to several questions: Why and how has this loose coalition grown in both influence and membership in Syria? And, how has it emerged under a regime that restricts private business and constrains religious activism and whose own principles and social base have depended upon the support of Syria's minorities and lower classes at the expense of the traditionally Sunni business class? More broadly, how does the existence of this sort of civil society grouping affect the existing theoretical understandings of the relationships between authoritarianism, processes of liberalization, and "civility"? In answering these questions, this chapter will examine how the selective economic and political liberalization undertaken by the Syrian state in the last decade, with the aim of consolidating power, has prompted significant transformations in both the nature of the country's civil society and in state-society relations while also throwing up new challenges for civil society actors, all in an environment that has remained, from a strictly institutional point of view, a closed one despite increasing contestation. As we will see, the Bashar al-Assad regime has also empowered civil society actors that would otherwise have been less dominant within a freer Syrian civil society.

Authoritarian Upgrading: Economic and Political Liberalization to Avoid Democratization

A recent trend among Middle East scholars argues that economic and political liberalization in the region has tended to reinforce authoritarian models of rule rather than lead toward democratization. Such processes of liberalization have been referred to as "authoritarian upgrading,"[6] "calculated decompression" or "selective economic liberalization,"[7] "modernizing authoritarianism,"[8] and "reform strategies."[9] With regard to the Syrian case, in particular, these notions describe the reform strategies undertaken by the country's populist authoritarian regime to adapt Syrian authoritarianism to new circumstances and thus to survive as a political entity without having to resort to full-fledged democratization. As Thomas Pierret and Kjetil Selvik write:

> "Authoritarian upgrading" is taking place in the Arab context whereby regimes adjust to pressures for reform by manipulating features of political and economic liberalization, such as pluralist elections and privatizations. In doing so, they minimize political constraints stemming from increased social participation and maximize their relative autonomy from society's less supportive sectors. The outcome, Heydemann claims, is an authoritarianism that is "stronger, more flexible, and more resilient than ever."[10]

In the Syrian case, authoritarian upgrading has gone through two distinct phases. In the 1970s and early 1980s, the regime of Hafez al-Assad faced a militant Islamic rebellion. It responded to that challenge with a set of tactics that accommodated willing and politically quietist Islamic groups and their business allies.[11] These tactics also involved saturating the public with state-approved Islamic religiosity, so as to marginalize or even overwhelm the political and religious discourse advanced by the Muslim Brothers. At the same time, efforts were made to mute Baathist secularism,[12] to reappropriate religious institutions and messages, and to co-opt Syria's bourgeois class with selective economic liberalization. This signaled a clear departure from the Baath's previously socialist agenda. More generally speaking, the regime adopted an overall plan aimed at broadening its social base of support in the active sectors of society that had lost the most under the secularist and populist early Baath policies: the religious and the bourgeois classes.[13]

The scale of the regime's response is a reflection of just how strongly its legitimacy was challenged by the conflict with the Muslim Brothers. The resulting legitimizing formula was initially successful,[14] to the point that al-Assad soon appeared to be in total control of the domestic scene and was able to focus most of his attention on the regional context.[15] Indeed, under the regime of Hafez al-Assad, the state apparatus was sufficiently secure and in control as to be able to make foreign policy decisions independently of domestic concerns and events. Even when the Islamic uprising was taking place, the formidable corporatist structure that al-Assad was presiding over gave the political ruling elites enough maneuvering space and confidence to continue to make unpopular foreign policy choices, such as siding with the Maronite-led coalition in Lebanon and backing the Iranians in their war against Iraq during the 1980s.[16]

At the same time, however, the survival measures that were meant to strengthen the authoritarian system in the aftermath of the Brothers' failed armed rebellion unintentionally opened up a large space for contestation by businessmen in alliance with religious groups. As a result, this new alliance could recruit members and popularize its message openly, while the rest of Syrian civil society—in particular, its secular wing—continued to be repressed by the regime. As a result, by the early 1990s, Syria's religious movement was the only nongovernmental sector that was growing in terms of number of members, institutional size, and influence. Such growth was something of a paradox given that, until the 1960s, religious groups and the Syrian Islamic Front (Syria's Muslim Brotherhood) had struggled in vain to attract a larger membership and had won no more than a few seats in what were then free parliamentary elections. Another result of the regime's provision of space for Islamic groups to legally and safely propagate their message and expand their membership at the expense of secular groups was the creation of a new bourgeoisie at the heart of the state, which was able to thrive as a result of its political connections.[17] The net effect of these developments was that the religious class and the bourgeois class were given space and resources that made it possible for them to grow at the expense of the more traditionally dominant elements in Syrian civil society, though on the condition that they remain politically quietist.

The new Syrian political command of President Bashar al-Assad faced a difficult situation as a result of Hafez al-Assad's first phase of authoritarian upgrading, one that was made even more difficult due to the radicalized Islamic regional environment in the wake of the 2003 Iraq War. The state's response was to launch a second phase of regime upgrading in order to avoid losing its political hegemony. This second phase continued Hafez al-Assad's reform measures, in the sense that the regime has also appealed to the bourgeois and religious classes by implementing further economic and political liberalization, while at the same time repressing the secular, politically driven civil society in favor of the religious, politically quietist elements in civil society.

Selective Economic Liberalization

When he first came to power, President Bashar al-Assad had a strong need to maintain and consolidate his ruling coalition. He thus initially kept in place the economic and social policies begun by his father, though he was soon forced to go further in terms of economic liberalization and accommodation of Islamic groups. The factors that forced him to do so are intrinsic to populist authoritarian regimes: in particular, the challenges of trying to mobilize yet simultaneously control popular participation, of maintaining popular support, and of embodying the popular will while also dealing with the rise of new classes—namely the capitalists—that have a vested interest in shedding the *étatist* features of the regime.[18]

The economic liberalization policies pursued by Bashar al-Assad were marked by a move away from state capitalism toward a market economy, as Bassam Haddad details in Chapter 4. Concretely, this meant a series of fiscal, monetary, and trade reforms that were largely in line with International Monetary Fund (IMF) recommendations. Other aspects included greater privatization, with private banks and insurance companies able to open for business in 2004 and Islamic banks given the green light in 2006; meanwhile, national bank credits to the private sector rose from 7 percent in 2004 to 46 percent in 2005. State farms and state holdings were also privatized.[19] The number of so-called essential products being subsidized dropped precipitously to include only such staples as bread and sugar. Larger structural changes were made to the Syrian economy, including trade liberalization, tax policy reform, and interest rate liberalization aimed at stimulating new "sources of growth" in concert with fresh streams of domestic and foreign private investment.[20] The Syrian investment law was also amended so as to modernize the economic aspect of the country's legislative and financial systems. Import restrictions were relaxed, as were some customs duties and protectionist measures. Several new free trade agreements were signed, notably the Greater Arab Free Trade Agreement (GAFTA) in 2005[21] and an agreement with Turkey in 2007. The middle of the decade saw an end to the remaining boycotts of companies dealing with Israel, which made it possible for Coca-Cola and Pepsi to enter the Syrian market.[22] The launch of a financial market in 2009 led to the creation of the Syrian Stock Market Authority, which set and now monitors the stock market's regulatory framework.[23]

As noted earlier, this liberalization of the Syrian economy was aimed at stabilizing the country's populist authoritarian regime. However, it also had some unintended consequences, of which one of the most important was increased unemployment. The heavy cuts in the public sector were particularly difficult because it traditionally had absorbed the workers that the private sector could not employ. Concretely, Syrian unemployment rose from 6.9 percent of the active population in 1994 to 12.3 percent in 2004, according to official Syrian reports.[24] The impact of unemployment was made even more severe by the generalized effects of the economic challenges during the late 1990s/early 2000s and by rapid population growth.[25]

One result of these economic developments has been increasing social stratification and marginalization in Syrian society. Indeed, the Gini coefficient's rise from 0.33 to 0.37 shows that despite economic growth, inequality in Syria has, in fact, climbed by 11 percent between 1997 and 2004.[26] This is partly because the level of foreign trade has remained static and because about two-thirds of the country's exports in that period were oil related, which disproportionately benefit the upper classes.[27] It is important to note that the economic opening arising from liberalization disproportionately benefits certain cities, such as Damascus and Latakia, while poverty rates are far above the national average in rural areas, and it is probably not a surprise that the Syrian uprising of 2011 began in forgotten rural towns and small cities. For example, in the rural northeastern region of the country, the percentage of people living on less than one dollar a day is more than ten times higher than in the country's urban areas.[28] This has accelerated processes of urbanization that were already strong in the 1990s.[29] Even apparently positive economic data turn out to be less positive upon closer examination. For instance, the World Bank estimates that Syria's real GDP growth averaged 4 percent per annum between 2001 and 2010, around one percentage point above the rate of population growth. Yet Syrian studies and UN reports affirm that when population growth and inflation are taken into account, the real growth rate is actually much less than that calculated by the World Bank.[30]

Overall, Syria's economic liberalization within a context of economic challenges has led to the creation of a powerful economic elite whose growth has come at the expense of the Baath's traditional supporters, namely the lower socioeconomic classes. This underlines the manner in which the structural economic reforms undertaken as part of the authoritarian upgrading are fundamentally changing Syrian society. As the Baath's traditional supporters grow increasingly disenchanted with their situation in today's Syria, they are turning toward the only sector of civil society that has been allowed to exist and grow within the country: the Islamic sector. At the same time, this process is also being driven from the other end, with Islamic groups utilizing a variety of successful outreach methods and putting in place well-funded social programs, often with help from wealthy Syrians living abroad.

Perhaps of most concern to the state is that the large number of institutes, mosques, and *zawiyas* (prayer rooms) controlled by the Islamic sector are growing ever more independent of state control, as will be further examined later in the chapter. The overarching pattern then is that Syria's Islamic groups, which were once unable to attract the subordinate classes to their cause, are today clearly surpassing the country's leftist civil society groups in terms of power and influence—particularly among the economically alienated and politically excluded Syrian youth—and they are doing so in part thanks to the regime's survival measures.[31]

Selective Political Liberalization

In addition to economic liberalization, the authoritarian upgrading pursued by Bashar al-Assad's regime has also involved selective political liberalization. Like its economic counterpart, this political liberalization has contributed to the flourishing of a religious civil society at the expense of the secular and socially liberal one. The reasons for this are rooted in the Baath Party's elimination of its secular opposition. This policy of elimination was briefly reversed during the so-called Damascus Spring in 2000, which saw the reemergence of a relatively vibrant secular and liberal civil society. But the associations and groups were not strong enough to survive the regime's subsequent crackdown. By contrast, the Syrian state both could not and did not choose to repress the country's religious groups in the same manner. There are two main reasons for this. First, Syria's Islamic groups have been shrewd players in the game of realpolitik since the Hama uprising of 1982, refraining from openly criticizing the regime and more generally remaining politically quietist. They have again begun, since the rise of Bashar al-Assad to power, criticizing the regime but have almost exclusively confined their comments to its secular orientation rather than its authoritarian nature, although during the repressive climate of 2011 and 2012 some groups voiced stronger opposition to the regime itself. Second, the regime made efforts to accommodate Islamic leaders in order to broaden its ruling coalition, and in so doing empowered these groups to such an extent that it became impossible to marginalize them without risk of destabilizing the regime itself.

In the face of such strength, the regime opted to further accommodate the country's Islamic groups. Thus the Syrian president promulgated bills allowing exiled Islamist leaders to return to the country and released long-serving Islamist prisoners accused of militant activity, such as Fateh al-Bayanuni and Khalid al-Shami. In 2003, the state lifted a longstanding ban on prayer in military barracks. And at the Baath Party Conference of June 2005, the regime declared that it is important to give domestic Islamic groups a platform to express their views in order to avoid their radicalization, given that exclusion only leads to fundamentalism, and also explicitly claimed to champion a moderate Islamic revival.[32] In 2007, the national military academy invited religious authorities to lecture cadets for the first time. The notorious Mazza political prison, which had become a symbol of the regime's repression and was strongly feared by political dissidents, was also closed down.[33]

More generally, the first years of Bashar al-Assad's rule saw the number of detainees fall to between 300 and 1,000, a significant decrease from the 1993 total of 4,000 political prisoners.[34] In February 2004, the Syrian state organized the country's first "religious" conference in forty years, renewing the religious message while also ensuring the moderation of Syria's religious environment.[35] The regime also issued decrees that led to the expansion of Syria's official Islamic institutions and schools in both Damascus and Aleppo.[36] Other significant moves made by the government included allowing the public to enter mosques outside prayer times for the first time since the early 1980s, which has resulted in an increase in the number of religious classes being offered, and allowing Syrians to organize public festivals and to post religious banners in the streets in celebration of the Prophet Muhammad's birthday, something which had not been done in the country for decades.[37]

Despite stopping short of including a political Islamic party within the ruling National Progressive Front, the authoritarian regime did allow an increasing number of prominent Islamic figures to compete for seats in the Syrian National Assembly in the last ten years. Observers claim that this was done to head off US pressure to effect a regional rapprochement with Saudi Arabia and possibly also an international rapprochement with Israel and France, which would have been hard to resist because Syria was weakened by allegations of its involvement in the February 2005 Hariri assassination. A number of Syrian observers have even claimed that the regime has entertained the idea of extending political participation to a Syrian Islamic party.[38] The logic behind doing so is that incorporating moderate Islamists into the Syrian political system would make it easier to control them and would allow the regime to consolidate its power and ally itself with domestically powerful groups.

Regional and International Imperatives

The regional environment was another reason for the new Syrian ruling elite's decision to initiate its second phase of survival measures. Indeed, while the formidable corporatist structure that was deployed under Hafez al-Assad had allowed the Syrian command to successfully keep its foreign policy choices and alignments separate from the domestic scene,[39] Bashar al-Assad had fewer options. This was for two reasons. First, the first phase of authoritarian upgrading weakened the populist corporatist structure that both kept the Baathist regime in power and allowed Hafez al-Assad to separate his foreign policy from the domestic environment. Second, Bashar al-Assad faced a regional crisis at the outset of his rise to power and thus had to deal with the added problem of operating in an unfavorable regional and international environment.[40]

The regional crisis that challenged the new president was due to the US-led intervention in Iraq in 2003. That intervention caused chaos in Iraq, and provided an opportunity for militant Islamists there to implement some of their political vision. This in turn gave rise to fears that Syria could become an easy target for the jihadists and prompted the Bashar al-Assad administration to further work with and to appease both regional Islamists and domestic Islamic groups. It did so by seeking to portray itself as the bastion of Arabism and the champion of Arab resistance, which concretely meant allowing Arab fighters and Islamic jihadists to pass through Syria into Iraq, on the condition that they not undertake any activities within Syria.[41] This move also sent a clear message to the United States that Syria's regional influence remained strong and thus that its regional interests were not to be lightly dismissed.[42] But enabling Islamists and allowing "foreign fighters" to enter Iraq from Syria angered the US-led coalition forces, which threatened to impose sanctions against Syria. It also prompted increased international rhetorical pressure on the Syrian regime to modify its economic and political system, pressure that culminated in the United States enacting the Syria Accountability Act in November–December 2003. Additional economic sanctions were also imposed by the Bush administration in May 2004 following the assassination of Lebanese prime minister Rafiq Hariri, which was initially blamed on Syria. The US ambassador left the country in 2006, and diplomatic relations remained severed until January 2011, when the Obama administration finally appointed a new ambassador to Damascus.[43]

The US invasion of Iraq and US-imposed sanctions have, if anything, reinforced the Syrian regime's existential fears and made it even more determined to strengthen its relationship with the most active and powerful domestic civil society actors, namely the Syrian Islamic movement and its business allies. Thus we can see that the rise of Islamist militancy in the region, coupled with economic challenges and international pressure on the Syrian state, has led the Syrian ruling elites to further cultivate an Islamic profile in domestic affairs. The logic behind this accommodating effort is that it would help to guard against attempts by the powerful Syrian Islamic camp, namely the Syrian Muslim Brothers, to topple the Baathist command and would make it possible for the regime to use co-opted Islamic shaikhs to educate Syrians about the "wrong" and the "right" Islam— that is, respectively, radical and moderate Islam.

The attempt to cultivate an Islamic profile has meant that the speeches of the Syrian political command and of the Grand Mufti went from asserting national secularism to stressing that nationalist Syrians know the right Islam and should pledge to fight off foreign radical innovations, a direct allusion to the Salafi militant movement that originated in the Gulf region. It has also meant greater accommodation of co-opted *'ulama' al-din* (religious scholars) and of their associations, who have been given more organizational space and allowed a louder voice in order to help the state bolster moderate and pacifist interpretations of Islamic beliefs. At the same time, the state has sought to use its Islamic proxies to underline the theological difference between jihad and *qital* (fighting), with pious Syrians urged to join with the state in resisting US neoimperialist ambitions in the region. Taken together, all of these moves highlight the manner in which the Syrian state has chosen to respond to regional pressures by adjusting its domestic policies and changing which civil society actors it accommodates and encourages.

Impact of Liberalization: Emergence of an Odd Civil Society

The selective economic and sociopolitical liberalizations pursued in the last decade have exposed and created a number of new realities within Syria's civil society. This section will explore how Islamic civil activists have affected Syrian politics more than have their secular counterparts, and how the latter have lost their momentum with the ending of open contention within the political arena in 1982. This will have inevitable repercussions on what Syria's institutions will look like once the country emerges from the crisis engulfing it since 2011.

Generation of a Larger and More Powerful Islamic Civil Society from Below

In the previous sections, it was shown how the selective political and economic liberalization undertaken by the regime in order to maintain its hold on power shaped Syrian civil society. The changes are stark: before 1982 it was overwhelmingly secular and leftist, but today Syria's most important and influential parts are overwhelmingly religious. Yet it is important to underline that this is not due only to the state's authoritarian upgrading. In fact, Islamic groups have strategically taken advantage of authoritarian upgrading measures to efficiently recruit members and to organize their civil activism. Indeed, today's Islamic movements have effectively broadened their base of support to the lower socioeconomic classes, an achievement that continually eluded the Syrian Muslim Brothers in the past. They have been able to do so because the economic transformations and the reforms that go against the Baath's initially populist policies have forced the workers who were once pillars of the regime to join new social networks in order to meet their various needs. These networks are almost exclusively run by religious associations, since religious groups are the only nongovernmental civic alternative allowed to flourish over the last twenty-five or thirty years. This observation is not meant to imply that increasing socioeconomic differences and rising poverty levels are in and of themselves causal reasons for religious activism in secular contexts, but rather that they *can* be so in the absence of other viable alternatives.

Islamic groups have also been successful at using their available resources to seize opportunities arising from the inherent limitations of the populist authoritarian political model. This has included adopting a number of new and different outreach tactics, such as giving well-advertised lectures; offering lessons; handing out books, pamphlets, and CDs; expanding the number of Islamic bookstores; attending book fairs; maintaining sophisticated websites; and even marshaling social pressure through families and friends. Generally speaking, their discourse has abandoned its combative and adversarial antiregime stance but has focused upon engendering gradual change from within[44] and has sought to turn individual difficulties into social problems for which all society then becomes responsible. To give a brief example of the latter: the individual challenges of finding a life partner or of keeping one's marriage strong in the face of increasing divorce rates are portrayed as socially induced problems, related to modern expectations regarding what wives/husbands should provide for and should be. Moreover, the Islamic civil network has grown to become widely dispersed, as well as informal and personal in nature. It is clearly identified with local aspects of the neighborhood, is both normative—in the sense that it aims at creating uniformity in the community rather than accommodating individual preferences—and is often portrayed as an organic part of Syrian society—that is, Syrians are told that they are intrinsically religious and that Islam is part of Syrian culture, while such ideas as secularism are not. The psychological and financial support that these groups provide to their members has also proven to be reliable and continuous. Psychological support in this context does not merely refer to praying and encouraging followers to be committed to the words of God but is rather an elaborate program in which the preacher helps or teaches his/her disciples to deal with life difficulties and to overcome personal problems of all sorts. The support covers a wide range of issues: from dealing with illness, a bad marriage, or a difficult boss, to accepting one's overall destiny instead of resisting it in instances where change within the confines of Islamic strictures is deemed impossible. Financial support helps committed members marry, pay to hospitalize the sick, and send children to private schools (public schools are free in Syria), and provides much-needed subsidized housing units.

Overall, half of Syria's charitable organizations are Islamic, while 80 percent of the organizations in Damascus are Islamic.[45] This ubiquity makes it possible to run a tangible support system, one that revolves around the provision of basic but vital social services and charity, and that has gained a membership initially attracted to the instrumental benefits of joining but then becomes increasingly attached to the emotional ones. The facilitating condition of ideological framing is, in this case, rising structural inequality—in other words, increasing economic disparities. That being said, all this institution building would not have been possible without the elite support or extension that these groups have benefitted from.

Civil Activism and Democratization

The actors examined within this chapter are not concerned with some of the more traditional issues that drive such activism, such as liberal human rights and political democratization. Rather, these groups have focused on economic liberalization and the ethical transformation of Syria's citizens. This is perhaps unsurprising given that those businesses and Islamic groups that are co-opted by the regime have helped to ensure a proregime and politically quietist movement and thus one that does not push the traditional prodemocratic concerns that would represent challenges to the existing political order. In other words, the rise of this coalition of regime–co-opted religious groups and businessmen—as opposed to nonregime–co-opted ones, which have not been allowed to prosper as civil society actors—is neither a symptom nor a sign of improving prospects for democratization. More particularly, the coalition's concerns are not civil liberties, equality before the law, or the common good, but rather the realization of their own particular agenda (whether it be increased Islamic religiosity or individual economic advancement). At the same time, however, if anyone can pose a serious and existential challenge to the regime today, it is these groups, as a result of their influence and size but also the fact that they have transformed Syria's national cultural fabric to reflect their own conservative and acquiescent approach. The groups have done so by successfully operating within the space available to them to advance a comprehensive cultural system and to expand their effective control over Syrian society, orienting it away from demands for political rights and civil liberties and thereby ultimately infringing on the country's secular and socialist heritage.[46]

And so an important question, given the wide-ranging impacts of this new civil society, is whether or not it might ultimately lead to democracy.[47] In general, if we look at the different Islamic groups allowed to form Syria's civil society, such as the ones led by Syrian shaikhs Sa'id al-Buti, Muhammad Habash, Muhammad Ratib al-Nabulsi, or Ahmad Kuftaro, we can see that their discourse superficially suggests the moral necessity of pluralist rule, with the family sometimes portrayed as an institution that is, ideally, organized democratically. However, upon closer inspection, it turns out that each family member is still expected to fulfill a specific, hierarchically defined role. To give a specific example, the Abu al-Nur foundation, which is Syria's largest religious organization, does not stress the need for an absolute Islamic state; yet, as Leif Stenberg argues, "it does have strong ideas about the importance of Islam in shaping an ideal society and the commitment of each citizen to living an Islamic life."[48] The tension here concerns the degree to which a diverse society like the Syrian one can be pluralistic while simultaneously having an Islamic understanding of morality as the primary moral imperative.

Conclusion

This chapter has argued that while consolidating power in a manner typical of populist authoritarian regimes, the Syrian secular authority that once fought aggressively against overt religiosity within the public sphere has felt compelled to create a viable space for a new Syrian Islamic movement to form a coalition with businessmen. The coalition's members have subsequently entrenched themselves as the only organic civil society actors. The roots of this move by the Syrian regime lie in its once radically secular and authoritarian nature, which led to the emergence of a powerful Islamic opposition that nearly set off a civil war in the early 1980s. The regime's strategy for dealing with that opposition created a vacuum in Syria's civil society, which had to be filled through the creation of new, powerful civil society actors that were not part of the country's previous civil society nor of its earlier democratic parliaments. This observation underlines the fact that the existing civil society activism in Syria is not a sign of increasing democratization.[49] Rather, it has been empowered from above at the expense of another, unwanted civil society activism and is thus a mechanism for upgrading the Syrian regime's authoritarian nature. This development constitutes an effective illustration of the phenomenon described in the introductory chapter of this volume:

> The type of activism that nontraditional actors are developing creates new dynamics of interaction between society and the regimes, leading to a reconfiguration of the role and objectives of activism. These new actors have emerged as civil society actors, but interests and work do not conform to a traditional understanding of activism linked to notions of liberalization and democratization. (p. 9)

One might argue that a dynamic and engaged civil society, no matter its nature, will eventually lead to political change. This certainly is the case in present-day Syria, where the civil society that was once under the total control of the state has gradually become more independent and is now causing the state to further compromise with it.[50] Having said this, whether the Syrian religious and business associations, in alliance as they are with the state, will lead the way to a pluralist political environment is a question that has yet to be satisfactorily answered. At the same time, it is important to recognize the fluidity of events in the country. For instance, the Syrian state has begun slowing down or even retreating in the last four years from a number of its accommodationist policies directed toward the co-opted religious groups. It did so in an attempt to reassert its own monopoly on power, thus sending a clear message to rising voices within such civil society that their social influence is ultimately a matter of regime choice or is at least contingent on the regime's support. It remains unclear whether such moves will lead the country's up-to-now politically quiescent civil society to join the prodemocracy movement. Now that the regime is literally fighting for its life, it is unclear if the business-religious grouping will abandon its patron regime and join the prodemocracy movement. We will have to wait on events that are presently playing out on the streets of Syria's towns and villages to know if this will happen.

Notes

1. Przeworski, "Some Problems"; Wiktorowicz, "Civil Society as Social Control"; Clark, *Islam, Charity and Activism;* Jamal, *Barriers to Democracy;* Sater, *Civil Society and Political Change;* Liverani, *Civil Society in Algeria;* and Cavatorta and Durac, *Civil Society and Democratisation.*

2. The Baath's actions toward Syrian *religious* civil society groups were considerably more aggressive, and it could well be argued that the aim was to eradicate them.

3. It is important to note here that opposition religious leaders—that is, those who actually expressed their opposition to the regime, such as the Syrian Muslim Brothers—have not been allowed to join Syrian civil society. Until the uprising of March 2011, their opposition activism took place outside the country.

4. Haddad, "The Syrian Regime's Business Backbone."

5. Batatu, *Syria's Peasantry;* Hinnebusch, "The Islamic Movement in Syria"; and Hinnebusch, *Syria: Revolution from Above.*

6. Heydemann, *Authoritarianism in Syria;* and Heydemann, "Upgrading Authoritarianism."

7. Hinnebusch, "The Political Economy of Economic Liberalization"; and Hinnebusch, "Syria: The Politics of Economic Liberalization."

8. Perthes, *Syria Under Bashar al-Assad.*

9. Brumberg, "Authoritarian Legacies."

10. Pierret and Selvik, "Limits of 'Authoritarian Upgrading' in Syria."

11. In Syria, there is a traditional rapport between business and Islamic religious leaders. For the Syrian religious class's links with the Syrian bourgeoisie, see Batatu, "The Syrian Muslim Brethren," and Hinnebusch, "The Islamic Movement in Syria."

12. Baathist secularism aims to restrict religiosity to the private sphere. In this sense, it is closer to the French *laïcité* than to the US or Anglo-Saxon models of secularism.

13. Khatib, *Islamic Revivalism in Syria.*

14. Ibid.

15. Salloukh, *Organising Politics in the Arab World.*

16. Ibid.

17. Hinnebusch, *Syria: Revolution from Above;* and Khatib, *Islamic Revivalism in Syria.*

18. Hinnebusch, *Syria: Revolution from Above.*

19. Ababsa, "Contre-réforme agraire et conflits fonciers cn Jazîɩa syrienne," p. 211.

20 International Monetary Fund, "Staff Report for the 2006 Article IV Consultation," August 2006, p. 38, www.imf.org/external/pubs/ft/scr/2006/cr06294.pdf.

21. The other GAFTA member states are: Jordan, United Arab Emirates, Bahrain, Saudi Arabia, Oman, Qatar, Morocco, Lebanon, Iraq, Egypt, Palestine, Kuwait, Tunisia, Libya, Sudan, and Yemen.

22. Vigual, "La 'nouvelle consommation' et les transformations des paysages urbains."

23. See "Syria Stock Market Starts Trade," news.bbc.co.uk/2/hi/business/ 7934644.stm (10 March 2009). For general information about the Syrian stock market, see www.syria-bourse.com. For a view of the economic challenges facing Syria, as well as of economic needs from a Syrian perspective, see Sikkar, "Hatmiyat al-Islah al-Iqtisadi fi Suriya."

24. Satoof, *al-batala fi suriya 1994–2004*, p. 32.

25. Laithy, "Poverty in Syria: 1996–2004," p. 26.

26. Ibid., pp. 9, 12. See also Zisser, *Commanding Syria*; the Syrian Central Bureau of Statistics, *al-Maseh al-'Unqudi Muta'aded al-Mu'ashirat 2006*, www.cbssyr.org/people%20statistics/Final_Report_Syria_ARB.pdf; and the United Nations Development Programme (UNDP), Syria Report, *The Impact of Subsidization of Agricultural Production on Development,* October 2006, p. 6, www.undp.org.sy/files/psia.pdf.

27. Laithy, "Poverty in Syria: 1996–2004," p. 9.

28. Ibid., pp. 16–17. See also UNDP Syria Report.

29. Leverett, *Inheriting Syria,* p. 36.

30. World Bank, http://data.worldbank.org/country/syrian-arab-republic; Zisser, *Commanding Syria,* pp. 113–114.

31. Khatib, *Islamic Revivalism in Syria.*

32. Zisser, "Syria, the Ba'th Regime and the Islamic Movement," pp. 61–62.

33. Ibid.

34. Landis, "The Syrian Opposition," p. 47.

35. Khatib, *Islamic Revivalism in Syria,* p. 117.

36. Ibid.

37. Moubayed, "The Islamic Revival in Syria," www.mideastmonitor .org/issues/0609/0609_4.htm.

38. Personal interviews. Discussions during the Tenth Ba'th Conference, June 2005. See also Moubayed, "The Islamic Revival in Syria."

39. Salloukh, *Organising Politics in the Arab World.*

40. Leverett, *Inheriting Syria;* Zisser, "Syria, the Ba'th Regime and the Islamic Movement."

41. Ben-David, "Jordanian Indictment"; and Gambill, "Syria Rearms Iraq."

42. This was not the first time that Syria made a tacit pact with Islamists. Indeed, Syria's position as a frontline state in the confrontation with Israel, one that still has a large part of its territory occupied by the Jewish state (the Golan Heights), has caused it to ally with regional Islamists such as Hamas and Hizbullah and to support their resistance activities against Israel.

43. The US ambassador subsequently left Syria when the Americans closed their embassy in February 2012.

44. Khatib, *Islamic Revivalism in Syria.*

45. Pierret and Selvik, "Limits of 'Authoritarian Upgrading' in Syria."

46. Hatina, "Restoring a Lost Identity," p. 194.

47. This is a different debate and one that really depends on the Islamic

group being examined and the way it would actualize its allegedly sacred principles once in power.

48. Stenberg, "Young, Male and Sufi Muslims in the City of Damascus," p. 84.

49. Brynen, Korany, and Noble, "Introduction: Theoretical Perspectives."

50. See Khatib, *Islamic Revivalism in Syria,* chapter 7.

3

Iran's Civil Society Grappling with a Triangular Dynamic

Ali Fathollah-Nejad

The headlong stream is termed violent
But the river bed hemming it in is
Termed violent by no one.
　　　　　　　—Bertolt Brecht[1]

The scholarly literature on the role of civil society in authoritarian states often focuses on the relationship between the state and civil society, examining the ways in which the former maintains power over the latter. However, in order to adequately assess the evolution of civil society, especially in countries of geostrategic importance and in conflict with great power interests, it is essential to explore the triangular relationship among global geopolitics, the state, and civil society. Thus, I contend in this chapter that a proper understanding of state-society dynamics must take into account external pressures exerted on the country and hence on the entire body politic.

The debate on "new authoritarianism" or "upgrading authoritarianism" revolves around the claim that today's authoritarian governments, rather than relying on the classic repertoire of totalitarian control, are using new and more sophisticated methods of control over and of co-optation of dissent.[2] Here, the use of new communication technologies and the political co-optation of the opposition often take center stage. However, such strategies might be successful also because external dynamics are exploited by the authoritarian

39

regimes doing the upgrading. Generally, however, the literature on political liberalization and democratization neglects, with some exceptions,[3] external influences, with the emphasis usually on domestic political culture, the dynamics and nature of civil society, and domestic political economy. Whereas most literature focuses on the regional or global diffusion of democratic models and discourses, the study of the infusion of external forces—for example, in the forms of economic globalization and foreign policies—has been widely neglected. In particular, little attention has been given to external pressures that might fuel authoritarian tendencies in the name of national security, especially in countries and/or governments beleaguered by the "West" (or, for that matter, any other great power with global ambitions), or, in other words, to "the complex interaction between external and internal variables in shaping the prospects for democracy."[4]

In the Iranian case, many studies display a blatant disregard of geopolitics as a factor in facilitating or constraining authoritarian rule, and in shrinking or widening the space available for civil society activism. Therefore, I suggest here that only an exploration of the triangular dynamics between the global level (in the case of Iran, the key actor is the United States, in particular, and the West, in general), the state, and civil society can provide useful insights to the space left for civil activism in the contested field of democratization and authoritarianism. Hence, I shall examine the impact of "external infusion" upon state-society relations, and its effect on authoritarianism and democratization.

First, I will identify the reasons behind the omission of external factors when discussing authoritarianism in strategically important countries not allied to the United States. Second, I will introduce the concept of space as a key dimension for civil society activism, impinging on its scope, limits, and form. Taking into account the geopolitical environment, I will assess the space for civil society in Iranian state-society relations. Third, I discuss the role of external infusion since 2002, in the context of US confrontational policies and the transatlantic "coercive diplomacy"[5] toward Iran. I will assess the consequences for the interaction between the state and civil society in Iran as well as for resulting forms of civic activism. Finally, I will examine the relationship between economic sanctions—the other salient pillar of the transatlantic coercive diplomacy—and the issue of authoritarianism and democratization.

The Authoritarianism Debate
and the Shadow of US Interests

Through a critical examination of the uses and misuses of the label of authoritarianism, its politico-strategic raison d'être is brought to the fore. Not unimportantly, a great number of studies conducted on authoritarian rule in Iran have been produced by agencies close to the US government and its European allies. They almost exclusively focus on authoritarianism in countries that are in geopolitical conflict with the United States (e.g., Iran, Syria, Venezuela, Russia, and China) or find themselves at critical junctures in this regard (e.g., Pakistan), while concealing the conditions in authoritarian countries friendly to US interests (e.g., the countries of the Gulf Cooperation Council). In that vein, a study on twenty-first-century authoritarianism by Freedom House, Radio Free Europe/Radio Liberty, and Radio Free Asia unequivocally explains the choice of its focus on Russia, China, Iran, Venezuela, and Pakistan as reflecting the countries' "fundamental geopolitical importance . . . integrated into larger economic, political, and security networks and exert[ing] a powerful influence on international policy at the regional and global levels."[6] Iran is defined as "a unique authoritarian polity ruled by Shiite Muslim clerics, loom[ing] over the Middle East."[7] While the study attributes to those countries "an important role in contributing to the global setbacks for democracy,"[8] the potentially negative effects of the policies pursued by the "established democracies"—as they are complacently called in the study—escape due consideration.

Often the authoritarianism debate on Iran is framed in a US-centered imperial narrative that discusses the "Iranian challenge" in regard to US interests,[9] thus reducing Iran's internal and external politics to its usefulness for US interests often disguised as that of the entire international community. The United States is therefore presented as an intrinsically benevolent actor when it comes to furthering the case of democracy in Iran. For instance, based on a peculiar reading of history, Abbas Milani argues that "promotion of democracy has been part of US policy in Iran for [the] better part of half a century," portraying the United States as the only outside force truly interested in Iranian democracy. It was only eclipsed in such a benign endeavor by the "exigencies of the Cold War,"[10] in which context, for Iran, "[a]uthoritarianism was deemed a reasonable, if not indeed necessary price to pay for the containment of communism."[11] Such a narrative totally ignores the fundamental question of how a democratic and independent Iran would satisfy US imperial ambition, or, inversely, undermine those very "vital interests," as has been powerfully illustrated in the context of the US/UK-designed 1953 coup d'état of Iran's democratically elected government of Mohammad Mossadegh. Concerning the situation today, it is along such an imperial framing that Milani suggests that an "'International Brotherhood of Authoritarianism' is emerging, with Iran as a junior partner to Russia and China"[12]—again simply reducing the complexities of political systems around the globe to their function of usefulness to US interests.

In contrast to the euphemistic description by the United States of friendly Arab dictatorships as "moderate," derogatory notions are deployed to describe the political systems of challengers to US domination: besides authoritarianism, the terms "dictatorship," "tyranny," and "despotism" often appear in government literature, the press, public discourse, and even academia. Such denominations have foremost a political purpose in US strategic thinking, as the 2006 US National Security Strategy illustrates when it discusses authoritarian politics in states that challenge US interests.[13] Therein, the alleged concern for the nature of domestic governance in those "tyrannical" countries is directly connected to their external anti-US behavior. Such a line of argument, primarily suggesting the external politics of a country as a mere corollary of its internal constitution, obscures the fact that geopolitical divergences might be driving countries to act in ways not in line with US interests.

Furthermore, in such literature, the claim that a democratic Iran is seen as the best hope for the United States to tackle the "Iranian challenge"[14] comes with the idea that Iran's perpetual quest for democracy, with its population described as the Middle East's most "pro-American" one, would inevitably bring the country back into the fold of the "international community," and concomitantly a strategic realignment with the West would materialize.[15] Such an assertion is flawed in many ways, not least because it portrays Iran's civil society as being pro-American as well as secular in the Western sense. However, Iran's diverse civil society cannot necessarily be captured within the frame of such "Western ideals." For instance, a groundbreaking Harvard University study on political and cultural dimensions of the Iranian blogosphere has shown that, aside from the secular-reformist camp (allegedly pro-Western), another major camp is conservative-religious (allegedly anti-Western) yet at the same time critical of the government.[16] In fact, a Western-centered perspective that largely constructs a division in the domestic sociopolitical scene along the schism of secular/pro-Western and religious/anti-Western forces is a profoundly inadequate representation of the politics of Iran.

Besides the benevolent, prodemocracy role ascribed to the United States, Milani's discussion of outside influences on a country's governance is reduced to a flawed argument about the power of conspiracy theories as an inherent dimension of the modern Iranian politics of paranoia. The externally stimulated 1953 coup was not a conspiracy, but a hisorical reality. And, whereas "conspiracy theories" in Iran might constitute a powerful "enemy of democracy," it should be emphasized that there is a powerful history of external meddling that justifies a degree of suspicion.[17] Certainly, both the many revolutionary moments in modern Iranian history and more recently the mobilization around the June 2009 presidential election can hardly stand as proof for Iranian citizens' passivity.

The previous perusal sheds light on the potential reasons behind the lack of a proper consideration of the geopolitical dimension in the analysis of authoritarianism in geostrategically important countries. In this, the framing of a benign (US) empire is pitted against a tyrannical state.

Space and Civil Society

This section will highlight the importance of space as an analytical tool for assessing the scope, limits, and contents of civil society activism. The concept of space is pivotal for examining the strength and influence of civil society. Therefore, analyzing the context and the reasons why space is shrinking or expanding, how this is done, and by whom should be at the heart of any discussion of civil society. In a number of studies, however, the discussion of civil society's space is framed solely as a function of state behavior or measured as a result of the interaction between civil society and the state. Hence, it ignores influences from outside the country, which also affect the space within which state-society relations take shape.

The Gramscian concept of space is theoretically useful for analyzing the triangular dynamics between geopolitics, the state, and civil society. In the Gramscian sense, space is regarded as an area in which civil society actors can create and organize counter-hegemonic projects and challenge state authority. There is a threefold dimension to this term: social, physical, and mental space.[18] If all these dimensions of space are being constrained, the very existence of civil society will be jeopardized. Social space, in this context, can be regarded as the setting for the entirety of relationships and networks of both individuals and collectives. Obviously, this setting can be subject to control and repression by the holder(s) of coercive power (i.e., mostly but not exclusively the state) by preventing certain groups or individuals to gather and thus narrowing the opportunities for public conventions. "In more concrete terms," Shmuel N. Eisenstadt writes, "the elites of these societies attempted to limit the contacts among the different units of the periphery and between them and the center to mostly adaptive or external relations."[19] Such preemptive measures are intended to thwart the creative outcome of the "great diversity of knowledge"[20] that is implied in social space. By only permitting selected parts of society to convene and seek collective action, state authority may succeed in shaping the creative outcome in its favor.

The control of physical space is indispensable for an authoritarian state apparatus, and Asef Bayat addresses the relevance of physical or public space for resistance in suppressed societies.[21] He argues that public space, such as streets, can potentially turn passive networks into active ones, with the previously anonymous actors taking notice of each other and their common aims. Iran's modern history provides numerous incidents of mass street protests, from the late-nineteenth-century Tobacco Revolt through the revolutionary upheaval in the late 1970s to the "Green" marches of 2009. Interestingly, in the run-up to the 2009 presidential elections, by allowing citizens to march in the streets and by offering for the first time in Iranian history live TV debates among the candidates, the Iranian state engaged in an effort to upgrade the legitimacy of the system by opening up the public space. This is when the reform-seeking part of the electorate took note of each other during the numerous and large gatherings. The street—as a physical or public space—appeared to be in its hands. As Augustus R. Norton points out, once authority loosens its grip on space for civic activism, it is likely that active parts of civil society step in to seek the shaping of politics.[22] Such a correlation—a zero-sum game—will hold true for all three dimensions of space.

In controlling the mental space, it is ensured that norms, values, and thinking patterns reproducing hegemonic structures are profoundly internalized, so that counter-hegemonic thought is prevented from spreading.[23] External geopolitical pressure upon the entire country, the state, and/or society is likely to shape the mental space for civil society activism. The following discussion will concentrate on mental space as a dimension in which development inherently depends on the triangular dynamics between global geopolitics, the state, and civil society. The condition of the mental space is likely to shape the two other dimensions of space, as it can define the normative framework of civil society activism.

Toward the Advent of Civil Society During External Détente: The Opening of Political Space

The eight-year war with Iraq (1980–1988) proved to be a heavy blow to the democratic aspirations of Iranians. During the war, political repression intensified and was often legitimized by invoking "national security" in the "Holy Defense" (Defâ-e Moghaddas) against the aggression by Iraq, which was heavily backed by the United States and its allies. "[T]he consequence of the Iran-Iraq war for Iran," Elaheh Rostami-Povey writes, "was the creation of a state of emergency, leading to a far more centralised and authoritarian state, which imposed further Islamisation and repression of women, the secular left and nationalists."[24]

The end of the 1980s saw two major events within a matter of months. In August 1988 the war with Iraq ended, and in June 1989 Ayatollah Ruhollah Khomeini died. The state's priority under the presidency of Ali-Akbar Hashemi Rafsanjani turned to the economic reconstruction of the country after the devastations of the war. Along with it came a pragmatically motivated period of political liberalization, both internal and external. The international relations of Iran were marked by détente, including neutrality in the 1991 Gulf War, pragmatism in its dealings with conflicts erupting in post-Soviet Central Asia and the Caucasus, and rapprochement with European countries and Arab neighbors.

Détente in external relations was a crucial prerequisite for a relaxation of the domestic political scene. In other words, the postwar extinction of an imminent external threat paved the way for a more liberal political climate. On the domestic scene, according to Majid Muhammadi, one of the most influential voices in Iran's civil society discourse, the previously mentioned twin events "resulted in the diffusion of social and political power into multiple centres, on the one hand, and the formation of new political sentiments and increasing

awareness among the various social forces on the other hand. . . .
Power is no longer the monopoly of any one group," he maintained,
"and what results from power is now a product of many efforts, trials,
bargains, and pacts."[25] It was in that context that the Iranian discourse
on civil society emerged.[26] At the same time, the 1990s saw the rise of
Iran's civil society and its constituent social movements, above all the
women's, students', and labor movements.[27]

In May 1997, civil society's power in relation to the state became
apparent:

> Despite the new political environment that emerged starting in the
> late 1980s, it was not until a second highlight, the presidential elec-
> tions of 1997, that discussions of civil society moved out of small,
> often timid intellectual circles and assumed national political cen-
> tre stage [when] Hojjatoleslam Muhammad Khatami . . . made the
> notion of civil society (*jame' h madani*) the centrepiece of his pres-
> idential campaign.[28]

With huge support from various civil society groups, Khatami,
who was from the Islamic Republic's reformist faction, scored an unexpected landslide victory in the presidential elections. His victory,
however, was based on support from a wide range of groups and
went beyond the traditional scope of civil society. Not only the youth
and women stood behind the reformist cleric, but even a majority in
the clerical capital of Qom, many if not most of the people inside the
Islamic Revolutionary Guard Corps (IRGC), and the traditional Islamic left, as well as business leaders hoping for an opening of the
economy, favored Khatami over the Supreme Leader's and the hardliners' favorite candidate, Ali-Akbar Nateq-Nouri.

The evolution of social movements throughout the 1990s signaled a widening of social space. In the international relations of
Iran, détente had an empowering effect on civil society. The Iranian
struggle against authoritarian rule and the concomitant quest for
democratic government began at the end of the nineteenth century.[29]
Back then, Iran was already finding itself in the midst of global
geopolitical competition, originally because of its central strategic location, but soon after boosted by the world's first-ever discovery of
oil there. Hence, Iran's struggle has persistently been a dual one: (1)
against domestic authoritarian rule and for democracy, and (2)
against imperial domination and for national independence.[30]

A hundred years on, by the end of the twentieth century, diametrically opposing trends could be observed. While the reform movement

celebrated its most important successes in the history of the Islamic Republic, Iran's nemesis, the United States, saw the political rise of neoconservatives. In particular, two events that took place in 1997 cast a cloud over years to come. The spring of 1997 not only saw the landmark election of Iran's first reformist president but also the creation of the neoconservative Project for a New American Century (PNAC) in the United States. In its Statement of Principles,[31] released on 3 June, PNAC made the case for a US offensive centered on the Middle East and based on military might. On the Iranian side, President Khatami in January 1998 called for a "dialogue of civilizations" with the United States. Despite his administration's call for improved ties with the United States, PNAC and its neoconservative allies continued to argue for a continuation and even deepening of the existing containment policy toward Iran, which finally influenced President Bill Clinton's Iran policy.[32]

External Pressure and State-Society Relations

Another Kind of Authoritarian Upgrading

This section will deal with the ramifications of the external pressure exerted on Iran by the United States, focusing on the last decade. The terrorist attacks of 11 September 2011 were immediately followed by the promulgation of the global war on terror. The rapid "regime change" in Afghanistan, for which the Islamic Republic was a key enabler, would soon be followed by the January 2002 State of the Union address by US president George W. Bush, in which he designated Iran as part of an "axis of evil." The message sent by the US neoconservatives that Iran had been chosen as a potential regime change target had a profound effect on both the Iranian state and civil society. From one day to another, the issue of Iran's "national security" made an extraordinary resurgence and remained center stage with the threat of a military attack by the United States and/or Israel looming.

In a first step, the "axis of evil" speech broke the back of the reformist government's foreign policy approach built on rapprochement with Western countries, heralding the reformists' loss of credibility in the crucial field of national security policy. Also, the foreign threats prompted interelite consensus to focus on safeguarding the system of the Islamic Republic. In the face of the danger posed to the security of the nation and that of the system, democratic aspirations took a back seat.[33]

As journalist Seymour Hersh reported, war preparations by the United States against Iran had already begun in 2003.[34] The de facto external threat to national security, amplified by the state's instrumentalization of the latter to disqualify dissent as consciously or unconsciously playing into the hands of Iran's enemies, limited the mental, physical, and social spaces left for civil society activism. Another important aspect that contributed to further limiting the space for civil society was the provision by US state institutions of hundreds of millions of dollars of "democracy promotion" money to Iran, which wreaked havoc in Iranian civil society organizations. In 2007, upon President Bush's request, the US Congress allocated $400 million for covert operations in Iran's strategically important border regions in order to destabilize the country through separatist groups, and to eventually bring about regime change.[35] Funds were also made available to nongovernmental organizations (NGOs) in Iran. In the name of funding democracy, in the same year, the US government allocated $75 million to existing propaganda efforts—such as for the Voice of America's Persian News Network (VOA PNN)[36] that established a twenty-four-hour news program (the first of its kind on VOA), and Radio Farda that was part of Radio Free Europe/Radio Liberty. Yet, even Milani acknowledges that the latter fund

> to support "regime change" in Iran helped the regime and undermined the genuine democrats. It created an atmosphere of confrontation between the two regimes [the United States and Iran], and the clerics used that atmosphere to further dismantle the rudiments of civil society. Moreover, it put the democrats in a kind of defensive position—needful of "proving" that they were not a recipient of the seventy five million dollars largesse.[37]

Coupled with US covert operations, such US "largesse" paved the way for the Iranian regime's post–"axis of evil" insecurity to turn into paranoia, and also facilitated repression against regime opponents. Genuine civil society activists and organizations were the first to bear the brunt of those US policies,[38] as they were now exposed to heightened state surveillance and faced frequent interrogations.[39] In other words, the talk of war emanating from Washington turned out to be a "gift from heaven" for the conservatives among the Iranian elite.[40]

The "democracy promotion" funds have been closely associated with the US "Greater Middle East Initiative" and its regime change agenda, as Thomas Carothers lays out the double standards underlying US behavior: "Washington's use of the term 'democracy promotion' has come to be seen overseas not as the expression of a principled American aspiration but as a code word for 'regime change'— namely, the replacement of bothersome governments by military force or other means."[41]

Even under the Obama administration, which had initially pledged diplomatic engagement with Iran, these programs have continued. New funds amounting to hundreds of millions of dollars were made available for US clandestine military activities in Iran, anti-Iran broadcasting, and support for underground militant movements and "civil society" in Iran.[42] As such, also under Obama the effects on democratization in Iran have continued to be negative as the Iranian regime can readily blame any dissent as a US-sponsored plot. The secret nature of these US funds has jeopardized the security and even existence of the entire civil society sector in Iran rather than protect the security of the actual recipients, as claimed by successive US administrations. Iranian activists and organizations can easily be blamed by the Iranian authorities as beneficiaries of US regime-change money to justify even further crackdowns against them.

Since the early 2000s, the stage has been set for a process of securitization inside the Islamic Republic resulting from constant threats of war emanating from Washington and Tel Aviv, the encircling of Iran by US troops, the military buildup of Israel and the Arab petro-monarchies of the Gulf Cooperation Council funded by the United States and European Union (EU) countries, and covert military operations going on in Iran since at least 2004. This situation facilitated a process of securitization if not militarization of state and society, with most notably IRGC figures acceding to the highest levels of state power. Hence, the IRGC developed into an indispensable actor for the country's defense while simultaneously assuming the role of crushing dissent at home and running the greater part of the country's economy. Ultimately, the authoritarian state has employed the credible foreign peril to the country's national security in order to increase its control over domestic dissent.[43]

On balance, it can be concluded that the term democracy promotion, used as a public-policy motto, is misleading, because it rather promotes the opposite—authoritarianism.

Iran's Civil Society "Double-Track" Approach to Carve Out Space for Activism

In light of the preceding, civil society activists opposed the kinds of external policies affecting both its *marge de manœuvre* and the forms of its activism. For instance, in mid-July 2008, roughly thirty representatives of Iran's civil society, in an open letter to the US Congress and president, asked for the suspension of democracy promotion funding "which has had an outcome completely opposite to [the] declared goals" and "has caused so much pain and stress to a significant part of Iranian civil society."[44] The letter further states, "The fund has undermined Iran's home grown civil society initiatives. . . . The fund has provided a pretext for distrust and suspicion, leading to narrowing of space for independent civil society."[45] The statement voiced a great deal of anger over US policy, asking for the cancellation of the funds while demanding greater freedoms from the Iranian government with which dialogue was still sought.

In another open letter, in early July 2008, a large number of Iranians also lamented the negative consequences that the US-led wars in Iran's immediate neighborhood had produced for their country: "Because of this external climate of threat coupled with internal shortcomings and policies that are [a] groundswell for domestic tension, Iran, although not directly at war, has suffered the negative impacts of a virtual war, that is, massive inflation, economic stagnation, and tighter political, technical and scientific restrictions."[46]

The letter further stressed the need for a peaceful environment so welfare and sustainable development could succeed. With an implicit reference to the stated US goal to promote democracy, the statement notes:

> Iranian academicians believe democracy, not as an imported and luxury commodity, but as a viable method of people's participation in major domestic and foreign decision makings . . . is the best method for governing the country [and] view avoidance and prevention of war, while protecting Iran's honour and integrity, as a national duty.[47]

Also in July 2008, a National Peace Council was set up, following a November 2007 call by the head of the Center for Defenders of Human Rights (Kânoun-e Modâfe'ân-e Hoghough-e Bashar), Dr. Shirin Ebadi, to unify and organize movements around the issue of peace. The objective of the movement was defined as "long-lasting peace" (*solh-e pâydâr*). Its aims were outlined as "creating and strengthening the basis for peace; preventing a military attack; abolishing the imposed sanctions and preventing any additional sanctions; ending the situation of 'neither war, nor peace.'"[48] The National Peace Council's founding committee included seventy-two prominent civil society, political, and cultural activists, including journalists from several banned newspapers and former political prisoners. Hence, in the face of the Bush administration's confrontational policies toward Iran, several independent movements and organizations for peace have been formed in Iran,[49] most of which criticized government repression yet sought dialogue with it.

In addition, conscious of an outside threat while advocating peace, for the first time in the history of the Islamic Republic, both secular and religious groups agreed to meet on a regular, two-week basis. A number of peace organizations and activists took part in meetings by September 2008, including the Society for Chemical Weapons Victims Support, the Revolutionary Cinema and the Sacred Defense (led by the well-known writer Habib Ahmadzadeh), the Children's Culture of Peace Council (consisting of thirty NGOs), Hamyaran (a capacity-building NGO headed by Dr. Baquer Namazi), the Council for Research on Children, and the Peace and Tourism Society. Whereas the first two groups are Islamic NGOs, which get funding and support from the government, the rest are secular. Reportedly, despite this difference, all groups showed great respect and support toward each other and used a common language and consensus to promote a peace movement. Furthermore, representatives of the National Peace Council were invited, including well-known Iranian filmmaker Rakhshan Bani-Etemad and Marzieh Mortazi-Lagaroudi from the group Mothers Against War. Women and women's rights activists were at the forefront of such peace initiatives by connecting the domestic and international contexts, hence exhibiting a profound consideration for the "triangular dynamics" at hand. Prominent among them has been Mothers for Peace, which began its activities in 2008 as a group of women with different ideological backgrounds who opposed the possibility of war against their homeland. On 25 November 2011, the International Day to Fight Violence Against Women, the group stated:

> We as a group of women's rights activists in Iran, are worried about the increasing violence against women and children [that is the result] of the polarized and hostile atmosphere [and] dead-end national

and international politics of tension and violence. As a result of these policies, violence against women and children infiltrates the deepest social and political and familial layers of Iranian society.[50]

In conclusion, the belligerent posture of the Bush/Cheney administration toward Iran has forced Iranian civil society to deal with this newly emerging situation and its ramifications. Not only was civil society's own well-being in jeopardy, in case a military attack on Iran had materialized, but the state seized upon this opportunity by pursuing a harsh crackdown against independent civil society actors in the name of protecting national security. In fact, the US "democracy promotion" and "regime change" campaigns became a perfect tool for promoting and upgrading state authoritarianism. Iran's civil society found itself in a state of siege between extreme imperial pressures and massive state repression. Hence, civil society activists adopted a double-track approach: condemning foreign pressures and the provision of aid, and opting for a constructive dialogue with the increasingly repressive state. This strategy can be understood as an effort to counter the shrinking of space for civil activism by carving out new spaces commensurate with the unfolding dire circumstances. At the forefront of this new form of activism were mostly women's rights activists who showed the greatest amount of sensibility and comprehension necessary to offer a framework in which civil and human rights activism could continue, although under precarious circumstances.[51] Accompanied by the unrelenting warmongering from outside, the state nevertheless carried on its crackdown against independent civil society. This was done in an effort to further the patriarchal sociopolitical agenda of the Islamist ultraconservatives. The latter depicted feminist activists as part of an outside plot to bring about the soft overthrow of the Islamic Republic.[52] As a result, many civil activists, particularly among the women's rights movement, were forced to flee the country.[53]

Economic Sanctions and State-Society Relations

In addition to politico-military pressures, Iran has also been subjected to a severe regime of economic sanctions. In this section, I will address the ramifications of coercive economic measures on state-society relations and the question of authoritarianism. I will show that economic sanctions affect mostly the civilian population from which civil society originates, while cementing the position of the powers that be in the targeted state. In contrast to widely held assumptions in policy circles, there is scant evidence for a positive relationship between economic sanctions and the weakening of authoritarian structures. On the contrary, both the empirical evidence in the specific case of Iran and the scholarly literature on the effects of economic sanctions suggest that sanctions widen the power gap between society and the state, with the former overwhelmingly paying the price of sanctions while the latter's hold on power remains firm or becomes even tighter. This occurs in a number of ways.

A Magic Wand to Decapitate Evil?
The Political Narrative of Empowering Sanctions

In the public and political arenas, confusion looms large when it comes to the effects of economic sanctions on issues of democratization and authoritarianism. Importantly, it is the terminology embedded in the debate that casts a long shadow on how the effects of sanctions on these issues are commonly assessed. The sanctions imposed are alternately adorned with the attributions "smart," "intelligent," and "targeted." Such sanctions, it is claimed, are designed to weaken the repressive regime while sparing the civilian population, thus having an empowering effect on civil society. These kinds of sanctions are presented as a quasi-peaceful tool, which is deployed with surgical precision, targeting the designated entity portrayed as evil. Much like smart bombs, however, the sanctions variant produces collateral damage, whose wider ramifications remain largely unnoticed. Moreover, this dominant political discourse presents the sanctioning countries as benevolent actors engaged in weakening authoritarianism while opening the way for a democratic transition. Hence, such a portrayal of sanctions has indeed attracted parts of the Iranian regime opponents, almost exclusively in the diaspora, to the extent of voicing support for them.[54] However, such claims that sanctions can or do help the cause of democracy in Iran have not been based on empirical evidence. Rather, such assumptions are mostly a sign of wishful thinking, be it as a result of political desperation and a perceived lack of viable alternatives to war and/or state repression, or a disregard for the social repercussions of sanctions. With the round of US and EU unilateral sanctions imposed for 2012, politicians from the sanctioning countries began to abandon the rhetoric that the coercive economic measures imposed were "targeted" and "intelligently" aimed at the leadership of the sanctioned country. In fact, US and some European politicians openly started highlighting the "crippling" nature of the sanctions on Iran. US president Barack Obama, for instance, admitted that Iran would face "unprecedented, crippling sanctions."[55] In the same breath, however, politicians have been quick to add that sanctions are not meant to target the civilian population. In a press release accompanying the announcement of its boycott of Iranian oil, the EU echoed the distinction well known from other US policy declarations on Iran: "The Council [of the EU] stresses that the restrictive measures agreed today are aimed at affecting the funding of Iran's nuclear programme by the Iranian regime and are not aimed at the Iranian people."[56]

The partial shift in the political discourse—that is, the increasing acknowledgment that the sanctions were, in fact, crippling—was a reflection both of a unilateral drive by the United States and the EU to ostensibly increase the economic pressure on Iran and, by so doing, of an effort to comply with longstanding Israeli demands for crippling sanctions in order to dissuade Tel Aviv from taking unilateral military action against Iran. Yet, as an analysis of the "smart sanctions" reveals, they have already had crippling effects on the entire economy of the sanctioned country, that is, Iran. Hence, it is suggested that smart, targeted sanctions must be comprehended as belonging to the field of political discourse and rhetoric rather than as reflecting an empirically deduced socioeconomic reality.

The Comprehensive Economic Sanctions Regime on Iran

Iran's economy—including manufacturing, agriculture, banking, and financial sectors—has suffered from almost three decades of sanctions.[57] However, the most recent rounds of sanctions imposed on the country during the so-called nuclear dispute has elevated the sanctions regime to an unprecedented level. Iran is very much connected to the global economy, with about half of its (nominal) GDP based on trade with the outside world. Not only does the export of oil play a dominant role here, but also the import of goods.[58] The sanctions imposed are both unilateral (by the United States and its allies, but, above all, the EU) and multilateral (by the United Nations Security Council since 2006), as well as both formal and informal. Especially since 2004, the United States has pushed for a number of important economic and financial sanctions against Iran, making the country unrivaled in terms of its isolation from the international financial and banking systems, while incrementally disrupting Iranian trade relations with the rest of the world. In June 2010, multilateral UN sanctions targeted insurance companies worldwide that insured Iranian shipping. Another set of sanctions targeted the sale of gasoline products to Iran.[59] The financial sanctions, arguably the most effective ones, have a wide-ranging impact on the whole economy, as they handicap the financing of any trade involving Iran, both for domestic and foreign parties. This impedes the country's ability to do business and leads to rising business operating costs and even the closing down of businesses. In fact, the sanctions on the financial and banking sectors constitute the eye of the storm that subsequently wreaked havoc on the entire economy.

The sanctions regime has placed Iran's economy in a vicious cycle. Before the stark tightening of the sanctions for 2012, the situation could be depicted as follows:

- The costs for buying raw materials and intersectoral industrial goods have risen at an estimated rate of 50 percent.
- Production has therefore been considerably affected, which in part crumbled due to lack of spare parts and equipment or their becoming more expensive.
- The effects on production have led to widespread price hikes.
- All of that has resulted in rising inflation (because of the price increases of imported goods and the lack of coverage in consumer goods) and in rising unemployment (as a result of factory and enterprise closures).

A crucial aggravating aspect has been that Iranian institutions in international trade, such as banks, insurance, and logistics, have been boycotted by Western countries and their allies, which has led to a considerable increase in overall costs.

This isolation was carried to extremes when, by the end of 2011, the United States imposed sanctions on foreign financial institutions engaged in oil-related transactions with the Central Bank of Iran, which caused the Iranian currency to lose half of its value against the US dollar and other major currencies.[60] According to Mehrdad Emadi, an EU economic adviser,

> this particular form of sanctioning a nation has been unprecedented in the history of the world. . . . In this framework, all monetary transactions, currency transactions and business credit accounts for

imports as well as exports and for the coverage and payment of insurance, which in every country falls under the responsibilities of the Central Bank of that country, will be made illegal in Iran.[61]

On top of that, as of 17 March 2012, in an unprecedented step, SWIFT (the Society for Worldwide Interbank Financial Telecommunication) disconnected Iranian banks from its system that handles global banking transactions, making it almost impossible for money to flow in and out of the country through official banking channels. In other words, Iran has virtually lost the ability to finance imports and to receive payment for its exports. The result is an almost complete isolation of Iranian trade and businesses from the global market.

As a matter of fact, the reality of the sanctions regime could not differ more starkly from the portrayal of benign, targeted sanctions. Grasping the core of the matter, Suzanne Maloney, a US expert on Iran's economy, commented: "It's not an overstatement to say that the sanctions we've put on Iran . . . constitute a full-fledged attack on the Iranian economy."[62] According to Trita Parsi, president of the National Iranian American Council, "Many in Washington acknowledge that we are conducting economic warfare. That means the entire Iranian economy is the battlefield—and ordinary Iranians are [seen as] enemy combatants."[63] At the very least, international sanctions have deepened Iran's economic crisis and made it extremely difficult, if not impossible, to get on the path of economic recovery.

The EU itself was fully aware of the major consequences of its unilateral sanctions imposed in June 2010, in the wake of UN sanctions (UN Security Council Resolution 1929) decided in the same month. According to Mehrdad Emadi, Brussels expected that in the course of the first twelve months following the imposition of EU sanctions, Iran's economic growth would become negative for the first time ever.[64] Against this background, it can be argued that the crippling of the economy has been within the scope of expectations of the sanctioning states, and has been carried to extremes in spite of the proclaimed concern for the well-being of the Iranian populace.

The Political Economy of Sanctions: Crippling the Economy and Bolstering the Authoritarian State

The sanctions imposed on Iran negatively affect its entire economy, but, due to stark imbalances in the domestic power structure, their effects vary from one societal sector to another. About two-thirds of the

Iranian economy is controlled by state and semi-state actors.[65] In general, economic entities close to the state have the means to access state resources, with which they can to some extent cover the higher operational costs resulting from sanctions. Alternatively, such actors can circumvent the sanctions by using "black channels" mainly for importing goods, as can be seen in the case of the IRGC. Originally a defense organization erected to counter Iraqi aggression in the 1980s, the IRGC has developed into an expansive sociopolitico-economic conglomerate that is believed to possess unrivaled economic and political power in today's Islamic Republic. Sanctioning countries proclaimed that "smart sanctions" would target the IRGC's grip on the Iranian power structure, but an analysis into the effects of sanctions reveals that the IRGC's economic power position, in fact, expanded in the wake of sanctions.

With much of the international trade involving Iran being illegalized through sanctions and economic actors largely cut off from importing goods, the IRGC and its economic empire have been able to benefit from this situation. Both due to its control over at least sixty harbors in the Gulf and a number of unofficial airports, and its presence at the borders, the bulk of imports have been monopolized by the IRGC while lucrative profits from rising cross-border smuggling have been secured. As such, the IRGC as a (semi)-state entity has been capable of expanding its economic dominance vis-à-vis the civilian economy, which does not have the same sort of privileges. Moreover, with the bulk of the Iranian economy now part of the IRGC's economic empire, the much ignored difficulty is that the targeting of IRGC firms will in the end affect the millions of civilians connected to these wide-ranging sectors. Seen in this light, the gigantic dimension of even truly targeted sanctions aimed at specific, yet wide-ranging entities comes to the fore.[66] As such, the IRGC is gaining ground vis-à-vis other domestic economic actors and is being fortified as a linchpin actor of the authoritarian state.

In addition to that, the dramatic weakening of the civilian economy makes the socioeconomic role of the state even more crucial. As the economist Djavad Salehi-Isfahani explains:

> Sanctions are likely to cement the authoritarian pact between the conservatives and the economic underclass and at the same time weaken the voices calling for greater social, political and economic freedom. Heavy sanctions are likely to strengthen the hands of the Iranian leaders who have opposed the liberal economic reforms of the Rafsanjani and Khatami era and favor a return to the controlled

economy of the 1980s, when the government rather than markets decided on the allocation of foreign exchange, credit, and even basic necessities.[67]

Hence, sanctions enhance the role of the state for the provision of public services and even basic goods, and as such contribute to a more centralized country.[68]

Taking another angle, if one were to interpret Iran's domestic crisis in the wake of the June 2009 presidential election primarily as an economic war of allocation between the old elite, particularly surrounding the figure of former president Rafsanjani, and the new elite, composed of the Ahmadinejad-IRGC faction,[69] sanctions turn out to be detrimental to the interests of the former.

With the sanctions punishing honest traders and rewarding corrupt ones, Iran's civilian economy—those firms and factories not benefiting from privileges derived from regime proximity—and thereby both the middle class (usually seen as the backbone for processes of democratization) and the urban poor have been affected by this further economic isolation of the country. In other words, Iran's increasing isolation from the outside world, a fundamental face of sanctions, in fact, significantly limits the social space available to its citizenry as the role and power of the authoritarian state is strengthened.

Sanctions and the Weakening of Iran's Civil Society Actors

The weakening of the entire economy adds to the hardship experienced by civil society. Hence, in addition to political repression, civil society also suffers from economic pressures.[70]

As I will show, the constituent groups of civil society's key social movements—women, students, and workers—are significantly affected. In addition, as Sussan Tahmasebi, a prominent Iranian women's rights activist, explains, activists in Iran get increasingly isolated from the outside world: "Those who carry on despite hardships inside the country are also feeling more and more isolated. Activists, like regular Iranians, cannot use banks to transfer funds for conference participation, hotel reservations and to attend training workshops abroad."[71]

Women. The impact of sanctions on women and gender relations has been thoroughly studied in the context of the sanctions regime against Iraq from 1990 to 2003.[72] Socioeconomic patterns similar to the Iraqi case regarding the ramifications of sanctions on women can be identified, with women being disproportionately affected. The rise in unemployment is likely to fuel regressive conservative social policies that aim to preserve the traditional social status reserved to the male population by externalizing the costs of sanctions onto the female population. These include measures that push women out of work, relegate them to the domestic sphere, and curtail their access to higher education. Even the next generation of women's rights activists may be drained when "school age girls are at risk as economic pressures may force families to make choices and opt for boys' schooling [that] may lead to diminished literacy rates among girls in the near future."[73] Hence, sanctions can serve as the political platform on which conservative politicians can go on the offensive in order to marginalize women from education and employment, which consequently also limits the space for women's rights activism. Moreover, widespread unemployment affects the entire family, but mainly women, and exacerbates dominant gender relations.

> Women will bear the brunt of dealing with their unemployed spouses and the men of the family within the home. These new dynamics are likely to lead to increased incidences of domestic violence and family conflicts, as men's ability to meet social expectations can lead to depression and attacks on women. Reduction in family income is inevitable forcing women to find new sources of income. Their coping strategies will likely include cutting back on their own health, well-being and dietary needs to provide for their dependents.[74]

As a result, both economic sanctions and the heightened securitization of state and society as a result of the external threat of war foster patriarchal structures and complicate, if not undermine, the women's rights struggle.[75]

Students. The youth (fifteen-to-twenty-nine year olds), which comprises 35 percent of the population, disproportionately suffer from sanctions as they account for 70 percent of general unemployment.[76] Facing increasingly deteriorating job prospects, students also face additional hurdles. Sanctions affect the ability of Iranian students to study in the West, as the sanctions have severed their access to visas and made it almost impossible to use bank channels to pay for their tuition fees. Also, Iranian students and academia in general are prohibited from accessing academic journals online. Furthermore, many

Iranians and even those of Iranian descent are banned from many academic science programs at US and European universities. These sanctions-driven discriminations, as well as limits imposed on the mobility of Iranian students, also negatively affect solidarity work with the outside world when it comes to civil activism.

Workers. Workers are harshly hit by the economic crisis affecting Iran. Despite the lack of studies on the impact of sanctions on labor in Iran, one can think of a number of ways in which sanctions negatively affect Iranian workers. For one, Iranian businesses and factories that have been dependent on importing items to sustain their operations but cannot do so anymore because of sanctions have reduced their costs by cutting down on wages, laying-off workers, or even completely closing down. Furthermore, sanctions and the crisis in domestic production paves the way for curtailing workers' rights and benefits. Such measures could affect the right to strike, the level of the wages paid, and large-scale layoffs. As such, sanctions can also serve as an excuse for economic problems that lie in structural problems, mismanagement, and other shortcomings or profit-driven motivations by the employers themselves.[77] Hence, sanctions add to the hardship experienced by Iranian workers who are suffering from both neoliberal economic policies and harsh state repression.[78]

Throughout the rise in labor activism in the 2000s, Iranian workers were both sensitive to their struggle against neoliberal economics at home and the threat of war from abroad that served as a justification for the state's repression against them in the name of national security.[79] The negative effect of sanctions on labor has also been understood by their US counterparts. In a March 2012 solidarity resolution, US Labor Against War voiced its opposition to war, but also sanctions against Iran "that primarily victimize civilians and strengthen the Iranian regime, which portrays itself as the defender of the Iranian people."[80] As a result, all three social movements experience indirect fallouts from the severe sanctions imposed on the country, which in turn weaken their struggle in various ways. It can also be noted that the Green Movement[81] has largely opposed economic sanctions.

Iranian Case as an Example of the Effects of Sanctions

In this section I shall present additional insights derived from the academic literature on the effects of economic sanctions and tested in the specific context of Iran.

Prolonging authoritarian rule. In a remarkable article from spring 2010, Emanuele Ottolenghi formulates the goals of crippling sanctions: "strategic sectors of the economy" must be targeted, among them the operation and development of refineries, the energy, petrochemical, and metallurgical industries, so as to undermine the regime's stability:[82]

> Iran must know that the West is prepared to exact a steep price and that sanctions are designed to cause economic damage that will undermine the legitimacy and credibility of the regime. Not least, Tehran should be told that the international community will support regime-change from within. *It must know that the West will work tirelessly to make Iran poor* and internationally isolated unless and until dramatic changes occur within the Islamic Republic.[83]

Despite the claim that crippling sanctions might undermine regime stability, all the evidence points to the fact that sanctions contribute to regime resilience.[84] As noted, sanctions undermine the well-being of the civilian population while actors who are part of or close to the ruling system find ways to accommodate themselves to the sanctions regime, even cementing their own position of power. As a result, the power gap between the state and society widens.[85] This is in line with findings from the academic literature on sanctions that coercive economic measures prolong rather than shorten the rule of leaders in authoritarian states, with sanctions often having a stabilizing effect on such rule.[86]

Increasing state-sponsored repression. Academic research offers a number of findings about the impact of economic sanctions on authoritarian structures which can be relevant in the Iranian context. It has been shown that economic coercion through sanctions (even targeted ones) is counterproductive as it stimulates the sanctioned state's political repression.[87] Economic sanctions, particularly multilateral ones, worsen the targeted country's human rights situation by reducing the government's respect for physical integrity rights, including freedom from disappearances, extrajudicial killings, torture, and political imprisonment.[88] More broadly, the effects of economic sanctions on democracy as a whole have been examined. It has been argued that sanctions decrease the level of democracy because the economic hardship caused by sanctions can be used as a strategic tool by the targeted regime to consolidate authoritarian rule and weaken the opposition. The findings show that both the immediate and longer-term effects of economic sanctions significantly reduce the level of democratic freedoms in the targeted state, with comprehensive economic sanctions having greater negative impact than limited ones. Moreover, it has been demonstrated that economic sanctions enhance government control over the free flow of information, while independent media outlets suffer from economic damage inflicted by sanctions. As such, economic sanctions also affected media openness in a negative way.[89] Lastly, various authors concur that the more comprehensive and multilateral (as opposed to unilateral) the sanctions regime is, the more harmful it is to various pillars of democracy.[90]

Conclusion

In this chapter, I have sought to explore the effects of external factors on state-society relations in the context of authoritarianism and space for civil society. First, it has been demonstrated that much of the conventional literature on authoritarianism in strategically important countries inimical to US or wider Western interests suffers from a politically driven selectivity when it comes to the identification of authoritarian states. The focus on countries like Iran or Syria are important cases in point, while allied countries such as Saudi Arabia often escape due scrutiny as authoritarian states. Second, it has been shown that since the Iranian revolution of 1978–1979, geopolitical détente mostly coincided with the opening of space for Iranian civil society, while, conversely, geopolitical tensions have boosted authoritarian structures and limited space for civil society. Third, it has been argued that, faced with the dual peril of foreign threat and meddling as well as increasing repression at home, Iran's civil society has reacted by adopting a double-track approach. This included condemning malign external factors, engaging in a kind of critical dialogue with an increasingly repressive state, and forming new alliances among a diverse range of civil society activists to bring about long-lasting peace as a necessary condition for the realization of their democratic demands. In other words, the externally induced shrinking of space for civil society activism, in tandem with increasing state authoritarianism, was countered in a number of ways that allowed for a carving out of new space(s) for activism. Fourth, I have shown that economic sanctions widen the power gap between the authoritarian state and civil society, cementing and even boosting existing power configurations while hollowing out social forces indispensable to a process of democratization, such as the middle class and various constituents of social movements such as women and youth. It can be observed that authoritarian states use economic sanctions to cement their hold on power, regardless of the severity of the economic costs.[91] In an interesting recent development, a great deal of Iranian civil activism mostly taking place in the West has indeed taken into account the triangular dynamics among geopolitics, the state, and civil society. A categorical rejection of war and sanctions has been a fundamental proposition by these groups in order to impact positively upon the space available for civil activism inside Iran and more broadly the human rights situation there.

Crippling sanctions as a prototype of economic warfare in concert with the seasonal flaring-up of war-mongering is a toxic mix as to prospects of democratization. One of the resulting dilemmas is that with increasing sanctions that can pave the way for war, the repressive state itself and its defense forces will be the main actors defending the country against foreign aggression, and in the process of doing so could expand their reach into the state and society with further detrimental effects for civil liberties and democratic aspirations.

It has thus been argued that Iran's civil society has been placed in a state of siege, caught between reinforcing pressures: on the one hand, external-imperial, and on the other, internal-authoritarian, predicated upon the authoritarian machinations of the state. The global war on terror and the coercive policy toward Iran have thus proved to be a significant obstacle in the struggle to lay the groundwork for overcoming authoritarianism in Iran. One could indeed suggest that the most promising midwife for democratization in Iran seems to be geopolitical détente, regional peace, economic prosperity, and social justice—all of which ought to replace the policies and atmosphere of enmity, compulsion, and domination. If the attempt to further isolate Iran continues, it is unlikely that the new space of activism created over recent years will have more fruitful results than traditional activism.

The efforts so far to encourage the process of democratization from the outside have utterly failed to bring about positive results, or even gradual ones. Rather, they have acted in a counterproductive manner insofar as they have emboldened the authoritarian machinations of the state by sustaining a "state of emergency" in the country and reduced the space for democratic activism in Iran.

Therefore, productive international support must be geared toward détente. Cornerstones for such a policy of détente would be both immediate measures for the resolution of the conflict primarily pitting the Islamic Republic against the United States, including steps toward deescalation and preparing on the ground for a reconciliation of interests through a sustained diplomatic process respectful of widely accepted standards of international law. A promising project here is the establishment of a Middle Eastern zone free of weapons of mass destruction, including nuclear weapons.[92] Finally, it is important to end a sanction regime that is utterly counterproductive when it comes to democracy promotion.

Notes

1. From "Über die Gewalt" (On violence) (1930s), trans. John Willett, in *Poems, 1913–1956,* revised edition (London and New York: Methuen, 1987), p. 276.
2. See, e.g., Heydemann, "Upgrading Authoritarianism in the Arab World."
3. For instance, Cavatorta, *The International Dimension of the Failed Algerian Transition.*
4. Brynen, Korany, and Noble, "Introduction," pp. 18–20. Also see Aarts, "The Longevity of the House of Saud."
5. Sauer, "Coercive Diplomacy by the EU." Also see Fathollah-Nejad, *Der Iran-Konflikt und die Obama-Regierung* (The Iran conflict and the Obama administration).
6. Freedom House, Radio Free Europe/Radio Liberty, and Radio Free Asia, *Undermining Democracy,* p. 2.
7. Ibid., p. 2.
8. Ibid., p. 3.
9. See, e.g., Milani, "Transition to Democracy in Iran," pp. 3–4, 13–14; and Freedom House et al., *Undermining Democracy,* pp. 29–30.
10. Milani, "Transition to Democracy in Iran," p. 15.
11. Ibid., p. 12; see also Milani, *The Myth of the Great Satan.*
12. Milani, "Transition to Democracy in Iran," p. 9.
13. White House, *The National Security Strategy of the United States of America,* p. 3.
14. Milani, "Transition to Democracy in Iran," p. 4.
15. See Fouad Ajami's foreword in Milani, *The Myth of the Great Satan.*
16. Kelly and Etling, *Mapping Iran's On-line Public.*
17. Milani, "Transition to Democracy in Iran," pp. 2–3; see also Pipes, "Dealing with Middle Eastern Conspiracy Theories."

18. Lefebvre, *The Production of Space.*
19. Eisenstadt, *Traditional Patrimonialism,* p. 30.
20. Lefebvre, *The Production of Space,* p. 73.
21. Bayat, *Street Politics.*
22. Norton, "Associational Life."
23. For that discussion of space, I am indebted to Adnan Tabatabai.
24. Rostami-Povey, *Iran's Influence,* pp. 215–216. Also see Fathollah-Nejad and Yazdani, "Das Verhältnis von Religion und Staat in Iran" (The relationship between religion and state in Iran), pp. 303–305.
25. Cited in Kamrava, "The Civil Society Discourse in Iran," p. 169.
26. Ibid., p. 168.
27. See, for example, Farhi, "Religious Intellectuals, the 'Woman Question,' and the Struggle for the Creation of a Democratic Public Sphere in Iran."
28. Ibid., p. 170.
29. See Azimi, *The Quest for Democracy in Iran.*
30. Dabashi, *Iran: A People Interrupted;* and Rostami-Povey, *Iran's Influence.*
31. Available at the Project for the New American Century, Statement of Principles, http://www.newamericancentury.org/statementofprinciples.htm.
32. See Katz, "The United States and Iran"; and Clawson, "The Continuing Logic of Dual Containment."
33. Haghighi and Tahmasebi, "The 'Velvet Revolution,'" p. 965.
34. Hersh, "The Iran Plans."
35. Hersh, "Preparing the Battlefield."
36. Previously it was called the Persian Service.
37. Milani, "Transition to Democracy in Iran," pp. 19–20.
38. See also Azimi, "Hard Realities of Soft Power"; US Department of State, "Update on Iran Democracy Promotion Funding"; and Parsi, "Denying Iran's Democrats."
39. Interview with an Iranian women's rights activist, formerly active in a leading Tehran-based women's rights NGO, London, November 2011.
40. See also Jafari, *Der andere Iran* (The other Iran), pp. 155–156.
41. Carothers, "The Backlash Against Democracy Promotion," p. 64.
42. For details, see de Vries, "United States Policy on 'Democratizing' Iran," pp. 7–8.
43. See also Warnaar, "So Many Similarities."
44. "Message of Peace and Friendship to the People of United States of America: Request for the Congress and President of USA," cited in Ong, "Iranians Speak Out on Regime Change Slush Fund."
45. Ibid.
46. Cited in CASMII, "Iranian Academicians Call for Long-Lasting Peace."
47. Ibid.
48. Cited in CASMII, "Iran's Civil Society Movement Sets Up 'National Peace Council.'"

49. CASMII, "Iranian Academicians Call for Long-Lasting Peace."

50. "Bayâneh-ye Jam'i az Fa'âlan-e Jonbesh-e Zanân dar Dâkhel-e Keshvar be Monâsebat-e 'Rooz-e Jahâni-e Mobârezeh bâ Khoshounat Aley-heh Zanân'" (A statement of a group of women's rights activists inside the country on the occasion of the International Day for the Elimination of Violence Against Women), *Focus on Iranian Women,* 27 November 2011, http://ir-women.net/spip.php?article9837; cited from the translation from Persian by the International Civil Society Action Network, "Killing Them Softly," p. 7.

51. See, e.g., International Campaign for Human Rights in Iran, *Raising Their Voices;* Esfandyari, "In Iran, Talk of Military Strikes from Above Raises Fears Below"; Esfandyari, "Iranian Women's Rights Activists Say No to War."

52. Iran Human Rights Documentation Center, *Silencing the Women's Rights Movement in Iran,* p. 9.

53. See Kian, *L'Iran—Un mouvement sans révolution?* (Iran—A movement without revolution?), pp. 66–72.

54. For an exposition of such a view, see Torfeh, "Sanctions Against Iran May Boost the Protest Movement."

55. Cited in Voice of America, "Obama."

56. Council of the European Union, "Council Conclusions on Iran," p. 2.

57. See Torbat, "Impacts of US Trade and Financial Sanctions on Iran."

58. Ravand Institute for Economic and International Studies, "Sanctions."

59. For an overview on Iran sanctions, see Katzman, "Iran Sanctions"; and Fatollah-Nejad, "Auf Kollisionskurs mit dem Iran" (On collision course with Iran), and "Sanktionsregime gegen den Iran" (The sanctions regime on Iran). See also Gordon, "'Smart Sanctions' on Iran Are Dumb."

60. See Collinson, "Obama Signs New Iran Sanctions." The Kirk–Menendez Iran Sanctions Amendment to the U.S. National Defense Authorization Act for Fiscal Year 2012 (H.R. 1540)—worth $662 billion—was signed into law by President Obama on 31 December 2011 and went into effect by the summer 2012. For the Iran-related sanctions, see "Imposition of Sanctions with Respect to the Financial Sector in Iran," sec. 1245 of H.R. 1540 (112th Congress), at http://www.gpo.gov/fdsys/pkg/BILLS-112hr1540enr/pdf/BILLS-112hr1540enr.pdf, pp. 350–353.

61. Cited in International Civil Society Action Network, "Killing Them Softly," p. 4.

62. Cited in Dreazen, "The U.S. and Iran Are Already Locked in Economic War."

63. Cited in Kamali Dehghan, "Sanctions on Iran."

64. See statements made by Mehrdad Emadi, an economic adviser for the EU, on BBC Persian TV (18 June 2010) and Radio (19 May 2010), and on *CNN iReport* (10 June 2010).

65. See Daraghi and Mostaghim, "Iran Hard-Liners Skirt Sanctions."

66. Fatollah-Nejad, "Collateral Damage of Iran Sanctions."

67. Salehi-Isfahani, "Iran Sanctions."

68. The same happened to Iraq while under sanctions. See Gordon, *Invisible War.*

69. Abdolvand and Schulz, "Elitenkampf um Ressourcen" (Elite struggle for resources).

70. See, e.g., Salehi-Isfahani, "Iran Sanctions"; "Iran and Sanctions," *The Economist;* Mehrabi, "Report from Tehran"; Kamali Dehghan, "Sanctions on Iran."

71. Cited in Kamali Dehghan, "Sanctions on Iran."

72. See Al-Jawaheri, *Women in Iraq;* Al-Ali, "Women, Gender Relations, and Sanctions in Iraq," "Gendering Reconstruction," and "A Feminist Perspective on the Iraq War"; and Campaign Against Sanctions on Iraq, *Sanctions on Iraq.*

73. International Civil Society Action Network, "Killing Them Softly," p. 5.

74. Ibid.

75. "Under these circumstances, with economic hardships and prospects of yet another devastating war, long-term planning and the development of sustainable programs to maintain the gains already made and push for basic rights are increasingly difficult, if not impossible" (International Civil Society Action Network, "Killing Them Softly," p. 7); Khanlarzadeh, "Iranian Women and Economic Sanctions."

76. Salehi-Isfahani, "Iran's Youth, the Unintended Victims of Sanctions."

77. See *Iran Labor Report,* "Radio Interview"; International Civil Society Action Network, "Killing Them Softly," p. 5.

78. See, e.g., *Iran Labor Report,* "New Year Begins with Fresh Layoffs, Protests."

79. See Malm and Esmailian, *Iran on the Brink.*

80. For the resolution adopted on 9 March 2012, see US Labor Against War (USLAW) Steering Committee, "USLAW Calls for More Diplomacy, Not the Military in Dealing with Iran."

81. For a good discussion on the Green Movement, see Kian, *L'Iran— Un mouvement sans révolution?* (Iran—A movement without revolution?), pp. 15–37.

82. Ottolenghi, "Setting the Sanctions Agenda," p. 25.

83. Ibid., p. 21, emphasis added.

84. Fatollah-Nejad, "Salient Sanctions and Regime Resilience."

85. Fatollah-Nejad, "Iran," pp. 9–12; Salehi-Isfahani, "Iran's Youth, the Unintended Victims of Sanctions"; International Civil Society Action Network, "Killing Them Softly," pp. 4–6; Khanlarzadeh, "Iranian Women and Economic Sanctions"; also, with a focus on Iraq, see Al-Ali, "Women, Gender Relations, and Sanctions in Iraq," "Gendering Reconstruction," and "A Feminist Perspective on the Iraq War"; and Campaign Against Sanctions on Iraq, *Sanctions on Iraq.*

86. Licht, "Falling Out of Favor."

87. Peksen and Drury, "Economic Sanctions and Political Repression."

88. Peksen, "Better or Worse?"

89. Peksen, "Coercive Diplomacy and Press Freedom."

90. Also see Morgan and Bapat, "Multilateral Versus Unilateral Sanctions Reconsidered"; and Bahrami and Parsi, "Blunt Instrument."

91. Bahrami and Parsi, "Blunt Instrument."

92. See Fathollah-Nejad, "Iran," pp. 13–14, and "Security and Cooperation in the Middle East."

4

Business Associations and the New Nexus of Power in Syria

Bassam Haddad

Despite a plethora of theorizing regarding the breakdown of authoritarian regimes, including prescriptive recipes for their eventual, if slow, demise, such regimes have endured for much longer than expected. Even the 2011 uprisings that rocked the Arab world have so far yet to produce anything resembling democratic governance at the time of writing, with the possible exception of Tunisia and, to a lesser extent, Egypt. In many cases, autocratic regimes persisted for so long *because* they themselves employed what was prescribed for their demise. One such prescription is civil society, with its democratizing correlates and implications. The realities of numerous authoritarian regimes with fledgling civil societies, however, tell a different story, as Chapter 1 makes clear in highlighting that civil societies have often actually served the opposite of their putative role. Particularly, the correlation between the growth/strength of civil society and increasing democratization did not stand the test of time and experience, and, even where it did, other forces/factors played a more significant role. Conversely, regimes such as Tunisia, with its muted civil society, were among the first to fall. Traditional assumptions about the historical role of civil society no longer hold water. It is therefore important to strip civil society of its putative normative dimensions, if only to leave more room for other factors that might better explain outcomes. This will open the door for cumulative knowledge on the relational dynamics, development, and resilience of authoritarian regimes.

69

The same applies to the social designations "middle class" or "capitalists" that were supposed to herald the calls for democracy or challenge dictatorships, according to similar traditional assumptions in the enthusiastic civil society literature. Much has been written to debunk such claims and explain the plethora of factors that render such assumptions erroneous.[1] More importantly, the same liberal ideological canon that produced such theorizing is employed to spur democratization through economic liberalization, seen also as a process that enhances civil society by increasing the size of the private sector. In turn, the assumptions go, this enterprising private sector is likely to form the centrifugal force around which a magnificent current of private initiatives is built in the form of associations and organizations—from business associations to those that serve as a buffer between the individual and the state.

Seeking to respond to the interests of their constituencies and members, such a body of independent social forces would gradually chip away at the powerful edifice of authoritarian rule by holding it in check and even pushing it back in some regards. This liberal, and more recently neoliberal, analytical narrative rests on a strong dose of ahistorical and apolitical accounts of societal relations and development. However, the ideological and normative drivers at work are fed by a status quo of international power relations that sustains their influence, no matter their fallibility. Ironically, two of the Arab states that were heralded by international financial institutions (IFIs) and the European Union as models of economic reform for the region were the first to fall: namely Tunisia and Egypt.

Falling well short of a comprehensive treatment of the origins of such ideological and theoretical trajectories, I will use the case of Syria to examine how, on the contrary, the development of the private sector and the growth of the correlate business actors have served the purpose of sustaining authoritarian rule by a combination of broadening dictatorship and undercutting possibilities of collective action among excluded sectors. This took place amid a steady increase of an ostensibly private sector that gradually gave rise to associations and organizations deemed part of a potentially fledgling civil society. On the other hand, in what might at first sight appear to be a paradox, I seek to debunk some of the long-held assumptions of supporters of the democratist aspects of the civil society argument—in particular, the putative causal link between the domination of neoliberal IFIs and the adoption of liberal economic prescriptions in domestic settings. In this regard too, the crucial case of Syria, which has no relations with IFIs and often antagonizes its patron countries, demonstrates that adoption of seemingly neoliberal policies (no matter how much it falls short of classical prescriptions) is a function of homegrown decisional processes that responded primarily to local interests. The structure of the global political economy facilitates the adoption of such policies by providing a context in which they *may be* nurtured but is not the only impulse or the determinant factor behind the policies. This is crucial for explaining the local (not just internationally imbued/imposed) rationale that drives incumbent regimes to promote civil society at particular points in their development.

The analytical narrative that tells this tale starts with the prolonged process associated with the unraveling of a state-centered, or central-command, economy, with its attendant dominant public sector and the political (turned economic) elite that midwife its transformation. It ends with the emergence of places and spaces where a diametrically opposed set of institutions and attendant actors emerge either to feed off, transform, or, in fact, prolong the demise of failing economic structures for a variety of purposes—that is, feeding off of them while postponing their demise and/or transformation, akin to borrowing money to prolong one's financial solvency. The new sites that emerge are essentially market mechanisms and institutions that not only do not function properly because of the absence of supportive legal and policy environments (e.g., the Damascus Stock Exchange), but also facilitate further the process of rent-seeking via unwarranted bank loans and privileged access to policy formulation. The fact that this process seems to be pulled in various directions indicates that notions of "regime," "state," and/or "business" are not monolithic, and that indeed various players are exercising their interests in different ways, even if the hierarchy of power remains somewhat predictable. There are those who are trying to set the new rules of the game to preserve the political status quo (top regime leadership); those who are trying to influence the new rules of the game in one or another direction (powerful public and private stakeholders); and those who are grabbing what they can in the process (everyone). This state of exploiting a seeming transition is theorized as being temporary, a way station on the road to transformation. In reality, research has shown that much of these transitions are in fact permanent states of being, at least to the extent that any political-economic formula is permanent.[2]

In the process, I will address the shift in state alliances, the different phases of liberalization, and the emergence of new business actors as well as the putative role of business associations—all as part of the unraveling of state-centered economies. I will start with a brief discussion of Syria's voluntary adoption of neoliberal policies that were presumably imposed on other developing countries. Such policies are best understood as a function of the very local interests that eventually lead to the development of a desire to promote civil society. The drivers for both the unraveling of the state-centered economy and the adoption of a new probusiness political-economic formula are the new socioeconomic groups that began to emerge in the late 1980s.

New Civil Society, IFIs, and the New Elite Preferences

The unraveling of state-centered economies gave rise to a new kind of civil society that reflected the interest of the "winners" in the process, within the rubric of authoritarian rule. These winners, or the new political and economic elite, developed political-economic preferences that coincided with IFIs' neoliberal prescriptions. In this sense, the Syrian case is quite instructive.

As opposed to a host of developing countries, Syria has had no binding relations with IFIs such as the World Bank and the International Monetary Fund (IMF) since 1985. Nonetheless, the homegrown set of economic reforms in Syria since 1986 has been similar to most of those prescribed by IFIs (e.g., trade liberalization, currency devaluation, fiscal reform and austerity, encouraging private business), even if the pace was slower. Generally, the deleterious developmental outcomes in Syria have been remarkably similar (e.g., high unemployment coupled with a demand for unskilled labor, concentration of wealth, socioeconomic polarization and growing poverty, dramatic expansion of the informal sector and the shadow/unregulated economy, stringent labor laws, and decline of education) to those in other developing countries. How might we account for such similarities and the decision to adopt IFI prescriptions in a country where the regime prides itself on being insulated from the tentacles of imperialism and the exploitative reach of globalization and its institutions?

Some may assume that this "coincidence" speaks to the sound nature of IFIs' prescriptions. However, a closer look at why such policies are adopted in cases like Syria attests not to their problem-solving validity but rather to the fact that the interests of IFIs coincide with those of the new indigenous elites, even of self-proclaimed "socialists."

Discussed in the literature as a "laboratory case," Syria is indeed instructive, even if the laboratory itself is not completely isolated from global trends. Syria remains relatively more impervious to such trends than, for instance, either Egypt or Jordan, not least regarding relations with IFIs. What, then, prompted the quasi-socialist Syrian regime to emulate reform conditionalities imposed on Egypt by global capitalist institutions?

My provisional answer is that local and global elites share similar preferences regarding choices of reform strategies. However, local elites exhibit variation as to the timing, scope, and pace of reforms. Egypt's reform, for instance, was initiated earlier than that of Syria and, by contrast, ultimately included an official IMF package, with conditionalities (not always official) and other trappings. Egypt long ago allowed for private banks to operate, established a stock market of sorts, and engaged in privatization of state-owned enterprises, all of which were unheard of in Syria until 2004–2005 (precluding on paper). Such variations, so far, have produced similar developmental consequences.

The source of differences in terms of developmental outcomes is governed by what can be termed "positionality" and resource endowments: local elites are simply differentially positioned vis-à-vis their own polities and the composition of state revenues. Local decision-makers must therefore approach the formulation and implementation of liberalization processes accordingly so as to preserve their political power. But all roads lead to Rome, it seems. A more structural factor is at work, one that explains similar outcomes despite differing starting points and contexts.

Civil Society, Capitalist Development, and Authoritarian Resilience

Consistent with the argument in this chapter, I contend that alongside the narrative of the unraveling of state-centered economies, we have been witnessing the unfolding of a new stage, not in economic development, but in the actual development of capitalist relations within peripheral countries such as Egypt and Syria. In this stage, a new elite (call it what you will) is coalescing from the remains of the old bourgeoisie, the new bourgeoisie/entrepreneurs, and the state bourgeoisie. We are concomitantly witnessing the transfer of assets not from the state back to society (empty/depoliticized categories in more than one way) but from the control of groups in their official public capacity to the same groups and their networks in their private capacity as citizens: new assets in the private sector are owned or controlled by the same individuals who run or control the public sector. That is, the form of ownership is undergoing change from public to private, while the social content (social carriers) remains the same but more consolidated in terms of political-economic preferences. We can also observe an order of unfettered capital accumulation that is resubordinating state and community to the preferences of its (capitalist) social carriers and their structural (if not official) links to global capitalist relations. After a period of state capitalism building in the mid-twentieth century, compelled by postcolonial social structural and political realities, capitalist development resumes with vigor, but now with a relatively more educated and skilled labor force capable of being turned into consumers and laborers in support of local and global capitalist relations.

The requirements of power and markets globally are mirrored locally: in both cases, the disempowerment of masses/constituents through the use of various mechanisms and technologies of power is a constitutive factor. The intervention of IFIs may catalyze the process of disempowerment but does not necessarily cause it: regardless, broader impersonal agents such as market relations in an increasingly globalized world are hard at work. In sum, one may observe that the development of global capitalism coincides with the development of state capitalism in peripheral countries (or perhaps with its demise and transformation to a yet unknown formula that remains guided by capitalist development). These processes are relevant to this chapter in how parts of the international community link economic liberalization, civil society, and democratization. The immutable faith in the impact of civil society emanates from the same ideological/theoretical canon that emphasizes liberalization and the private sector as the panacea to economic ills in developing countries. The new social forces that have emerged out of processes of economic liberalization are the same ones that are slowly becoming dominant in nascent civil society associations, such as the new business associations/groups. This development is far more likely to buttress

authoritarian rule than to challenge it given the mutual interests between the state and big business. The fact that Syria is completely
disconnected from any international institution that imposed similar
economic liberalization patterns on other countries reflects the power
and interests of local social forces, a fact that is lost on many critics
of globalization and imperialism. What remains is the deleterious impact on the overwhelming majority of ordinary citizens who are losing out both in the economic and political spheres. The culprit has
been the manner in which power circulates locally and internationally, and how it is embodied in a set of exclusionary policies but-
tressed by an increasing coalescence of interests between the local
political and economic elite. This new nexus of power seems to satisfy parts of the international community as it "reforms" the Syrian
economy and builds "civic" and "civil" associations. The Syrian
regime still had an interest in appearing as though it was "reforming"
its economy in order to maintain or restore economic agreements
with, for instance, European partners. The intended or unintended
consequence has been the resilience of authoritarian rule since the
late 1990s.[3]

The Unraveling of the
State-Centered Economy in Syria

The emergence of business actors as part of the now legitimate—and
growing—civil society in Syria has its roots in the post-1970 political-economic transformations that Syria underwent. Over the past
four decades, as regime alliances have gradually shifted from labor to
business, new powerful actors have emerged, primarily business actors associated with the Syrian regime through informal economic
networks that helped shape economic decisions since the early
1990s.[4] As a result, calls for the expansion of civil society increased
from nearly all actors on the spectrum: the top regime leadership,
state officials, business actors, opposition leaders, Islamist organizations, and human rights advocates. The regime benefited precisely
because some parts of "civil society" benefited the regime (e.g., business associations), and other actors benefited because they hoped that
civil society would shield them from the regime. Granted, some of
these calls are genuine[5] and actually comport with the putative role
of civil society in much of the literature. I will focus on the calls for

civil society that emanate from unusual suspects, including business actors, who wouldn't otherwise embark on such campaigns. Why did they start doing so in the early 2000s? How do such calls as well as the establishment of civil society associations, particularly business associations, serve their interests? What do the answers tell us about the literature on civil society, authoritarianism, the private sector, and economic reform?

The context within which the shift in alliances takes place is the unraveling of state-centered economies. Although this unraveling is often understood as a function of international pressure, it is primarily a local development that reflects, among other factors, the changing class structure of Arab economies, including Syria, especially among the political elite or the "state bourgeoisie."[6] But bringing business back to the political-economic equation is risky business, especially in Syria where the business community showed its ability to make a dramatic comeback and recapture power, as it did in 1961 when the liberal order was restored after the army generals dissolved the United Arab Republic. Thus, the challenge for the regimes overseeing this transition was to prevent new wealth from being transformed into political power. In Syria, as elsewhere, one avenue for bringing business back in was to do so informally and selectively at first, without venturing into a full-fledged institutional reincorporation of private business interests. As such, what can be called informal economic networks bringing together state officials and business moguls (and later lesser private sector actors) mushroomed around the inflow of capital from the Arab Gulf states in the aftermath of the celebrated 1973 war with Israel.[7]

Both the private elements of the networks and state officials needed each other: the state provided ample patronage and the ability to transgress laws and regulations while businessmen (old and new) provided entrepreneurship, capital, and/or skills. Throughout the 1970s and 1980s, this formula persisted while economic networks were maturing, giving rise to new interests among both the private and public elements thereof. Within the private sector, there was a growing bifurcation between the few privileged elements that are beholden to the state and the rest—a split that undermines possibilities of effective collective action among the business community as a whole.

In the 1990s a new business class emerged with ties to the state and external powers (states and agencies), and possessed relational

characteristics that shaped its further development, such as its proximity to, and dependence on, the regime. This class benefited tremen-
dously from rents (privileges, distinctions, and exemptions that are
not based on reciprocity) at the expense of the health of the Syrian
economy and the average Syrian consumer, let alone citizens. In
short order, some new private sector elites went into politics (via parliamentary participation and other venues) and launched their own
media outlets (first, print; then, to a lesser extent, satellite television).
The new business elites do not share the ideological profile of previous business elite generations. Generally, they are economically liberal but not nationalistic, socially liberal, politically disinvested, pro-
West, pro–"peace" with Israel irrespective of nationalist/political costs,
profligate in their consumption, and exhibit ostentatious behavior.

Fusion of Power and Capital

On the other hand, state elites in Syria went into business beginning
in the 1970s, but much more markedly in the 1980s and 1990s (when
their offspring matured in the latter decade) for at least two reasons.
First was the simple desire for personal gain. More importantly from
a strategic perspective, they went into business as a collective to ensure the dominance of the new private sector by friendly economic
players. This phenomenon, which I term "fusion," is notorious in
Syria. It refers to the combination of decisional power and capital in
the hands of one person: the state official. Though not particular to
Syria, such instances of fusion increase dramatically in contexts
where the state bourgeoisie is distrustful of the business community
or unable to develop durable alliances with it. The effects of this phenomenon, especially when rampant, as in Syria, are invariably negative for both the economy and the institutional context.

To the extent that decisional power and capital are fused in the
hands of officials, state-business relations tend to develop initially
along idiosyncratic, as opposed to institutionalized, lines.[8] Laws, rules,
and regulations tend to be used, issued, and manipulated in an instrumental manner to achieve goals that serve particular individuals. Finally, although this type of fusion is not uncommon in less-developed
countries, it is exacerbated in cases with a history of adversarial state-
business relations based on the initial sociopolitical and socioeconomic
dissonance between power holders and capitalists (which manifests itself in Syria between the originally rural-minoritarian power holders

and the urban Sunni-majority business elite). In such cases, we find that politicians are even quicker to go into business, and lay capitalists are eager for a political representation of sorts when conditions permit, as discussed. These two moves in opposite directions reflect both parties' need for social legitimation: the state bourgeoisie wants to acquire social status independent of their role as state elite, while the new rentier bourgeoisie seeks to acquire a social-political base of sorts that both legitimizes their source(s) of wealth and improves their leverage with the regime. Ultimately, in such context, both parties tend to reproduce the economic status quo in the short run. In the long run, it is the private partners who are reaping the social and political benefits as their capital and power accumulate. When capital accumulation in the private sphere (by both state officials and private businessmen) reaches a threshold of sorts, both the state and private business actors develop an interest in establishing responsive institutions either to protect their interests (from the perspective of private capital) or to monitor them (from the perspective of the state elite, even if they are also in business). In due course, these desires spill into the realm of civil society proper, where these economic actors begin to be legitimized by civil society.

From Individual Relations to Networks to Associations

Thus, state-business relations develop from selective personal relations to networks and finally to associations, reflecting the simultaneous growth of accumulated capital and the structural power of capital.[9] Though unintended consequences (e.g., eventual business empowerment) might appear in the long run, state-business relations continue to be predictably within the regime's control in the meantime. Until 2011, Syria was witnessing such a period where, despite the apparent changes in terms of the nature of business actors and market-institutional environment, it was not a puzzle where true power resided—within the regime. However, this formula is likely to begin acceding to other political economic forms as capital accumulation begins to play a role in determining power relations and balances, even in a less autocratic Syria. In this context, the discussion on unusual civil society suspects infuses itself, with the caveat that the resultant outcome bodes ill, rather than well, for democratization. The unraveling of state-centered economies comes full circle in terms of expanding dictatorship, shifting alliances, and undermining collective action on the part of the business community as a whole.

In the long run a new nexus of power develops between the political and economic elite. This is by no means an automatic process but is wrought by challenging historical junctures that have given form and content to the process of unraveling. The empirical referent here is the record or phases of economic liberalization that Syria underwent since 1986 (informally) but, more credibly, since 1991, when former president Hafez al-Assad heralded what is called the strategy of economic pluralism. That strategy acknowledged officially for the first time the importance of the three sectors (public, private, and joint sector) to the national economy. The second phase is associated with the transition of power from Hafez al-Assad to Bashar al-Assad, a process that opened the door for a more fundamental economic shift. The third phase represents the ongoing final stages in the unraveling of the state-centered economy in Syria.

Syria's Official Phases of Economic Liberalization

First Phase: The Legitimation of Private Capital Accumulation

The first phase of liberalization represents the post-1991 jolt when Syria had its first official all-around "opening" since former president Hafez al-Assad's assumption of power in 1970. Set against a background of a lost decade of development in the 1980s when severe shortages and "newspaper toilet paper" were the order of the day for unfortunate Syrians, every molecule of opening seemed like a breath of fresh air. The consumption boom that followed in the 1990s reflected untapped savings and consumerist hunger but camouflaged a decrepit economic and administrative infrastructure firmly lodged in the late 1960s. Still, the air seemed fresher, until, that is, an economic crisis hit in the mid-1990s, putting a damper on the excitement.

During this period, new upper-middle social formations began to develop around the public-private partnership arrangements or networks—formations that soon procured a stake in the social, if not the political, order in Syria. These new strata served the state and frustrated most Syrians because they added to the perception of transgressions by the powers that be, such as special economic privileges and distinctions. Soon, and for more than a decade to come, these entrepreneurs and their partners in officialdom came to dominate the commanding heights of the Syrian economy and set the stage for the transformation of Syria's official economic identity in 2005. Syrians experienced an era of openness hitherto unseen, where even some of the red lines—the legacy of the Baath Party—were open to some discussion, within reason. This is when Syria began to see semifree parliamentary elections, civil society resurgence, and courageous events like the Tuesday Forum, held yearly by the Economic Sciences Association during spring, where relatively open discussion was the norm.

Second Phase: Change Within Continuity

After Hafez al-Assad's death in 2000, the gaze of citizens and observers of Syria turned to the helm of the Baathist regime to see what would transpire: principally, whether power would transfer smoothly to his son Bashar. Equally important, though, Syria analysts focused on post–Hafez al-Assad events to answer a plethora of questions about the nature of the regime that they had been asking and "answering" without much certainty for the previous three decades. Within a couple of weeks after Hafez al-Assad's departure, it became obvious that transfer of power to Bashar proceeded smoothly—smoother than most analysts predicted. What remained to be seen is whether the posttransition period would be as peaceful, and whether the transition of power to Bashar was indeed complete.

Bashar al-Assad was handed a tough job and was surrounded by a tough crowd whose interests were often tied to the then-existing political-economic arrangements. Any change in any area was likely to damage the interests of some power center; hence the importance of strategy and the organization of reform stages according to, first, the priorities of rule, and, second, to establish the infrastructure of reform (e.g., law, administration). Ultimately, Bashar was able to accomplish both: the new regime was consolidated within three to four years, and the "social market economy" was adopted in 2005 at the tenth Baathist Regional Command Conference. The "social market economy" was an odd mixture of market and state-centered economic policies, a move that reflected the growing power of capital in Syria as well as its proximity to, if not its existence within, the regime. As matters stood, Bashar had the loyalty of all heads of the security branches and the army chief, as well as of the party and bureaucracy, with minimal and, ultimately, insignificant reservations here and there. Bureaucratically, Bashar surrounded himself with a team of younger technocrats who were eager for change. The new cabinet that was formed henceforth reflected this new spirit in most instances.

However, at the point of transition/succession, expectations for Bashar were high, and a "Damascus Spring" seemed on the horizon in the first year after 2000. Damascus especially, but also other cities, witnessed a hitherto unseen mobilization of voices and spaces, calling for a new era of openness and freedom (in all regards) without the threat of emergency laws, arbitrary arrests and rulings, or stifling laws regarding organization and mobilization. However, it did not last long because the opposition was somewhat disarrayed, and the "new-ish" civil society movements, forums, and initiatives seemed to overplay their hands from the perspective of the regime hardliners, if not Bashar. Severe crackdowns ensued, led by hardliners within the regime. There is still speculation regarding the extent to which Bashar concurred with the hardliners from the start or was pressured to move in their direction by the force of unfolding events and proclamations that targeted the Baathist legacy of the former president and sometimes the former president himself. Nonetheless, it was during this phase that the groundwork for the third and crucial phase was established: whatever legislation, policies, or decrees were adopted after 2005, they originated in behind-the-scenes deliberations of influential state actors and some of the private sector moguls. Everything had to wait for Bashar to consolidate his rule and for the regional turbulence to settle, namely, the Iraq War of 2003 and its aftermath.

Third Phase: The Establishment of Market Institutions

Since the adoption of the social market economy in 2005, the economic face of Syria began to change decisively, no matter what observers might have criticized about the nature of the transformation, namely its crony-capitalist dimensions that perpetuate the status quo but with an aura of (decreed) legality. What Syria has witnessed since 2005 is irreversible (less so in the civil society sphere, though the economic and political spheres are not totally separate). The question is whether or not change is moving in a direction that benefits most Syrians. So far the answer is not mysterious: though many Syrians have seen and benefited from a more vibrant economic environment, most have yet to taste its fruits, and a growing number are approaching the poverty line as a result of reduced government spending and subsidies.

To be sure, the economic landscape in Syria is indeed different compared to anything Syria has seen since the mid-1960s. After 2005, Syria saw a number of private banks mushroom, hard currency everywhere (after being taboo for decades), the emergence of holding companies, a flurry of market-supporting organizations and institutions, a Damascus stock exchange (2009), new business councils (2007) and joint business associations (2010), and a steadily widening door for foreign direct investment, with emphasis on regional investors. As discussed earlier, change was always couched in the language of continuity in the late 1980s, throughout the 1990s, and even during the early years of Bashar's presidency. This "couching" has eroded recently as market forces (however imperfect) have steadily advanced and the distributive infrastructure of Syria's state-centered economy has further unraveled. The reasons are primarily structural, and the new team of technocrats that Bashar empowered realized this. In an interview with the star of this process of economic change in 2007, Deputy Prime Minister for Economic Affairs Abdallah al-Dardari told me that Syria is "running out of alternative sources" of revenue after the late 1990s, and that "we can no longer depend on oil revenues as we once did."[10] Something had to be done. Regarding the sensitive and thorny issue of the Hafez regime, he further stated that, "our slogan is 'change within continuity,' but the dangers of persistence [continuity] have become greater than our ability to manage them."[11] In the Syrian political context, this attitude is revolutionary despite falling short of the aspirations of most Syrians.

The third phase of liberalization is actually not as cosmetic as some may claim. In this period political and economic power became consolidated on firmer grounds. But there are built-in limitations as to how far changes can lead to serious reform, especially in the realm of independent civil society and politics. The built-in limitation is simply that, at some level, continuity will not be sacrificed, particularly in terms of the emergence of alternative centers of power. Economic change can proceed so long as the biggest players support the status quo and roam within its orbit, even if this is not infinitely sustainable. So long as economic wealth is not converted to political power, economic change will proceed, "neoliberally" or otherwise. But here is where economic change and fundamental political change part ways. The prime beneficiaries of economic change, given the path it has taken, have been small in numbers and beholden to the existing social and political order. However, the beneficiaries of fundamental political change would be a majority, and have other plans for the political order, though there is little cohesion among them, as was seen during the short and dizzy period of the Damascus Spring in 2000/ 2001 (noting that even that string of efforts represented the secular left more than other sectors of society).

This limitation, or the awareness that real political change is undesirable from the regime's point of view, does not stop all political liberalization. The extension of some civil and political rights has proceeded at various levels, and public space has been selectively widened, but no power-sharing measures or precursors are in sight (e.g., the introduction of laws that allow for the emergence of *independent* political parties). The first lady, Asma, has been a major force behind such change, and it seems that there is some room for the safe and depoliticized expansion of civil society associations and initiatives. In fact, one can argue that this expansion in civil society associations is in part a function of the emergence of new social strata, notably those who benefit from ongoing economic liberalization and who are invariably interested in protecting the infrastructure of personal property, freedoms, and economic action. On the margins, too, there is some genuine change that is affecting certain groups with no ties to economic and political power, visible to the extent that they are less politically oriented if at all. Such change manifests itself in the ability of some groups to organize and speak out so long as they stay under the regime's political radar. Activists have been pushing to include beneficiaries more broadly in this ongoing march, but they collide with the limitations imposed by a risk-averse regime that is unwilling to tolerate independent power centers. At the time of writing, Syria is being rocked by continued uprisings that might well change the rules of the game, if not the regime itself.

The Embryonic Existence of Business Associations and Their Institutional Precursors

The manner in which economic institutions were established or rejuvenated in Syria in the late 1980s, along with the rules of participation, inclusion, and operations that pervade them, reflects the interests of those actors that stood to benefit from the impending formalization of reforms.[12] More significantly, these institutions, primarily the Chambers of Commerce and Industry, represent the organizational expression of maturing economic networks seeking both to secure and to legitimize past, present, and future gains.[13] By 2005, much of these representative institutions had outlived their purpose and were considered dated in terms of their mode of operations, types of sectors to which they were limited (e.g., they did not represent the "new economy" sectors associated with information technology), and even their active leadership, who were viewed as part of the bygone business community. After 2005, Syria began to see a host of new formations, from holding companies to business councils, both of which emerged in 2007 under various guises. By 2010, the first business associations were established, largely in the form of joint ventures between local businesspeople and foreign countries. This development has had its share of criticism as most such associations did not represent the business community as a whole.

The political-economic logic that governed the emergence of earlier business institutions under the tutelage and semicontrol of the public sector continues to govern the emergence of new business associations, with two important exceptions. First, the players are different and their collective power is more potent. More importantly, however, whereas the earlier institutions reflected the interests of maturing economic networks, the variety of institutions, councils, and associations that have emerged, and continue to emerge, since 2005 reflects the growing structural power of capital, allowing independent (but not subversive) capitalists to forge ahead in the business community without the kind of state stewardship that was, in effect, required in the 1980s and 1990s. It is too early to provide a comprehensive evaluation of the emerging institutions, but one can glean a particular path of dependence from the evolution of business institutions since the late 1980s.

Private sector representative institutions such as the Chambers of Commerce and Industry were rejuvenated in the mid- to late 1980s, just when economic networks began to consolidate. These institutions constituted the primary funneling bodies in which identification, initiation, and/or recruitment of potential business allies occurred. *Official* negotiation and bargaining within these institutions and between them and the government does occur but on a limited scale and often concerning the most banal of issues (e.g., what time to close the market in the afternoon during the summer). Generally, the chambers are not (yet) taken seriously as representative institutions by prominent members of the business community:

> The Chamber of Commerce has approximately 50,000 members, but less than 9,000 actually vote. Why do they join if they don't vote, given that these chambers are supposed to serve their interests? . . . Also, artisans are registered with both the Chamber of Industry and the Artisans Cooperatives Union. There is no separation between industrialists, professionals, and artisans. There are sectors that are not represented and sectors that are represented more than once. My business [auto dealer] is not represented. There are a thousand reasons why people join or avoid the chambers.[14]

However, the chambers constituted, and continue to be, latent arenas of mobilization where, for good or for ill, businesspeople come together. There, private sector power centers may be lured, co-opted, or manipulated by some regime strongmen—or they play their cards right with the backing of their capital and themselves penetrate the regime elite and state institutions alike. Alternatively, the chambers represent the strategic arena for those who wish to independently carve out space for themselves in preparation for the coming stages of Syria's liberalization or turmoil.[15] It is these individuals and their partners who were among the pioneers to establish more independent representative business organizations after 2005, including the prominent Joud family.

The context of state-business relations began visibly to change as Bashar consolidated his power and his new economic team began to facilitate the overt entry of business, from a big front door, into social and political life. By 2007, well-connected businesspeople found expression in the two holding companies (Sham Holding and Syria Holding) that were perhaps organized well in advance. According to Haitham Joud, one of the leading figures of Sham Holding and a top businessman in Syria, "We felt that existing institutions are out of step with the economy. . . . There are entire sectors, such as Information Technology, that are wholly unrepresented"[16] within existing business associations. Joud and many of his partners and colleagues consider the holding companies to be the new face of the private sector.

While it is true that these new bodies are more up-to-date and modernized than the chambers, private sector observers are skeptical on two counts. First, they do not deem holding companies to be institutions in the first place, much less "representative" institutions of the private sector, as most businessmen are not, nor are they likely to become, associated with them.[17] Thus, and perhaps consequently, they view this development more as a club than as an institution. Second, it is public knowledge that both holding companies are either wholly dominated by regime officials or by individuals who are ultimately beholden to the regime. Yet, another brand of economists sees a potential for such endeavors whereby they might assume a more productive role under changing circumstances.[18] More meaningful at face value are the sixty-eight business associations that the government gave licenses to in February 2010, most of which, however, are joint trade associations with particular countries, which do not explicitly aim at organizing or representing the domestic private sector.[19] But now the terrain is clearly open for the further emergence, on a larger and more legitimate and even semi-independent scale, of local business associations akin to those that have been operating in Egypt since the 1970s and 1980s, for example, the Egyptian Businessmen Association. It is noteworthy that these new associations, and their future incarnations, are also confined sites that the regime can easily control, that is, they still operate within a low glass ceiling in terms of the changes they might seek. It is not at all surprising, therefore, to see members of the political elite extol the virtues of such institution building on part of the business community.

As for the impact and side effects of the development of a new brand of business associations, we must turn to another type of social resistance. Though most business actors make do with the existing decrepit institutions like the chambers, some have turned to the ostensibly cultural and religious charities realm, which nurture the formation and development of informal groups and organizations capable of collective action in due time (see Chapter 2). The facade of such groups seems innocuous, but by 2010 their power and associative nature in virtually every metropolitan city in Syria could no longer be ignored by the regime. Under changing circumstances, such social networks can be transformed quickly into political ones, as we have seen of late during the 2011–2012 uprising. Short of responding with any explicit and regulatory action, the regime reduced its appeasement of "cultural" Islam, especially in major cities, certainly Damascus, as part of what seems to be a more long-term campaign to reassert the "secular" aspects of society and polity in Syria. Such maneuvers were not ubiquitous at the time of writing, but the proliferation of liquor stores that dot the Mazzeh freeway in Damascus as well as stringent rules on *niqab* and other forms of what is viewed as "excessive" veiling are beginning to roll back the regime's flirtation even with establishment Islam. Ironically, the cultural concessions made to conservative values in March and April of 2011 by way of winning conservative social forces during the uprisings speak of the instrumentality of all such maneuverings.

Conclusion

In May 2010, the Syrian magazine *al-Iqtisadi* (The Economist) published a series identifying the hundred most prominent businessmen in Syria.[20] This exposition is symbolic of the post-2005 business-friendly atmosphere in Syria, a development that was unthinkable just a few years ago. Until the end of 2010, however, the stigma that was associated with the usurping classes has been transformed into the new normal, the status quo, though the uprisings interrupted all such developments, and it remains to be seen to what extent class politics will play a role in the near future.

In any case, the legitimation, and indeed celebration, of capital accumulation by private sector actors in Syria was one of the most significant outcomes of the unraveling of state-centered economies. It ushered in a new era in which the vestiges of Arab semisocialism seemed to have finally been put to rest, dissipated under the weight of new realties that have been fermenting for nearly three decades. Time will tell whether such burial will endure the uprisings now under way.

The causal mechanism at work was not simply the dynamics of an authoritarian regime fending for itself, trying to survive no matter what sort of alliances it must sacrifice (i.e., labor) or new social forces it must foster (i.e., a new business elite). Rather, it was the simple and crude development of the process of capital accumulation. This process reflects a rational choice for the reproduction of power by the political elite under conditions of global capitalist development. As junior partners, initially, private sector members of privileged state-business networks took what they could get from the regime by way of policies and distinctions as they accumulated capital, when no alternative to state patronage existed. With the passage of time, this new business elite began to develop a modicum of independence (in term of capital accumulation and sources of financing) as the privileges associated with public sector patronage (in terms of contracts and tenders, as well as supply of goods) began to dry up. This process was supported by the regime because the political elite assumed they could control it. The reality, however, is that the regime's ability to control the process diminishes to the extent that the state grows dependent on business and capital accumulation beyond the confines of the public sector. As a result, the leverage of the state declines vis-à-vis the segments of the business community who are members of state-business networks. This new equilibrium or ostensible balance of power—between the holders of power and the carriers of capital—takes place as capital accumulation in the private sector slowly becomes an irreplaceable engine for the health of the national economy. Thus, the interest of the state as state, and the regime elite, becomes increasingly dependent on the provision of favorable investment conditions for loyal economic actors, within and outside the state.

For more than three decades now, the processes described here have been unfolding at various rates and in varying degrees, and represent the coalescence of a new and systemic nexus of power between the political and the economic elites. The enduring aspect of this nexus of power is its systemic quality: the basis of the partnership and mutual interests are based less on a politically expedient coincidence of interests and more on the common interests of the political and economic elites in sustaining the systemic conditions of capital accumulation and hence on opposing whatever forces that may disrupt that process. For the most part, this explains the lack of a neat alliance and some of the contradictory outcomes and skirmishes that analysts try to explain away by reference to changing political circumstances or leaderships in this or that ministry or security apparatus. In reality, the bond between the political and economic elites grew stronger at a deeper structural level while intermittent conflicts over economic spoils and fiefdoms occurred at the surface, reflecting mundane self-interest in maximizing profit. But with the erosion of the socialist basis of the now defunct populist distributive formula, this new pursuit of profit and self-interest requires a legitimation of another sort—one that helps to reproduce existing patterns of control (i.e., authoritarian rule) while gradually satisfying international norms.

The claims put forth in this chapter reinforce the central themes of this book, particularly in reference to the need for doing away with the transitology literature that overgeneralizes the import of related topics (e.g., civil society) based on the experience of some cases. As indicated in the introduction to this book, this literature focused excessively on particular objects of study associated with "reform," notably that of civil society as conduit. The premise of this book is to shed constructive doubt on the correlations established in some of the mainstream literature between civil society, reform, and democratization more generally. In keeping with this endeavor, I demonstrate that no connection exists between the growth of civil society and democratization. More significant is the fact that the development of a class-biased civil society contributed to the resilience of authoritarian rule.

Up until the spring of 2011, it is within this context that we could best understand the impulse behind the promotion of a civil society in the developing nexus of power between the political and economic elites; hence, the futility of tracing the impact of such a civil society to pushing back the boundaries of authoritarianism. Civil society in this and other contexts is not an automatic agent of democratic change. It is a constructed arena that can serve various ends based on the conditions of its emergence and development. In the Syrian case, it is an agent for the legitimate reproduction of power. As part of civil society, the mushrooming and development of business associations reflect less the power of an independent business community and more the common interests of the political and economic elites to legitimize capital accumulation, even when preferences diverge at a superficial level. In effect, they become a part of the new nexus of power between the political and economic elites. During the first months of the Syrian uprising, there had been no significant upheaval emanating from the touted civil society circles that were developed in the last decade, particularly among big business. In fact, some of the most robust support of the status quo (if not the regime) has come from sources associated with the development of Syria's "civil society"—namely, big business interests that can be considered one of the regime's and civil society's backbones.[21] By fall of 2012, the violence gripping Syria disrupted all such alliances, save those that are organic to the regime.

Notes

1. Bellin, "Contingent Democrats."
2. See, e.g., Heydemann, "Upgrading Authoritarianism"; and Carothers, "The End of the Transition Paradigm."

3. After the Arab uprisings of 2011, the argument of authoritarian "resilience" was severely conflated with authoritarian "permanence." This conflation reflects more a desire to debunk than to analyze or engage these arguments. Authoritarian resilience refers to the decades in which authoritarian rule in various parts of the developing world flourished beyond the expectations of analysts, especially after the fall of the Soviet Union. These arguments pointed out the social, economic, and institutional reasons (locally and internationally) that maintained the resilience of these regimes, not their permanence.

4. Haddad, "The Formation and Development of Economic Networks."

5. See *New York Times,* "Doors Open to Activists in Syria," 28 August 2010.

6. Other factors include the growing inefficiency, sometimes near collapse or failure of the public sector, and the resultant inability of the state to meet its redistributive commitments.

7. Haddad, "The Formation and Development of Economic Networks."

8. Evans, "State Structures."

9. To be sure, networks continue to exist but fade into the background as they become thinner, albeit effective in terms of high economic policy.

10. Interview with Deputy Prime Minister for Economic Affairs Abdallah al-Dardari, Damascus, 25 July 2007.

11. Ibid.

12. Actual economic reforms, which began in 1986, preceded their officially proclaimed variety in Syria. Economic reform as an official policy—defined as a minimal acknowledgment by the government for a need to liberalize the economic system—was not pronounced until 1991, when the government rejuvenated what came to be known as "economic pluralism" (*al-ta'addudiyya al-iqtisadiyya*). This term, used extensively in official statements by Hafez al-Assad upon his assumption of power in 1970, refers primarily to the actualization of the complementary formula that brings together the public, private, and mixed sectors under the service of the "national economy" (*al-iqtisad al-watani*). For a review of such early statements, which are repeated in nearly every speech or printed text on economic change, see the yearly reports by the Chambers of Commerce and Industry in Damascus and Aleppo, and President Hafez al-Assad's inauguration speeches in 1992 and 1999. Also see (virtually all) papers on the topic of economic reform presented at the Economic Sciences Association since 1991. Even papers by otherwise critical writers and economists have adopted one dimension or another of the *ta'addudiyya* discourse. See, for instance, papers by Nabil Marzouq ("Development and Labor" [*al-Tanmiya wa al-'Ummal*], Conference Series, no. 17 [Damascus: Economic Sciences Association, March 1998]); Sa'id Nabulsi ("Correcting the Problems of the Labor Market" [*Tasheeh al-khalal fi suq al-'amaalah*], Conference Series, no. 6 [Damascus: Economic Sciences Association, 23 March 1999]); and Raslan Khaddour ("Tax and Customs Exemption Policy," *Buhuuth Iqtisaadiyyah 'Arabiyyah,* June 1996) from 1996 to 2000. It is noteworthy that the power of the economic pluralism discourse rests in the fact that parts of

it (e.g., division of labor between the public and the private sector) coincide with progressive economic thought worldwide in the 1990s, albeit only in form. Thus, repeating some of its tenets (e.g., that the public and the private sector ought to complement each other) may be intended to reflect the conditions of sound economic policy, but the unintended outcome, especially when particular vocabulary is used (e.g., *al-iqtisad al-watani*), is to reinforce Assad's discourse.

13. A more detailed discussion of private sector institutions and their role is discussed in Haddad, "The Formation and Development of Economic Networks."

14. Interview with Ihsan Sanqar, Damascus, 29 December 1998.

15. Parliament member and prominent industrialist Riad Saif is a prime example of such personalities.

16. Interview with Haitham Joud, Damascus, 24 July 2007.

17. Interview with prominent economist Nabil Marzouq, Damascus, 22 July 2008.

18. Interview with a seasoned economist and head of a leading business consulting agency in Syria, SCB (Syrian Consulting Bureau), Damascus, 23 July 2008.

19. See Hamidi, "Damascus Rises Economically"; and Mansour and al-Tawashi, "Business Associations," http://all4syria.info/index2.php?option=com_content&task=view&id=29394&pop=1&.

20. See "Abraz 100 rajul a'maal fi suriyya" (The 100 most prominent businessmen in Syria), *al-Iqtisadi* (The Economist), special issue (19 June 2010), http://aliqtisadi.com/PDF/Aliqtisadi95.html.

21. Haddad, "The Syrian Regime's Business Backbone."

5

The Ambiguous Role of Entrepreneurs in Iran

Peyman Jafari

In recent years, "private sector" (*bakhsh-e khosoosi*) and "privatization" (*khosoosi sazi*) have become buzzwords in Iran's political discourse. The roots of this development can be traced back to the presidency of Ali-Akbar Hashemi Rafsanjani (1989–1997), who initiated a shift toward economic liberalization. Privatizations continued under President Mohammad Khatami (1997–2005) but gained real momentum under President Mahmoud Ahmadinejad following the revision of Article 44 of the Constitution in 2005, which in its original form represented a legal obstruction for further privatization. In February 2007, Supreme Leader Ali Khamenei urged the full implementation of the revised Article 44 and even called on the authorities to regard this duty as a kind of "jihad."[1]

Privatization is promoted for different reasons. While some regard it as a panacea for the country's economic misfortunes, for others it represents a potential road toward democratization. The latter logic, which will be scrutinized in this chapter, is popular among many Islamic and secular reformers who take their cues from liberalism. The renowned prodemocracy journalist and activist Akbar Ganji, for instance, writes: "A free [market] economy must become a central demand in the republican movement in order to open the way for an independent sphere from the state (civil society)."[2] Similarly, two Iranian scholars and policy advisers have argued that "while the ownership of industries and companies are transformed, the bases of civil society will be changed. In a patrimonial government-centered econ-

93

omy, civil society is neither meaningful nor useful. But in a liber-alised economy, with a powerful private sector, civil society can be empowered, consequently creating the bases of democratisation."[3]

These claims, of course, are not new. "No bourgeoisie, no democracy," Barrington Moore asserted famously.[4] And Seymour Martin Lipset stressed another correlated variable in explaining this assumed causal relationship between capitalist development and democracy, when he wrote that civil society organizations "are a source of countervailing power, inhibiting the state or any single major source of private power from dominating all political resources."[5]

These claims, of course, are part of the transitology paradigm, which is critically discussed in Chapter 1. A number of authors challenged the assumption that the expansion of the free market gives birth to a bourgeoisie and a civil society that are inherently prodemocratic forces.[6] For instance, Eva Bellin persuasively argued that entrepreneurs, used here interchangeably for "bourgeoisie" and "capitalists" in the private sector, are in fact "contingent democrats." Their enthusiasm for democratization depends on two key variables: state dependence and fear. "State dependence" refers to "the degree to which private sector profitability is subject to the discretionary support of the state. Such support is typically delivered in the form of subsidized inputs, protected market position, close collaboration in the definition of economic policy, and state containment of labor and the capital poor."[7] "Fear" refers to entrepreneurs' concern that "inclusion [of the lower classes] threatens to flood politics with 'the logic of distribution' rather than the 'logic of accumulation.'"[8] Poverty and inequality, labor, and, more generally, social unrest are factors that could increase the perception of fear among entrepreneurs.

If state dependence and fear perception give us an indication of entrepreneurs' inclination to oppose authoritarian states, we also need to measure their ability to do so effectively. Hence, another variable should be added to the equation: the collective power of entrepreneurs, which relies on structural and organizational factors. The question of civil society activism is closely related to the organizational collective power of entrepreneurs, which is a complex issue in the context of Iran. With this theoretical orientation we can now approach the main question of this chapter: What is the role of Iranian entrepreneurs in the changing nature of state-society relations? In order to provide an answer, I first analyze the location of the private sector in the overall economic structure. The second section concentrates on the contingency factors that affect state-business relationships in the context of authoritarianism: the entrepreneurs' structural and organizational collective power, state dependency, and fear perception. The third section focuses specifically on the role of the Iran Chamber of Commerce, Industries and Mines (ICCIM) as the largest organization of entrepreneurs. The last section draws some conclusions and provides a critical theory to contextualize them.

The Private Sector in the Iranian Economy

Following the 1979 revolution, the private sector was squeezed between the semistate or semiprivate sectors and a large number of companies owned by the state. The dominance of the state sector was enshrined in Article 44 of the Constitution, which divides the economy into state, cooperative, and private sectors and relinquished to the state, before the article's revision, all strategic activities such as large-scale production, foreign trade, banking, insurance, power generation, communication, aviation, and shipping. The semiprivate sector mainly comprises the *bonyads* (foundations), most of which were set up after the revolution to provide charity to the poor and the victims of war, but which rapidly developed their own economic activities through a large number of firms.[9] The bonyads are exempted from taxation, operate outside the jurisdiction of the government and parliament, and are only accountable to the Supreme Leader (see Figure 5.1).

During the 1980s, a severe economic decline disrupted the private sector as capitalist market relations unraveled.[10] The war with Iraq (1980–1988) led to the destruction of industries, diverted resources to the military sector, and further intensified the economic role of the state. The private sector also suffered from the postrevolutionary ideological climate that was antagonistic toward capital and promoted redistributive policies.

As Iran entered the 1990s, many of these trends began to reverse. The relative economic recovery after the war rejuvenated the private sector as price controls, tariffs, and restrictive regulations were partially lifted and some companies were privatized as part of Rafsanjani's economic liberalization (see Table 5.1).[11] This resulted in a relatively freer business climate for private sector entrepreneurs in the following decades (see Table 5.2). In addition, in the ideological climate after the fall of the Berlin Wall in 1989, many politicians and

Figure 5.1 Economic Sectors and Capitalist Social Classes

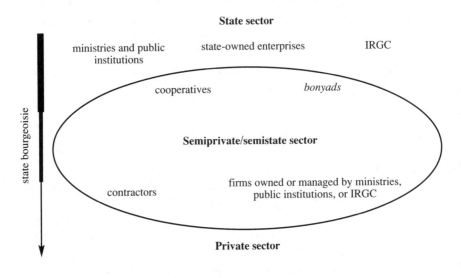

Table 5.1 GDP per Capita, Purchasing Power Parity

1981	1986	1991	1996	2001	2006	2009
6,484	6,249	6,930	7,192	7,822	9,721	10,496

Source: World Bank, International Comparison Program database, www.databank
.worldbank.org.
Note: Data are in constant 2005 international dollars.

intellectuals dropped their statist economics and gravitated toward economic liberalism. This process had its linguistic corollary, with "entrepreneur" (*karafarin*) slowly substituting "capitalist" (*sarmayeh dar*) in the narratives of the media and academia.

The rehabilitation of the private sector that started under Rafsananjani received a real boost under Khatami. The introduction of the Third Five Year Development Plan in April 2000 was a crucial moment in this regard. It aimed "to reduce the system of subsidies and protection, to reduce the administrative red tape, to increase the role of the private sector and to depart from the redistribution policies of the earlier period."[12] The speed of privatization was accelerated as four private banks, two private credit organizations, and two

Table 5.2 Index of Business Freedom in Iran, 1996–2011

1996–2000	2001–2005	2006	2007	2008	2009	2010	2011
55	40	56.1	55.4	55.8	60.6	69.9	69.4

Source: Heritage Foundation, *Index of Economic Freedom* annual publications, http://www.heritage.org/index/download.

Note: The Heritage Foundation measures "business freedom" by looking at different variables, most notably the effort it takes to start a new business, in terms of time, procedures, and costs. It also includes the minimum capital that is required to start a new business. In the table, 0 represents no freedom; 100 represents maximum freedom.

private insurance companies were licensed for the first time.[13] Khatami also approved changes to the Labor Law in order to exempt small businesses from rules that protected workers against dismissal. Private sector activity also benefited from high economic growth rates in 2000–2005, which approached an average of 6 percent per year.

The election of Ahmadinejad in 2005 seemed to turn the tide against the private sector, as bureaucrats and military men moved up the economic and political hierarchy and with economic populism making a comeback. However, the private sector proved resilient and found new opportunities to expand its activities. According to Vali Nasr, "Despite the setbacks of the Ahmadinejad years, many of these [private] companies are growing fast, even expanding into regional markets. Many have benefited from the president's mass expulsion of seasoned state-officials, a fair number of whom are now private sector managers. Others have taken advantage of untapped markets and innovative technology to grow new businesses."[14] Increased private sector activity is reflected in the growth of its share in employment. In 2006 three-quarters of the workforce was employed in the private sector, up from two-thirds in 1986.

Although private sector activity has increased in recent years, it is still constrained by Iran's political, economic, and legal structures that privilege monopolistic capital in the state and the growing semi-private sector. It is estimated that both sectors together control 70 to 80 percent of the economy. This leaves 20 to 30 percent in the hands of the private sector, which includes domestic and foreign trade, small industries and mines, and a growing number of services.[15] It should be noted that the private sector is characterized by a large number of small enterprises with few employees. Thus, in 1996, for instance, more than 95 percent of the private sector enterprises had less than ten workers.[16]

Important players in the semiprivate sector are the bonyads, the Islamic Revolutionary Guards Corps (IRGC),[17] public organizations, and ministries, which run their own economic activities through their enterprises or operate as shareholders. The largest Iranian bonyad, the Foundation of the Oppressed and War Veterans, has 200,000 employees and 350 subsidiaries, and an estimated value of more than $10 billion in assets.[18] Its enterprises are involved in domestic production and foreign trade and investment, with an estimated 10 percent contribution to the GDP. Bonyads have the financial assets to buy privatized companies or a considerable part of their shares. Public institutions like pension funds and the Social Security Investment Company are major players as well. The latter, which manages the financial reserves of the Social Security Fund, oversaw $8.4 billion in investments in various companies in 2009 (2.5 percent of the GDP).[19] Ministries operate in the semiprivate sector as well: "The procurement department of a given ministry would function as a company, selling supplies acquired with the ministry's funds to the ministry, for profit. The profits were then distributed among shareholders, who were mostly the same ministry's personnel."[20]

The IRGC in particular has become an important player in the economy. "From laser eye surgery and construction to automobile manufacturing and real estate, the IRGC has extended its influence into virtually every sector of the Iranian market," asserts one extensive study.[21] In 1990, many of its construction companies were brought under the umbrella of Khatam al-Anbiya (or Ghorb), which has acquired more assets since, benefiting from the close ideological and personal relationship between its commanders and Khamenei.[22] According to estimates, the IRGC has increased its direct and indirect share of the GDP from 5 percent in 1989 to 25 percent in 2010. This process was accelerated after Ahmadinejad became president in 2005 and, paradoxically, by the international sanctions regime against Iran, as Ali Fathollah-Nejad highlights in Chapter 3.[23] In September 2009, for instance, the IRGC bought a 51 percent stake at nearly $8 billion in Iran's biggest telecommunications operator.[24]

As the examples illustrate, privatization has become the main mechanism for the expansion of the semiprivate sector; thus it is also referred to as "pseudo-privatization." It can be concluded that the private sector in Iran is situated in a complex web of economic relations that involve the state and semiprivate actors. This complexity is aggravated by the political structure, which is fragmented between competing centers of power and highly factionalized by formal and informal groups with diverging social, economic, and religious views.[25] It is in this economic and political context that we must identify the Iranian entrepreneurs as a social class. As Figure 5.1 illustrates schematically, the Iranian economy is shaped by three overlapping sectors: state, semiprivate, and private. This economic structure has a social corollary. The commanding heights of the bureaucracy and the military and the management of state-owned companies and the bonyads constitute a state bourgeoisie. Here I define entrepreneurs as capitalists (owners and/or controllers of capital) who operate in the private sector, but I am especially interested in the big entrepreneurs. There is a large group between the capitalists and the big entrepreneurs in the semiprivate sector. This group comprises both those layers of state and military bureaucracy that have developed their own economic activities and those entrepreneurs who are directly dependent on their political connections as contractors or suppliers of the state, and many of them share the same ideological worldview that is promoted in the economic and management departments of various universities.[26]

Contingency Factors: Collective Power, Dependency, and Fear

Entrepreneurs' relationship with the state is, of course, not only shaped by their position in the overall economy. As explained earlier, it is contingent on three main variables: collective power (in terms of structural and organizational factors); state dependency; and perception of fear. Entrepreneurs' will and capability to challenge the authoritarian state and engage in civil society activism in order to achieve political reforms largely depends on these factors.

Structural Factors of Collective Power

The last three decades have witnessed the reconfiguration of the capitalist class in Iran. Adapting the definition provided by Farhad Nomani and Sohrab Behdad, "Capitalists are the owners of physical and financial means of economic activities and employ workers,"[27] they can be divided into the occupational categories of modern (managerial-administrative or professional-technical) and traditional (clerical, sales and service, agricultural and production).

In the 1980s, the number of capitalists decreased, and the shift to petty commodity production created a large number of small producers (see Table 5.3). This trend started to reverse in the 1990s when the number of capitalists increased from 528,000 in 1996 to 1,530,000 in 2006.[28] There has also been an important shift inside the capitalist class. While those in modern occupations constituted 6.5 percent in 1986, they accounted for 17.3 percent in 2006.[29]

The overall structural power of the capitalist class remains limited because of its fragmentation. The majority of the new capitalists employ one or two workers. This is borne out by the average concentration ratio of 3.1 paid workers and 0.5 managerial and technical employees per capitalist.[30] However, the concentration ratio is much higher in big enterprises with more than fifty paid workers. The number of big enterprises rose from 1,252 in 1986 to 2,433 in 1996. In that year, the big enterprises constituted 0.8 percent of the total private enterprises and accounted for 68.8 percent of their output and employed 53.5 percent of their paid workers. These percentages show an increase since 1986.[31] Although the data for 2006 are not available, it is reasonable to extrapolate this trend, as the underlying processes of economic recovery and privatization have continued. As Nomani and Behdad conclude, "While the number of very small firms increased at a very rapid rate, the number of large, modern private firms, with a complex management organization and a high requirement for skilled workers, has also been increasing."[32] These large private enterprises have enough economic leverage to seek political influence.

Table 5.3 Number and Percentage of Capitalists in the Total Workforce (n = 1,000)

	1976		1986		1996		2006	
	Number	%	Number	%	Number	%	Number	%
Capitalists	182	2.1	341	3.1	528	3.6	1,530	7.5
Modern	23	12.8	22	6.5	75	14.1	265	17.3
Traditional	159	87.2	319	93.5	453	85.9	1,266	82.7

Source: Sorhab Behdad and Farhad Nomani, "What a Revolution! Thirty Years of Social Class Reshuffling in Iran," *Comparative Studies of South Asia, Africa, and the Middle East,* Vol. 29, No. 1, 2009, pp. 84–104.

Note: Modern refers to managerial-administrative or professional-technical, and traditional refers to clerical, sales and service, agricultural, and production occupational categories.

One important structural change concerns the traditional bazaar. The mercantile bourgeoisie of the bazaar was one of the main beneficiaries of the revolution. The expropriation of pro-Shah capitalists and the enormous expansion of the black market in the 1980s created ample profit-making opportunities. Most notably, those sections that were well connected to the clerical establishment of the state benefited from export and import licenses, subsidized exchange rates, and contracts. However, as A. Keshavarzian has convincingly argued, the bazaar no longer maintains the internal cohesion and the economic power it had during the revolution.[33] The bazaar is not a homogeneous social force that influences state policies, as it is often perceived. During and after the revolution, only sections of the bazaar became politically active as supporters of Khomeini. Subsequently, they became incorporated into the state. It lost its autonomy and became dependent on a variety of state-controlled and state-regulated networks.[34] Hence the private sector has lost one of its sources of structural power vis-à-vis the state, and the bazaar's importance has dwindled with the growth of the industrial and modern service sectors in the private sector.

Organizational Factors of Collective Power

As the private sector started to recover from the blows of the revolution, it became more vocal in advocating its economic views to policymakers and started to develop civil society activities. The emergence of various newspapers, websites, think tanks and collective organizations is a clear sign of this development. Private sector organizations include the Confederation of the Iranian Industry (Majma'e San'at-e Iran), the Society of Producers (Anjoman-e Tolidgaran), the Association of Industrial Managers (Anjoman-e Modiran-e Sanaye), and the House of Entrepreneurs (Khaneh Karafarinan Iran). The biggest and oldest organization, however, is ICCIM, with 20,000 members in Tehran and another 35,000 in the rest of the country. While many of them are entrepreneurs who are or were active in the private sector, other members belong to the semiprivate sector. In 2006 "an estimated $67 billion in goods and services passed through the hands of the [ICCIM's] just over 3,200 charter members. In addition, by law, its chairman or one of his deputies can sit on, join in deliberations or vote for several key financial and economic bodies, including the Money and Credit Bureau, the Stock Market Council, the Imports

Council, the Centre Against Smuggling of Goods and Foreign Exchange and several others."[35]

The organizational power of the ICCIM, however, is limited because in some important respects it is subordinated to state control. This lack of autonomy makes the categorization of ICCIM as a civil society organization problematic, at least if we define civil society "as the realm of organized social life that is voluntary, self-generating (largely), self-supporting, autonomous from the state, and bound by a legal order or set of shared rules."[36] However, it is equally wrong to describe ICCIM as a fully state-controlled organization, because, as we will see, it serves to articulate the interests of entrepreneurs and lobbies state officials and politicians. This ambiguous character has much to do with the level of state dependency among entrepreneurs. As the description of the private sector in the economy made clear, entrepreneurs find themselves in a web of economic relations that makes them directly or indirectly dependent on the state bourgeoisie. However, it also creates antagonism. Because of their privileges, state and semiprivate sector conglomerates are obstacles for the expansion of the private sector. Hence many entrepreneurs advocate policies that undermine the monopolies and their ties with the state. They also resent the lack of transparency that enables networks of patronage to function in the interests of the monopolies. At the same time they seek access to the networks of patronage in order to outmaneuver their competitors. Thus antagonism and dependency are two poles of the same state-business relationship.

Entrepreneurs and State Dependence

The existence of state dependency, which mainly but not only operates through networks of patronage, places the entrepreneurs in a contradictory position. Those who are in these networks and benefit from them experience political constraints when they strive to become independent economic actors. On the other hand, those who are excluded or placed less favorably in these networks experience the economic disadvantage of their situation. Entrepreneurial dependency on the state has two main sources: (1) the patronage networks based on political and social relations and (2) the general state policies that influence the business environment.

Because of the major economic role of state and public institutions, the bonyads, and the IRGC, those who are politically well connected to them are favored as contractors, suppliers, and recipients of low–interest rate loans and licenses. As we will see later, the Society of Islamic Coalition (Jamiyat-e Motallefeh-ye Islami, in short Motallefeh) and its sister organization, the Society of Islamic Associations of Guilds and Bazaars of Tehran, provide a good example of how certain private bazaar merchants have used political connections to their economic benefit.[37] Political connections are also important in the modern industrial and service sectors. As the state increasingly outsourced its activities, well-connected contractors and suppliers have benefited. In 2004, for instance, the state ministries employed more than 10 percent of their personnel through contractors.[38]

According to Nomani and Behdad, "Many of those who gained access to state power found lucrative opportunities for personal gain. . . . With their political power and their leverage at the nodes of rent-seeking activities, and little fear of any political risk, they successfully managed a high rate of capital accumulation and constituted the nucleus of the new elite capitalist class in the newly formed oligopolistic structure surrounding bonyads, state-owned enterprises, and government bureaucracy."[39] These "lucrative opportunities" could also be illegal. In 1995, for instance, the brother of the director of the Foundation of the Oppressed and War Veterans, Mohsen Rafiqdoost, was found guilty of embezzling $450 million.

Social connections, which are often intertwined with political power, form another mechanism for economic profiteering. Kinship and intermarriage were constitutive factors in the emergence of the political elite during the revolution. Most notably, clerical families and their relatives have used their family connections to develop or expand economic activities, often through the bonyads and religious organizations. The term *aghazadegan* (the offspring of the gentlemen) refers to this stratum. The Rafsanjanis are a case in point. They have transformed into

> commercial *pashas*. One brother headed the country's largest copper mine; another took control of the state-owned TV network; a brother in law became governor of Kerman province, while a cousin runs an outfit that dominates Iran's $400 million pistachio export business; a nephew and one of Rafsanjani's sons took key positions in the ministry of oil; another son heads the Tehran Metro construction project (an estimated $700 million spent so far).[40]

Although political and social connections are important, a more general practice leads to state dependence for a much larger group of entrepreneurs: the state's economic policies. After the revolution, the

import-substitution strategy under the Shah was by and large continued, mainly by state control on foreign trade and the exchange rates.
This resulted in the decline of consumer imports, as a percentage of
all imports, from 25 percent in 1978–1980 to 14 percent in 1996–
1998.[41] Although the trade policy has become more open since the
1990s, many entrepreneurs are still dependent on the state for import
licenses, economic protectionism, and contracts. Gaining access to
subsidized products, especially fuel, is an important factor as well. In
2007–2008, private industries with more than 150 workers accounted
for nearly 40 percent of the total industrial energy consumption.[42]
The degree of state dependency becomes clear when we take into account that between 1997 and 2007 energy subsidies hovered between
15 and 20 percent of the GDP.[43] These subsidies and other "rents"
are, of course, financed by oil income.[44]

It is important to note that the paths to political influence are
shaped by a specific institutional environment. State institutions are
fragmented into competing centers of power, and the political environment is highly factionalized by formal and informal groups that
try to control the various state institutions. Hence, entrepreneurs use
political factions and different institutions to influence policies. Entrepreneurs, members of political factions, and institutions are
brought together in networks of patronage that are based on political
and personal loyalties.

Fear Perception

This contingency factor refers to the perception of instability and insecurity resulting from the (potential) social and political struggles of
the lower classes. This fear is especially tangible in a country that has
experienced a revolution with strong anticapitalist sentiments, which
still resonate within the working class. The consolidation of the Islamic Republic was a crucial factor in containing working-class rad-
icalism, as independent trade unions and socialist organizations were
suppressed and banned. Islamic Labor Councils were established
under the umbrella of a state-controlled union, Khane Kargar. The
populist arrangements of the 1980s and the pressures of the war
aligned sections of the working class to the state or at least pacified
them. However, with the economic liberalization that started in the
early 1990s, the populist coalition started to unravel. After the Islamic left faction started to lose its position in the state institutions

and then embraced free market politics, the lower classes lost one of their official channels to influence policies. Even Khane Kargar was increasingly alienated, for example, by the reform of the Labor Law during Khatami's presidency and started to lose some of its control over labor activism. The perception of fear among entrepreneurs is especially important in Iran because inequality is relatively high—the Gini index floats between 40 and 45—and at the same time the demand for social justice is firmly rooted in society. Hence many entrepreneurs are conscious of the fact that any struggle against the state might also create a space for the lower classes to demand redistributive measures and to create independent, potentially confrontational organizations.

Although it needs more rigorous scrutiny, this perception apparently played an important role in determining entrepreneurs' attitude toward the political reform project under the Khatami presidency. Generally, entrepreneurs tended to support the reformist faction around Khatami and the pragmatist faction around Rafsanjani in opposition to the (neo)conservative forces aligned with the monopolies. Hence they tend to resist the authoritarian state and demand transparency. However, once street protests threatened to lead to political destabilization and labor activism was revived, entrepreneurs started to waver in their support.[45] Paradoxically, privatization and economic liberalization started to hinder political liberalization as the state antagonized the lower classes, reinforcing the authoritarian nature of the state in order to contain social unrest.[46]

One close observer of Iran's private sector, Albrecht Frischenschlager, believed that domestic and foreign businessmen were relieved when the political crisis in Iran ended, after the conservatives won the municipal elections in 2003.[47] Saeed Hajjarian, one of the strategists of the reform project, made this point more explicit in May 2005:

> During Khatami's first term, the private sector was a mainstay of the reformist movement, but that is no longer true. The private sector is more concerned with stability and order than with democratic reform, and some elements of it have now formed links with the conservatives. . . . The private sector is now part of the problem facing democracy in Iran.[48]

What this evaluation of the contingency factors makes clear is that Iranian entrepreneurs are weak in structural and organizational terms, are largely dependent on the state, and fear the working class and the potential disruption of the poor.

Iran Chamber of Commerce, Industries and Mines

Having looked at the contradictions and trends that characterize the economic sector in Iran and its actors, we can now turn to examine in some detail their biggest organization, the ICCIM, in relation first to civil society activism and then in relation to democratic political reforms. ICCIM was established in March 1970, after various local chambers of commerce merged with the national chamber of industries and mines.[49] The 1979 revolution brought it to the verge of collapse, but it was revived by a council that Ayatollah Khomeini appointed to supervise it. Its members were mainly supporters of Motallefeh, including Asadollah Asgarowladi and Alinaghi Khamoushi.[50] Asadollah Asgarowladi, whose brother, Habibollah, is a leading member of Motallefeh and a former minister of commerce, became a leading member of ICCIM and president of several of its international chambers. Alinaghi Khamoushi, himself a leading member of Motallefeh, became president of both ICCIM (1980–2007) and the Tehran Chamber of Commerce, Industries and Mines (TCCIM) (1980–2002).

While initially ICCIM was under the total control of the state, it started to develop a life of its own after the introduction of elections for its Council of Directors in 1988 and the revival of the private sector in the 1990s. As previously described, this process created a new entrepreneurial class that increasingly wants to assert itself in the political arena. ICCIM is structured around three bodies: the Supreme Supervisory Board, the Council of Directors, and the Board of Delegates. It has branches at the provincial level, which operate autonomously and have their own Council of Directors and a Board of Delegates. The elections for these bodies are held every four years. The members in each province elect fifteen people for the Board of Delegates—six from commerce, six from industry, and three from the mining sector. As an exception, the TCCIM's Board of Delegates has sixty members. The Board of Delegates of each branch elects, according to its total membership, a number of representatives for the ICCIM Board of Delegates.[51] These representatives, together with one delegate for each syndicate or union that is part of ICCIM, constitute the Board of Delegates that functions as a parliament. The

Council of Directors, which functions as the executive body, and its president are elected by the members of the Board of Delegates. ICCIM's Supreme Supervisory Council is responsible for formulating an overall strategy and oversees its execution. It has to ratify the regulations on membership and it has the right to dissolve chapters of ICCIM.

The autonomy of ICCIM is constrained by two mechanisms. First, there is the membership of three ministers (commerce, economy, and finance; industry and mines; and agriculture) and the director of the Institute of Standard and Industrial Research (Sazman-e melli-ye standard), along with the president and the two vice-presidents of ICCIM in the Supreme Supervisory Council. Second, the government is allowed to appoint twenty representatives to the Board of Delegates of TCCIM—the biggest and most influential chapter of ICCIM in the country. The other forty are elected by the membership: twenty have to be active in commerce, sixteen in the industrial sector, and four in the mining sector.

The organizational structure of ICCIM allows entrepreneurs to organize debate and elect their representatives but within the constraints enforced by state representatives.[52] However, it is important to note that the role of the government inside ICCIM is contested by its members, which reflects a real degree of civil society activism. In fact, ICCIM's strategic program aims to "strengthen the position of ICCIM as a nonstate, knowledge-based and inclusive organization."[53] Various members of ICCIM have also publicly challenged the role of the government in its internal life. As one of its leading members has argued, "The Chamber of Commerce is, like other civil society institutions, not independent from the state. . . . However, the existence of this kind of institution is better than their absence, because they have been able to achieve some positive results despite their shortcomings."[54]

Historically, the activities of the chambers have been more oriented toward commerce than industry. Concomitantly, pro-bazaar conservative forces, Motallefeh in particular, have dominated ICCIM. The economist Ahmad Roosta points out that "the activities of the Chamber are more oriented to trade instead of production and industry. This stems from the history of economic activities and the structure of the economy, which have created a situation in which there is more attention for import and import factors than export."[55] In the last decade, however, ICCIM's membership from the industrial and mining sectors has increased, and its elected officials originate increasingly from these sectors, creating tensions between "traditionalists" and "modernists" during elections.

In functional terms, ICCIM's structure facilitates two different processes. First, it allows members to develop a collective identity and organization that can represent them to the public in a positive way and increase their bargaining power vis-à-vis the state. This function can be defined as civil society activism. Thus ICCIM provides training for its members on issues ranging from human resources management and marketing strategies to e-commerce and labor laws.[56] It allows members to articulate their views and lobby for them by organizing expert commissions, seminars, and conferences; and by conducting research and producing publications such as a monthly magazine. In order to influence politics, it organizes meetings for its members and parliamentarians on a provincial and national level. Representatives of ICCIM participate in various governmental councils and institutions, increasing their numbers from 44 in 2008 to 120 in 2010.[57]

The specific policies for which ICCIM has lobbied the government are instructive for the economic interests that it represents—those of the private sector. It pressured Khatami's government to reform the Labor Law in order to exempt small enterprises from some of its provisions. In February 2000 all enterprises with five or fewer workers were exempted, and in January 2003 the right of nonobservation was extended to those enterprises with ten or less workers.[58] It tried to mitigate the negative effects of energy subsidy reforms on its members in 2010–2011 by lobbying the state.[59] ICCIM is a strong advocate of the implementation of Article 44 and privatization. It has produced reports that criticize the emergence of a semiprivate sector through "pseudo-privatization." At a meeting between members of ICCIM and Minister of Health Care Vahideh Dastjerdi, the president of the syndicate of chemical and medical producers complained that Iran's medical market is worth 2,500 billion tomans (more than $2.4 billion), but companies that belong to the Social Security Fund, the public organization that finances and provides welfare programs, have a share of 40 percent in the medical market, while the Sobhan and Shafa holdings that belong to the national bank each have a 10 percent share. That leaves only 40 percent for the private sector. He concluded: "The medicine mafia is in the hands of the state."[60]

The second process that ICCIM facilitates is more informal: it provides access to patronage networks. This can be viewed as a form of social capital building associated with civil society. Networks of patronage are, by definition, not transparent. Although this lack of transparency is an obstacle for outsiders, it provides opportunities for insiders and increases social capital, although a form that is normatively negative. For instance, in September 2010, the government announced that parts of the bazaar, especially the sellers of gold, had to pay more tax. In response, the gold sellers went on strike, and, after meeting with their representatives, the government announced that they had to pay only 15 percent more tax instead of the announced 70 percent. The website Alef, which is close to Ahmadinejad's neoconservative faction, claimed that "in the recent protests of the traditional Tehran bazaar a certain influential and famous political organization was involved."[61] This was a reference to Motallefeh, due to the involvement of its high-profile member Habibollah Asgarowladi in the negotiations.

ICCIM, Political Reforms, and Factions

Despite important changes in its leadership since 2002, ICCIM has not developed any explicit program to promote political reforms or democratization. Its internal politics suggest that it is divided on this issue and that those who promote political reforms do so in order to carve out a bigger space for their own economic activities in an arena that is dominated by politically well-connected actors. As a result, like Iran's political system, the internal life of ICCIM is factionalized. Hence ICCIM's internal life has transformed more or less in accordance with the shifting balance of power between factions, but it has been also influenced by the developments in the private sector and the changes in its relationship with the state.

The first sign that something was changing in the internal life of ICCIM and its relationship with the state came with the elections for TCCIM in 2002. The reformist government's explicit support for private business, along with the changes it introduced to the electoral regulation of the chambers and its invitation to entrepreneurs, helped boost the election turnout. For the first time, the leadership of the pro-bazaar conservatives was seriously challenged. Conservative Alinaghi Khamoushi had been president of both TCCIM and ICCIM since 1980. The pro-bazaar conservatives also had a strong base in the Ministry of Commerce, especially through members of Motallefeh. Habibollah Asgarowladi and Yahya Al-Eshaq, both leading members of Motallefeh, have served as ministers of commerce and have close relations with ICCIM. Habibollah Asgarowladi's brother, Asadollah, is a prominent member of ICCIM.

However, in 2002, a group of entrepreneurs and technocrats oriented toward a modern and industrial economy entered the elections to oust Khamoushi. This group was headed by the young engineer Mohammad Reza Behzadian, who was explicit about his antitraditionalist and proreform program:

> Creating economic development and economic democracy in the country is one of the fundamental plans of the change and reform aspiring group inside the Chamber [of Tehran]. . . . Iran's economy needs the participation of all entrepreneurs and economic thinkers. . . . Therefore, one of our priorities in the future is to establish syndicates, organizations and non-governmental institutions.[62]

Under Behzadian's leadership, the proreform candidates won the majority of the Board of Delegates in TCCIM.[63] According to Jamshid Edalatiyan Shahriyari, one of the reformist candidates who was elected to TCCIM, the reformists and conservatives agreed on the importance of the free market and the necessity of competition and integration into the world market. They diverged, however, on the issues of "open politics" and "transparency." "Reformists want to increase the participation of the private sector in its own destiny, while the traditionalists prefer lobbying [the government] to achieve their own goals."[64] This critique probably reflects the resentment among entrepreneurs who are not so well connected to the networks of patronage.

After the elections, the diverging views between the reformists and the conservatives led to conflicts. Khamoushi used his power as president of ICCIM to undermine and outmaneuver Behzadian until he was removed in 2005 and replaced by Mohammad Nahavandian. Nahavandian received the votes of the members on the Board of Delegates of TCCIM who had been appointed by the government, which was now controlled by the neoconservatives around newly elected president Ahmadinejad. Even so, the arrival of proreform entrepreneurs in TCCIM meant that new concepts such as transparency, meritocracy, freedom of speech, and civil society entered its discourse.

The next important development came with the election for the chambers on 21 February 2007. This time, the turnout was even higher. An estimated 6,000 to 7,000 of the 19,000 members of TCCIM went to the ballot box in 2007, in contrast to the 1,700 members who had participated in 2002.[65] This reflected a defensive response among entrepreneurs who sought to both increase their collective power and position themselves closer to the corridors of political power and networks of patronage, as the neoconservatives around Ahmadinejad were reviving the anticapitalist rhetoric of the 1980s.[66] The reformists regarded the chamber elections as an opportunity to win back some ground after they had lost parliament and the presidency to the neoconservatives.

The result was not only increased participation but also increased competition as three groups vied to win seats on the TCCIM Board of Delegates. The Pursuers of Change (Khastaran-e Tahavol), headed by Behzadian, represented the views of the reformists. The modern right was represented by the Renewers (No Afarinan), headed by Nahavandian. Khamoushi and Asadollah Asgarowladi were the prominent leaders of the traditional right or the conservatives, running under the banner of Activists for Development (Fa'alan-e Tose-e). The reformists and the modern right scored a big victory, although the demarcations between the three groups were not always clear, as many candidates appeared on two lists.[67]

The election outcome strengthened those who wanted a more independent course for the chambers as civil society institutions of the private sector. Mohsen Safa'i Farahani, the most prominent candidate of the reformists after Behzadian, was elected to TCCIM as a staunch defender of the private sector. Notably, he was also a member of the central committee of the biggest reformist alliance, the Islamic Iran Participation Front. He emphasized that the chambers should try to get their members into state institutions like the parliament in order to represent the interests of the private sector.[68] Not surprisingly, Safa'i Farahani was one of the prominent reformists arrested during the political fallout of the presidential election in June 2009. In his election campaign, Ahmadinejad accused him of "economic corruption."

The conflict between the neoconservative government and the proreform members of TCCIM was also manifested in the outcome of the election of its Council of Directors. Although the reformists had won the elections for the Board of Delegates of the Tehran chamber, the government interfered to keep them out of the Council of Directors. The twenty representatives appointed to TCCIM's Board of Delegates by the neoconservative government voted as a block and in alliance with the traditional right minority against the reformist candidate Mohammad Reza Heydari.[69] As a result, Yahya Al-Eshaq, who had been a leader in the Motallefeh Party and the Foundation of the Oppressed, and a minister of commerce during Rafsanjani's presidency, was elected as the president of the TCCIM.

The next stage in this conflict came with the election for the Council of Directors of ICCIM and its president in June 2007. The incumbent president of ICCIM, Alinaghi Khamoushi, headed the conservative list, which also included Asadollah Asgarowladi and Manuchehr Gharavi (former director of Iran Khodro). "In my view the Chamber needs no change! The meaning of change is wrong, what does change mean?" declared Asgarowladi on election day, expressing the fear of the conservatives for the new forces.[70] The reformists had put forward Mohsen Mehr Alizadeh, but Khamoushi's main challenger was Nahavandian, who had become the president of TCCIM in 2005. He had the image of an able state manager, by serving as an adviser to the minister of commerce during Rafsanjani's presidency and leading the National Center for Globalization Studies when it was funded in 2003. His education at George Washington University was another factor that made him an attractive figure for those who wanted to strengthen the private sector and promote the modernization of the economy, while maintaining good relations with the state.

Although the neoconservative government, through its position on the Supervisory Board, interfered to block Nahavandian's candidacy by changing the regulations, it had to undo this after protests. Before the election, Nahavandian declared his fourteen-point program, which included full support for the implementation of Article 44 of the Constitution in order to strengthen the private sector; empowerment of the chambers as independent organizations from the state; active presence of the private sector in the negotiations to join the [World Trade Organization]; and the expansion of Iranian enterprises in world markets.[71]

On 12 June 2007, Nahavandian won the election after receiving 165 of the 305 votes on ICCIM's Board of Delegates and after many of the proreform members had made an alliance with the modern right reformists to drive out Khamoushi. Also the government gave tacit support to Nahavandian, realizing that it was time for Khamoushi to go and fearing a reformist winning the election. After his victory, Nahavandian declared: "The period of thinking in terms of a statist and centralized economy has ended, because the groups and tendencies that stressed the intervention in the economy during the first decade and parts of the second decade after the revolution, now have accepted that a centralized and statist economy is not working anymore."[72] He also expressed, diplomatically, his view about the relations between the ICCIM and the government: "The proximity of the state and the people is not bad; it even has to be a goal. However, we have to prevent that the Chamber repeats the views and politics of the government instead of expressing the views of the entrepreneurs."[73]

Conclusion

From the analysis in this chapter, we can conclude that the contingency factors point in the direction of an ambiguous attitude among entrepreneurs in Iran toward civil society activism and democratization. The structure of the economy makes the semiprivate sector not only a competitor for entrepreneurs, but developing good relations with it or even becoming part of it provides profit-making opportunities. On the one hand, many entrepreneurs find themselves in an oppositional relationship with economic monopolies tied to the state and the semiprivate sector. Hence they have an interest in political reforms that undercut the authoritarian structures that privilege the monopolies. On the other hand, however, the entrepreneurs exhibit a high level of state dependency. While challenging networks of patronage is one option to conquer a bigger economic space, becoming part of those networks remains an attractive alternative that meets less resistance from the state.

The second factor that reduces the entrepreneurs' potential to become agents of democratization is their fear of perceived political and social instability. Finally, entrepreneurs' collective power (structural and organizational) remains still weak vis-à-vis the state. Because of this situation, entrepreneurs have an ambiguous relationship with the authoritarian state. This explains why the space in which entrepreneurs operate is a mix of civil society and patronage networks, although one in which the latter element is dominant. Hence business organizations' activities are centered more on lobbying than activism. This dynamic is reinforced by state actions, which, resembling the Syrian case, are aimed at controlling business associations through direct and indirect interventions

This contention is supported by the analysis of the nature and actions of the ICCIM. First, while it opposes the power of economic monopolies, it has not developed a prodemocratic agenda. However, it should be emphasized that its factionalized internal dynamics reflect the heterogeneity of entrepreneurs regarding political reforms. There are certainly advocates of democratic reforms in and outside of ICCIM who challenge the power of the state and its economic allies, but they have not been able to play a decisive role until now. Second, the nature of ICCIM as a civil society organization is itself ambiguous, as it is a playing field for both state and private actors. Hence, it not only functions as a transmission belt to articulate the demands of the private sector to the state but also functions in the opposite direction. The state uses ICCIM to disseminate its views in the private sector and the civil society at large. It also seeks to build a base of social support among sections of entrepreneurs by institutionalizing dependent state-business relationships.

It would be unsatisfactory to conclude this chapter without addressing the objection of those adherents of the "no bourgeoisie, no democracy" theorem who argue that the entrepreneurs' ambiguous position is merely transitory. Thus they argue that genuine privatization would strengthen the private sector as a prodemocratic force. In *The Rise of Islamic Capitalism,* Vali Nasr argues that the "momentum for reform will become unstoppable only if the private sector and the middle class grow bigger and stronger."[74] He draws his inspiration from Europe's Industrial Revolution that spawned "a new intellectual class of the likes of Adam Smith and David Hume, who gave voice to the aspirations of the rising commercial classes. Commerce and the social changes it requires and stimulates changed mind-sets, not the other way around."[75]

This logic reveals the lasting influence of the modernization theory that views the historical development of capitalism as a progressive, unidirectional, and homogenizing force in a global context. It is informed by the Weberian meta-dichotomy of "tradition" versus "modernity." In its wake follow other dichotomies such as "authoritarianism" versus "democracy," "state" versus "private," and "nationalization" versus "privatization." Consequently, phenomena that lie between these poles are regarded as "grey areas" of hybridity, which are supposedly in transition to one of the poles. This transitology paradigm has been criticized in Chapter 1 and elsewhere.[76]

As the editors suggest in Chapter 1, it is more fruitful to analyze the ambiguous nature of Iran's semiprivate sector, civil society, and "pseudo-privatization" in its own right. A fruitful course in this direction could be taken by applying the insights of international historical sociology, which have further developed the concept of "uneven and combined development" pioneered by the Russian Marxist revolutionary Leon Trotsky.[77] This perspective "takes its starting point from world economy, not as a sum of national parts but as a mighty and independent reality which has been created by the international division of labour and the world market and which in our epoch imperiously dominates the national market."[78] When we analyze the development of entrepreneurs, the private sector, and civil society, and their relations to democratization, the historical and international context of development becomes crucial. Thus the assumed pro-democratic role of entrepreneurs, civil society, and social capital involves an extrapolation from the experience of Western industrial countries to the realities of developing countries, without considering the different spatial and temporal conditions.[79] Developing a research program that takes into account these conditions of global capitalism is indispensable for understanding the nature of civil society and business associations in countries such as Iran, Russia, and China, where capitalism does not necessarily equate the free market.[80]

Notes

1. The Office of the Supreme Leader, "Ayatollah Khamenei Instructs Authorities in Charge of Article 44 Drive," 19 February 2007, http://www.leader.ir/langs/en/index.php?p=contentShow&id=3597.

2. Ganji, *Republican Manifesto,* p. 99.

3. Molavi and Salimi, *Privatise to Democratise?* p. 9.

4. Moore, *Social Origins of Dictatorship and Democracy,* p. 418.

5. Lipset, "Some Social Requisites of Democracy," p. 84.

6. On the role of the bourgeoisie, see Therborn, "The Role of Capital and the Rise of Democracy"; and Rueschemeyer, Stephens, and Stephens, *Capitalist Development and Democracy.* The notion that the relationship between the bourgeoisie and democratization depends on the temporal and spatial context of the social formation in which this relationship is rooted goes back to Marx and two of his Russian followers, Parvus and Trotsky, although they are almost never mentioned in this context. See Day and Gaido (eds.), *Witnesses to Permanent Revoluton.* On the role of civil society (organizations), see Kleinberg and Clark (eds.), *Economic Liberalization, Democratization and Civil Society;* and Mercer, "NGOs, Civil Society and Democratization."

7. Bellin, "Contingent Democrats," p. 180.

8. Ibid., p. 181.

9. On the bonyads, see Maloney, "Agents or Obstacles? Parastatal Foundations and Challenges."

10. Nomani and Behdad, *Class and Labor in Iran,* pp. 191–192.

11. For accounts about Iran's economic postrevolutionary trajectory, see Behdad, "From Populism to Liberalism"; Hakimian, "Institutional Change";

Salehi-Esfahani and Pesaran, "The Iranian Economy in the Twentieth Century"; and Salehi-Isfahani, "The Oil Wealth and Economic Growth in Iran."

12. Alizadeh, "Iran's Quandary," p. 276.

13. Amuzegar, "Iran's Third Development Plan," p. 52.

14. Nasr, *The Rise of Islamic Capitalism,* pp. 80–81.

15. Khajehpour, "Domestic Political Reforms and Private Sector Activity in Iran."

16. Nomani and Behdad, *Class and Labor in Iran,* p. 91.

17. Also known as Sepah-e Pasdaran-e Enqelab-e Islami or simply as "Pasdaran."

18. Ilias, "Iran's Economic Conditions," p. 8.

19. Harris, "Pseudo-Privatization in the Islamic Republic."

20. Karbassian, "Islamic Revolution and the Management of the Iranian Economy," p. 37.

21. Wehry et al., *The Rise of the Pasdaran,* p. 55.

22. Hen-Tov and Gonzalez, "The Militarization of Post-Khomeini Iran," p. 49.

23. Ehteshami and Zweiri, *Iran and the Rise of Its Neoconservatives.*

24. Ilias, "Iran's Economic Conditions," pp. 8–9.

25. See Moslem, *Factional Politics in Post-Khomeini Iran.*

26. Articles 21 and 48 of the Fourth Development Plan (March 2005–March 2009) stimulated the establishment of new entrepreneurship departments and created a common programmatic framework for these and older departments.

27. Nomani and Behdad, *Class and Labor in Iran,* p. 87.

28. Behdad and Nomani, "What a Revolution!" p. 91.

29. Ibid., p. 101.

30. Ibid.

31. Nomani and Behdad, *Class and Labor in Iran,* p. 91.

32. Behdad and Nomani, "What a Revolution!" p. 94.

33. See Keshavarzian, *Bazaar and State in Iran.*

34. Arjomand, *After Khomeini,* p. 122.

35. Yasin, "New Era for Iran's Private Sector."

36. Diamond, "Rethinking Civil Society," p. 5.

37. See Keshavarzian, "Regime Loyalty and Bazari Representation."

38. "A Problem Called Contract Workers" (Masale-i be name karkonan-e Sherkati), *Iran Economics Monthly* (Mahnameh Eghtesad-e Iran), January–February 2007, http://www.iraneconomics.net/fa/articles.asp?id=2657.

39. Behdad and Nomani, "What a Revolution!" p. 99.

40. Klebnikov, "Millionaire Mullahs."

41. Amid and Hadjkhani, *Trade, Industrialization and the Firm in Iran,* p. 49.

42. Sharif Institute for Economic and Industrial Studies, *Evaluation of the Consequences,* p. 108.

43. Ibid., p. 36.

44. For a broader discussion of "rent-seeking mechanisms," see Bjorvatn and Selvik, "Destructive Competition."

45. Moghissi and Rahnema, "The Working Class."

46. For a comparative study of this mechanism, see Ehteshami and Murphy, "Transformation of the Corporatist State in the Middle East."

47. Farhadian, "Beyond Khatami's Reform Era," p. 7.

48. Khojasteh Rahimi and Sheibani, "Gathering of Intellectuals for Democracy."

49. However, its history can be traced back to much older precursors that go back to the 1880s. See Ashraf, "Chamber of Commerce"; and Saeidi and Shirinkam, *Moghe'iyat-e tojjar va saheban-e sanaye dar Iran-e dore-ye Pahlavi.*

50. Other members were Ali Nasab, Hajj Tarkhani, Mir Fendereski, Mohammad Ali Navid, Abolfazl Ahmadi, and Alla Mir-Mohammad Sadeghi. For an account of this early period, see the interview with Sadeghi by Mehrjoo in *Shargh* (n.a.).

51. A provincial chamber elects one delegate for its first 150 members and one delegate for every 100 members above that.

52. For a discussion of ICCIM's internal organization, see Heshmati Mola'i, "The Pathology of the Position and Function of the Chamber of Commerce."

53. ICCIM, "Strategy of the Iran Chamber of Commerce, Industries and Mines," http://www.iccima.ir/fa/index.php?option=com_content&view=article&id=46232&Itemid=888.

54. "Dolat pedarkhande-ye otagh-e bazargani."

55. Ibid.

56. ICCIM, *Two-Years Report,* pp. 64–66.

57. Ibid., p. 33.

58. Malm and Esmailian, *Iran on the Brink,* p. 56.

59. Center for Economic Studies and Evaluations of ICCIM, "Opinion Poll Among Private Sector Entrepreneurs. Theme: The Subsidy Reform Bill" (Tarhe Nazarsanji Az fa'alan-e Bakhshe Khosusi Keshvar. Mozu' Nazarsanji: Laye-he Hadafmand Kardan Yarane-ha), Tehran: ICCIM, Azar 1388/ November–December 2009, www.iccim.ir/fa/images/stories/DATA/research center/nazar_sanji_hadafmand_sazi_yaraneha_site.pdf.

60. *San'at va tose-e,* "The Medicine Mafia Is in the Hands of the State," p. 11.

61. *San'at va tose-e,* "The Bazaar Under the Threat of the New Principalists," p. 16.

62. Hassan Nia, "A Chamber for Development and Political Democracy."

63. Ibid.

64. *Etemad Meli* (9 November 2004).

65. *Kargozaran,* "The Elections of Iran's Capitalists Took Place."

66. Reed and Pirouz, "Election Aftershock in Corporate Iran."

67. Mehrjoo, "Piruzi-ye eslahtalabane."

68. *Shargh,* "The Chamber Is Not a Political Arena."

69. Heydari went on to become consul in Oslo in 2007 but resigned from his post in 2010 in protest against the violent reaction of the government against participants and leaders of the Green Movement.

70. *Kargozaran,* "The Elections of Iran's Capitalists."

71. *Donya-ye Eghtesad,* "Asman-e abi-ye Nahavandian va khaterat-e khakestari-ye Khamoushi," 24/03/1386 (14 June 2007).

72. *Donya-ye Eghtesad,* "Doran'e eghtesad-e dolat mehvar be payan reside ast," 13/04/1386 (4 July 2007).

73. *Dony-ye Eghtesad,* "Nemigozarim otagh-e Iran dolati shavad," 26/03/1386 (16 June 2007).

74. Nasr, *The Rise of Islamic Capitalism,* p. 83.

75. Ibid., p. 254.

76. Carothers, "The End of the Transition Paradigm"; and Cavatorta, "The Convergence of Governance."

77. For discussion of this theory, see the special issue of *Cambridge Review of International Affairs,* Vol. 22, No. 1, 2009; and Davidson, "From Uneven to Combined Development."

78. Trotsky, *Permanent Revolution,* p. 146.

79. See Mercer, "NGOs, Civil Society and Democratization," for a critical discussion of the relationship between the three; and LiPuma and Koelbe, "Social Capital in Emerging Democracies," for a critical discussion of social capital in developing countries.

80. Examples of these attempts are: Chaichian, "Structural Impediments of the Civil Society Project in Iran"; Liodakis, *Totalitarian Capitalism and Beyond;* and Canterbury, *Neoliberal Democratization and New Authoritarianism.*

6

The Internet and Civil Activism in Syria

*Roschanack Shaery-Eisenlohr
and Francesco Cavatorta*

The advent of Al Jazeera and other Arab satellite channels in the mid-1990s progressively undermined the monopoly on information of state-run media in the Arab world, leading to a lively debate among political analysts and policymakers about the impact that this technological transformation might have on the wider Arab public and its political choices. The so-called Al Jazeera effect indicated an appetite among citizens of the Arab world for information untainted by state propaganda and, in turn, affected how ordinary Arabs perceived international politics and how they related to the information that their own governments were providing, since the new channels did not shy away from hosting opposition figures and views railing against authoritarian rulers in their respective country. The seismic change that Al Jazeera and Arab satellite television brought about was quickly linked to its potential for democratization. Thomas Friedman, for instance, labeled the station a "beacon of freedom in the Arab world" in February 2001.[1] By the 1990s, most scholars and policymakers had become convinced that the authoritarian exceptionalism of the Arab world could be reversed if the right policy ingredients could be found and mixed together. The privatization of media and the arrival on the scene of pan-Arab media nominally outside the control of states was hailed as one of the necessary ingredients.

Accordingly, it is no surprise that the arrival of new media in the region in the early 2000s strengthened the belief that new social media, technological developments, and democratization were connected. The expansion of Facebook and Twitter in the region seemed to hold even more promise than independent satellite channels because new social media accelerated the exchange of information in a much faster and less-controlled manner. Philip Seib argued that "new media are affecting democratization within the Middle East. . . . This Al Jazeera effect is a relatively new phenomenon but may become more significant as the number of regional satellite television stations grows, along with the proliferation of other new communications technologies, such as the Internet and cell phones."[2]

Far from being a minority view or an argument marginalized in academic and public debate, the belief in the potentially revolutionary role of social media in the realm of politics has been often reemphasized over recent years. As Malcolm Gladwell highlights in his analysis, there is widespread enthusiasm and belief in the revolutionary potential of social media, with political mobilization through Twitter held responsible for events such as the Green Movement's protests in Iran or demonstrations in Moldova, where protesters seemingly took to the streets against the respective regimes buoyed by the extent of online dissent.[3] Even more recently, in a *Jeune Afrique* editorial following the departure of Zine El Abidine Ben Ali from Tunisia in the wake of widespread demonstrations in January 2011, Marwane Ben Yahmed lauded the role of social media in the so-called Jasmine Revolution.[4] In fact the Arab Spring seems to be intimately connected to the use of new social media, and their role during the uprisings has been praised in many political quarters, with a number of bloggers and Internet activists coming to prominence. The organization of demonstrations, the ability to circulate information quickly, and to counter the propaganda of the regime owe certainly a lot to new technologies and new social media, particularly because they provided the opportunity to internationalize the struggle against authoritarianism.

However, the enthusiasm with which the spread of satellite TV, the Internet, mobile phone technology, and social media as potential agents of democratization has been received is tempered by a growing literature arguing that new media and technologies do not necessarily contribute to political liberalization and, in the case of the Arab Spring, by accounts that argue that their role should not obscure the vital importance of off-line social networks. In terms of the Al Jazeera effect, Moahammed Zayani points out that pan-Arab TV channels might actually stifle political liberalization because they give the impression of freedom and therefore postpone real political change.[5] Furthermore, as Shanthi Kalathil and Taylor Boas claimed, there is no necessary causal relation between the advent of new media and political liberalization.[6]

This more skeptical attitude has three broad explanations. First, the belief that privatization of media would be inherently beneficial to democratization and political liberalization seems to be misplaced. For instance, over the last decade, a number of private media entered the audiovisual market without undermining the regimes in power. A recent study of Tunisia's changing media landscape highlights how, from the perspective of the regime, media reform and, in particular, the introduction of private economic actors on the media scene, was an important element of the authoritarian upgrading strategy[7] necessary to ensure the survival of authoritarianism.[8] Second, the Al Jazeera effect did not alter domestic power dynamics within Arab states. It took more than fifteen years since the launch of Al Jazeera for uprisings to occur, and when they did, demands had much more to do with socioeconomic grievances than outright political change. Thus, while it is true that an international Arab public opinion on political matters affecting the region has been formed and that important and divisive issues are indeed discussed on Arab satellite television,[9] demands for change came years after the launch of the station and are not connected to the Al Jazeera effect, which might be best understood as a facilitator of protests rather than the cause. While the Tunisian and Egyptian uprisings have been broadcast on Arab satellite channels, the impetus for change did not come from the coverage but from the creation of horizontal formal and informal social networks among ordinary citizens. Third, a more general skepticism informs the manner in which social media function. As Gladwell indicates, social media, with their loose and weak links, are not revolutionary or politics-changing per se, because what is needed to create "revolutionary" political change are strong social linkages (face-to-face mobilization) and hierarchical organizational structures that can drive such change, particularly if the challenge is to be sustained over a longer period of time. Gladwell states that "Twitter is a way of following (or being followed by) people you may never have met. Facebook is a tool for efficiently managing your acquaintances, for keeping up with the people you would not otherwise be able to stay in touch with. That's why you can have a thousand 'friends' on

Facebook, as you never could in real life."[10] This means that there is an inherent weakness in social media related to the absence of strong personal ties, which contradicts findings about what it takes to mobilize citizens for radical change. The mass demonstrations against Bashar al-Assad might have been facilitated by social networking sites, but what is crucial is the extended formal and informal networks of mobilization that occur in mosques, coffee shops, universities, and workplaces. It is the face-to-face interaction and the off-line mobilization that puts the Syrian regime under pressure.

Thus, this recent skepticism reflects some of the wider disillusionment with democratization and its theoretical assumptions, particularly the ones linked to the privatization of media and access of citizens to new and social media as tools for political mobilization. This has significant implications for civil society activism in general and the tools activists can and do use. There is little doubt that activism across the globe has profoundly changed with the technological revolution, as Peter Hajnal highlights when discussing technology's role "in the functioning and impact of civil society."[11] It is precisely on the outcomes of such use that differences emerge. On the one hand, we have the conviction on the part of many activists and scholars that new technologies are fundamental in bringing about a new political order, whether in democracies or authoritarian regimes, and have almost revolutionary potential to affect politics. On the other hand, less enthusiastic authors and activists argue that the users of technology and not the technology itself bring about political mobilization and change. Whatever the case, it is important to analyze how new media and new technologies, with a particular focus on the Internet and social media, affect civil society activism because it can help explain how new civil actors, whether individuals or organizations, utilize these new technologies and what kind of influence, if any, they are having on traditional political structures. This is doubly important in a country like Syria where authoritarian rule is remarkably strong, where repression of dissent is particularly violent, and where these new technologies and media arrived quite late. The relative novelty of the Internet in Syria, the dynamics that develop between activists and the regime in the cybersphere, how such dynamics might be translated into off-line cooperation or confrontation, and the increasing relevance of the free flow of information in a rather closed society make for an interesting exploration of how activists operate and what kind of influence they have.

The Internet in Syria

On 24 February 1996 the Syrian prime minister authorized the Syrian Telecommunications Company (EST) to enter the Internet age. He was encouraged to do so by Bashar al-Assad, who was president of the Syrian Information Technology Association from 1995 to 1999 before becoming president of Syria in 2000. Thus, on 11 March 1996, the prime minister signed a collaborative agreement with the association, whose president had "put such immense efforts into bringing the Internet to Syria, and Internet culture to all of Syrian society."[12] Under the terms of this agreement, the two parties were to cooperate in implementing a pilot project that would allow public institutions to use the new communication technology. The project's first objective was to assess the usefulness of the Internet, its appropriateness for Syrian culture, and any security issues related to its use. Although the evaluation was not very informative in terms of technical and economic usefulness, it appears to have occupied an important place in the minds of the project's pioneers from the political arena. Those in power were already aware of the "dangerous nature" of this hard-to-control tool. As we can see, the security-related concerns of the authorities highlight how authoritarian systems tend to be proactive when it comes to the Internet and access to sites they wish to block. This contrasts sharply with democracies, where concerns about security are usually raised after the fact and tend not to focus on banning sites.

On 13 March 1996, the period of assessment resulted in a report on the technical and administrative aspects of Syria's connection to the Internet. Its authors concluded that "Syria should establish a connection as soon as possible."[13] They also listed the main reasons in favor of encouraging the Syrian authorities to allow ordinary Syrians to enter the virtual era. Among these justifications were

- The incalculable wealth of information and services available online for students and researchers, the Internet having become a pillar of research worldwide, especially through online databases
- The importance of the Internet as a means of commercial promotion and electronic trade
- The opportunities of the Internet for Syrian companies to promote their products and publicize Syria's cultural history as well as its archaeological heritage and tourist attractions

- The possibility of publicizing and supporting the stance of the Syrian political establishment, defending the rights of Syrian Internet users, correcting lies about Syria, and repairing damage to its international image.[14]

At its inception in 1997, the pilot project had a maximum capacity of 150 subscribers. Various authorities were connected—including the president's departments, the prime minister, local and national leaders of the Baath Party, ministries, military departments, state-owned companies and institutions, the universities, and Arab and international organizations—as were news agencies, hospitals, and chambers of commerce. That same year an information technology (IT) communications specialist, Amr Salem, published an article on the introduction of the Internet to Syria.[15] Salem, headhunted in the United States and presented in the state media as a "manager" at Microsoft and "modernizer," offered then-president Hafez al-Assad his services in banning any new technology that might threaten the "security and stability of the country." The development of the new technology in Syria went therefore hand in hand with clear attempts to closely monitor its use and prevent access to what the regime believed to be sensitive information. In 2006 Salem was appointed minister of communications and technology, indicating that he had been rewarded for his ability to place the Internet under a certain degree of control in Syria.

It is no surprise that the climate of distrust on the part of Syrian authorities vis-à-vis the new technology made Syrians look elsewhere for the provision of Internet services. Thus, Syrians in search of information used Lebanese, Jordanian, and Turkish Internet providers. Over 65,000 Syrians were "illegally" connected to the Internet even before the pilot project was implemented. These connections were expensive, which restricted them to the wealthy and led to a system of several people making collective use of a single access point. Since the authorities were unable to control this practice, they banned it. Threats to users ranged from simply cutting off their phone lines to being summoned to one of the security services. Human Rights Watch found that "until 1999, Syria was one of the rare countries in the world which was connected to the global Internet network but did not allow its citizens to access it, in spite of official speeches and declarations praising this tool."[16] This was part of the political logic of a government that wanted to prevent the development of an information source that might become a threat.

In early 1999 the pilot project was launched with the provision of e-mail services inside the country. Soon afterwards the authorities also allowed access to international e-mail and other services offered by the Internet, such as browsing the Web and file exchange via FTP (file transfer protocol). Two types of subscriptions were already available: e-mail-only or e-mail plus surfing the Web. The authorities increased the number of those "entitled" to an Internet connection and accepted subscriptions from private companies (both commercial and industrial), tourism agencies, doctors, engineers, and lawyers. However, the process was slow, since it entailed bureaucratic procedures to obtain papers that granted legal access to the Internet. It also opened the door to a scam that involved people falsely obtaining documents certifying their membership in an entitled profession, thus adding a new outlet for corruption to the hundreds of profitable outlets already in existence. This widening of access also rendered a great service to educational establishments, where the national program of IT teaching was being applied since enrolments and access increased. Since its inception, the Internet had been the sole domain of the EST, which is answerable to the Ministry of Communications and Technology. In 2001 the Syrian Information Technology Association entered the market with subscription offers that were more flexible than EST's, while still complying with the regulations: namely, the requirement for users to belong to specific professions. The year 2005 saw increasing growth in the Internet sector with the arrival of two other private service providers on the market: Aya and CEC, along with the Italian satellite Internet provider Best-Italia. In 2007, mobile phone operators Areeba (later MTN) and Syriatel also entered the Internet market. As a result, the Italian company had its contract suspended that same year. In 2006, Minister of Communications and Technology Salem stated his determination to distribute to citizens one million affordable computers with Internet connection. He also proposed easier access to credit to encourage users. His third measure was to remove customs duties on IT hardware. Finally, the Syrian government envisaged creating several high-tech parks in Syria in order to attract foreign investment in IT. In official speeches, the government frequently referred to wanting to develop IT, and Internet and specialist institutes have been created in a number of locations. Universities have offered special subjects in which students from all disciplines are taught the principles of computing. From these same universities, specialist faculties have emerged, and the state started to speak of e-government. Partly for efficiency's sake and partly for appearance, all public corporations as well as the authorities have invested in IT and training their staff in its use. Managers as well as ministers appropriate IT jargon in their speeches and frequently use IT tools in their presentations, even when they are not absolutely necessary. As part of the government's drive to offer Internet access to a maximum of users, in 2005 it permitted the sale of Internet access cards without any restrictions as to the buyer's identity. However, broadband access is still reserved for the privileged and especially for those who manage to obtain the approval of the security services. Requests for derogations from such approval have to be made to the management of EST.

In parallel with this proactive policy of spreading computer literacy and widening Internet access, all forms of state control over IT have been reinforced. Until 2003, all international sites offering e-mail service were blocked. This was intended to force users to subscribe to only local providers, which made them easier to monitor. Since then, with the ban on international providers, it has been a game of cat and mouse. Some IT specialists have managed to bypass the ban by using special software. But this has not been widespread enough to enable the populace to use addresses hosted abroad, even though the business cards of many politicians feature e-mail addresses hosted outside Syria by such providers as Yahoo! and Hotmail. The use of free e-mail sites became possible at the end of the 2000s. This "liberalization" followed a major investment in sophisticated hardware that allowed the state to monitor e-mail even on these free sites. The authorities' highly sophisticated technology blocks access to specific websites it deems antiregime so effectively that even knowledgeable users have been unable to break through the barriers. According to expert observers, new software programs imported from the Netherlands and Germany are able to monitor the entire process from the moment a user logs in, making it possible to know what sites the user visits, and when.

New Media and New Activism?

The history of the development of new media in Syria already points to the paradoxes and problems that exist for civil society activists to express some form of dissent. The Internet, by virtue of what it is, permits users to access whatever information they want and, conversely, allows them to disseminate worldwide whatever they wish. This has important repercussions for authoritarian governments, which, traditionally, have held the quasi-monopoly on information. Because the Internet fundamentally undermines this, authoritarian regimes have attempted to regulate access, monitor users, and ban sites through a number of administrative procedures and technological controls. Thus, an interesting dynamic has developed in Syria whereby activists and authorities are continually "testing" each other in the cybersphere in order to explore the limits of what can be said and accessed. In the process, the Internet has become another arena where many Syrians push the infamous red lines and test the boundaries. Unlike the very strict Press Law of 2001 (particularly Articles 50 and 51), which gave the state full authority to license newspapers and magazines, cancel existing licenses, and imprison journalists for publishing so-called false news or forged documents, no laws manage electronic media, although legislation is being drafted to regulate this as well, raising fears that its restrictions will be similar to the Press Law.[17] It follows that through trial and error new ways of transgressing boundaries were created. When the government blocked websites, activists learned about proxies that can access those websites through other servers. When the security services were able to crack their e-mail, dissidents changed e-mail addresses constantly or maintained at least two or three e-mail accounts.

But the Internet has done more than simply providing a new field to extend old debates with new practices. In the view of many civil society activists—and optimists—this new medium allows them to provide a counterweight to the culture of fear and to propagate the possibility for new state-society relations, which have a concrete influence on how the regime responds. Three examples help clarify how activists believe they resist the atomization of society and the isolation from the international community despite the authoritarian constraints they operate under.

Thara is an online magazine that defines itself as a "weekly review of scholarship, culture and literature on women's issues." Based in Syria, its goal is to provide a reliable resource of international, regional, and local documents—for example, laws and conventions—concerning women. It also aims to monitor social ills and practices that violate rights and freedoms, especially those of women, who are the most vulnerable and suppressed sector of Syrian society. The review tries to expose these problems and propose alternative courses of action.[18] *Thara* is part of Etana Press, which maintains strong ties with the international community by receiving funding from a variety of international organizations and by facilitating visits of foreign journalists and academics to Syria. In addition, it organizes a number of exhibitions and seminars. In the view of Maan Abdul Salam, the owner of Etana Press, "The internet is really important, but it doesn't make any change in the end, because the hand of security is still so strong. People can get information now, but they can't do anything with the information. Maybe you have a window on the world, but you don't have a window on what's going on inside, and that makes you blind."[19] However, despite his view, journalists and writers of *Thara* work around the clock to put information online, to respond to e-mails they receive, to provide legal advice (over e-mail), and to expand their readership. In the view of Yahya, a journalist charged with responding to the flood of e-mails the magazine receives, *Thara* is a de facto social institution. He says that the magazine caters to a small section of the population due to the high illiteracy rate among women and their limited access to the rather expensive Internet, but many readers discuss the articles with their friends, families, and neighbors, so ideas are disseminated.[20] More significantly, many women have heard that *Thara* cares about women's issues, so women from all sectarian backgrounds contact the office to ask for help, Yahya explains. Some have run away from their homes, some have been victims of domestic abuse, and a few even come to drop off their own or their daughters' illegitimate children. *Thara* has tried to help these women to find shelter and lawyers. Yahya concludes that "the implications of the Internet are larger than the Internet and its readers itself."[21]

Thus, while Maan Abdul Salam might be right that the Internet does not lead to political openings, the consumers of this e-magazine have viewed *Thara* as a social network outside the direct control of the state and Islamic charity organizations. As a women's organization or a place that women can turn to receive help, *Thara* has contributed to the creation of a counter-hegemonic space and has helped counter the atomization of the society. The intentions of the information producers to inform women through an e-magazine of their rights and to raise consciousness by providing them with legal documents has taken its own local form in Syria—of the importance of networking to improve one's plight. The example shows that civil society actors do in fact change state and society relations, even if not in the ways originally intended. What is also interesting is that the terrain of activism through social media can be activated by a "spark" that can mobilize society as a whole. In the final instance it is off-line mobilization and face-to-face social networks that allow a "revolutionary" movement to grow and sustain itself.

The second example is a monitoring organization that both monitors Syrian official media and reveals to the public what these official media have omitted in their news on human, children's, and women's rights in Syria. In addition, the organization trains journalists "to push the red lines further and show the government that we are here and that we see you and that we keep writing even if you censor it."[22] The result of this monitoring is published in the form of annual reports online. Because their website is blocked in Syria, their reports are sent as e-mails to subscribers. In "N"'s (name omitted) view the Damascus Spring failed because it focused only on political reform, which does not lend itself to more contact with citizens: "We now think it was a mistake to focus on political reform. We need to focus instead on mass contact and on social issues first. We have therefore about 11,000 subscribers who get our e-mail news."[23] This organization tells stories that official news sources omit and that would place unwanted attention on the shortcomings of the state in terms of protection of individual rights. Communicating with society, providing it with alternative news, and exposing the regime by telling individual citizens who might share the story with others is the goal of this institution. N said that the government uses a variety of methods to communicate with society, such as the Baath Party events, popular organizations, the education system, military, and others. Similarly, the Islamists have extensive ways of communication such as mosques, Sufi networks, Quran lessons, radio, charity, TV, and other channels of communication. However, secular civil society activists lack funding, institutions, and a popular base. Therefore, in his view, the Internet is important because it enables the activists to communicate and create networks reaching wider sectors of society.

Similar to the philosophy of *Thara* magazine, the Internet is believed to be an educational tool to make people aware of their rights by providing information and facilitating the creation of networks of like-minded people who would resist an oppressive regime. The Internet, in N's view, enables readers to share political views and exchange ideas. The advantages of the Internet, N believes, are threefold: its speed, the potential to gather information about those who are arbitrarily arrested, and contact with the people. "We get sixty to seventy e-mails per day as a response to our news e-mails we send out. Some say go to hell, you spy, and that we are American agents; some others write e-mails and thank us for our activities. None ever say let us please join your organization, though."[24] Fear of dissent has characterized Syrian society for a very long time, although the uprising of 2011–2012 has taken down the wall of fear. Through the use of the Internet, N and his colleagues produce new discourses on citizenship and position themselves as mediators between Western humanitarian organizations and ordinary citizens. N's organization thus competes with the regime, which until recently depicted itself as the only "voice" of the people. In this counter-hegemonic space, the organization offers new ways of thinking about state-society relations, whereby citizens hold the state accountable for its actions, and subsequently a state must respond to the citizens' demands. This stands in stark contrast to the regime's presentation of state-society relations in familial and organic terms, as if they were all part of a singly body with a unified purpose and vision for the country as dictated by the Baath Party.

The third and final example is that of another human rights organization in Damascus. The example shows how a human rights activist with the organization has domesticated the Internet in his social network and views its powers as enabling the maintenance and even improvement of the quality of this social network. "B" defines his mission as one of publicizing a culture of human rights among ordinary people through the use of social media.[25] In his view, "Many Syrians do not want a regime change; they rather want economic and social security. They do not care much about democracy. They want a symbolic gesture. We, as the leaders of the people, want a plural political system. We need to give people education what their rights are. They have lived for forty years under dictatorship; they need to learn."[26] B explains that his organization is not permitted by the government to publish any material that has the words "human rights" (*huquq al-insan*) in it. He does not have a business card because he cannot find a print shop that would dare to print the words "human rights," because the term has a Western connotation that is highly problematic. When the Internet became available, B remembers that "we began to surf the Net to get information about human rights. We wanted to know what it is exactly, what we have to do, for example, when someone is put on military trial and what can our lawyers say to defend them. What vocabulary should we use? How do we make a case? We had heard the words human rights, human rights, but we had no idea what it was exactly, and we still need training in it."[27]

The group's official statements are put online, and their communication with members is mainly through e-mail. B explains in detail how he and his colleagues publicize arbitrary detentions and locate missing persons:

> We got members in each city and everybody knows "this is the guy associated with the human rights," so when they have detained a person, family members run to me, and our contact visits the family of the victims and asks them to recount exactly what happened and who took the person, as there are five different types of security services. Before the Internet it used to take months before we heard of arrests. Now our contact e-mails us all this information, and we immediately telegram the Interior Ministry and ask about the whereabouts of this person and the reasons for his detention. This is what we call writing a statement. At the same time we e-mail this information to our contact in the United Nations in Geneva, who immediately gets in touch with the Syrian embassy abroad, who then gets in touch with the foreign ministry, who has no clue about this incident, so they telegram the *maktab al-amn al-qawmi* (Baath National Security Office), which then asks all its five branches to find out where the person is held, and they might then get back to us after two or three days, two or three weeks, or never. If we hear a message we e-mail it to our contact, and he visits the family and tells them about the situation, so you see, time is of essence. Without the Internet it would have taken us months to even hear that some person was detained; now within hours we have the news and we can take some action.[28]

Whether through this method a culture of human rights is propagated is debatable, but what is obvious is that the families of the victim make use of this network to find out the whereabouts of their family members, and the way the activists use the Internet facilitates a quicker way to locate the victims. In the view of B, the new media, particularly satellite TV, has also enabled the creation of a community or a network of people who, prior to the advent of the media, either did not know each other or did not trust each other. In fact, the issue of trust is essential in a society where the fear of being reported to the security service is always present. B recalls that his cell phone did not stop ringing after he had been interviewed on Al Arabiyya TV about human rights conditions in Syria. Although people had heard his name and knew about his organization, it was the fact that an established reputable TV station, which many Syrians watch, had interviewed him that solidified his credentials as a trustworthy dissident. He was obviously not a *mukhabarati* (security official) in disguise.

From then on, he received e-mails and phone calls regularly and, with each case, others heard about his organization and consequently about the concept of human rights. In this case, the media also functioned as an authentication mechanism. Building networks of people who trust each other even when they do not know each other well is the first step to countering and breaking the regime's politics of fear. Similar to *Thara* magazine, it may be that this human rights organization also functions as a social institution that offers people ways to create some minimal boundaries to resist arbitrary state actions. More than learning about human rights or women rights through online articles, people primarily seek help from these organizations as individuals. This should not be discarded as a political act, although it should also be underlined that it is far from being systemic and institutionalized, as Gladwell outlined.[29]

The antiregime protests that have rocked Syria in 2011–2012 might not have their roots in social media and are likely to have more to do with the deteriorating economic and social conditions of a large part of the population, but the impetus for the demonstrations and the subsequent ability to quickly spread the word about them was facilitated certainly by new technologies. The ability to show the world the crackdown in real time is a significant change when compared to the silence that characterized the Hama massacre of 1982.

Social Networks and Blogging as Political Engagement

More broadly, it should also be underlined that similar trends appear when one analyzes the phenomenon of social networks such as Facebook and blogging. Millions of Arabs are registered with Facebook, and while it is formally banned in Syria, Facebook members are numerous. What clearly emerged from the uprisings across the region in the spring of 2011 is that many members use the site for social and political goals, engaging with issues that affect their societies and political systems, debating such issues, and organizing off-line activities. Thus, it appears that a significant segment of Arab users employ Facebook to advance political goals, with dozens of dissenters, human rights defenders, journalists, and other civil society actors using social networks to promote their agendas—operating both from inside Syria and abroad. Prominent journalists such as Ziad Haidar and Ayman Abdel Nour use Facebook to promote their online magazines, *Al-Watan* and *AllSyria,* respectively.[30] New emerging movements are being formed on the social networks: Popular Change Movement,[31] Syrian Reformist Middle,[32] Syrian Centre for Media and Freedom of Expression,[33] and Arab Democratic Centre for Strategic Political and Economic Studies,[34] among others. Some of these movements have between 1,000 and 2,000 members, and posts are relayed to a wider audience when members repost the articles on their profiles. These movements report instances of corruption and violations of human rights, and/or lobby for change in Syria according to their specific agendas. The Atassi Forum for Democratic Dialogue was reopened on Facebook in December 2009 after its office had been closed physically in 2005.[35] "Our goal is simple," said Suheir al-Atassi, the forum's president, "we want to pursue the dialogue, which had been interrupted, in order to reach a deeper understanding of our causes and find solutions together." In addition, many news services have started recently on Facebook, such as Syria Tribune Shabab,[36] Syria Today,[37] Syria Story,[38] Syria Now,[39] Syria News,[40] Syria Tribune Culture,[41] and Syria News Station.[42] According to Zeina A, a young journalist and blogger, "Media is controlled in Syria, and satellite televisions cannot report on Syria, unless what they report is in line with the government's policies, because otherwise their offices would be shut down and they would not be allowed to work again from within Syria. So the only source of credible news on Syria is through the Internet and especially blogs." She adds, "The Internet has become the ultimate source of news for most Syrian intellectuals."[43] Syria is number two in the top ten countries using Opera Mini, a software application used to surf the Internet on mobile phones.[44] Table 6.1 shows the top ten sites visited.

Interactive websites using Web 2.0 technologies are among the top websites accessed by Syrians on mobile phones, followed by information websites, such as the leading interactive source Wikipedia.org and independent news sites. According to a study conducted by the Berkman Center for Internet and Society on mapping Arab bloggers,

> Syrian bloggers are located almost exclusively in Syria and write primarily about domestic issues, including politics. Syrians are among the least likely to express support for domestic political leaders compared to other clusters. The discussion of religion in

Table 6.1 Top 10 Websites in Syria

1. google.com
2. facebook.com
3. youtube.com
4. live.com
5. hotmail.com
6. my.opera.com
7. wikipedia.org
8. kooora.com
9. yahoo.com
10. Syria-news.com

Source: Compiled by the authors.

Syrian blogs is dedicated predominately to personal religious thoughts and experiences, as well as religious poetry and Sunni Islam. This cluster has the second largest concentration of known male bloggers on the map, at 87%, while only 13% are female. Half of all bloggers in this cluster are in the 25–35 age range, making it slightly older than other clusters and the blogosphere on the whole, but not by much. Coders found that this group was more critical of Western culture and values than other clusters and one of the least likely to discuss movies and television.[45]

This overview of blogging and social networks appears to confirm the assumption that the Internet helps promote what are called alternative or counter public spheres that can offer a new, empowering sense of what it means to be a citizen.[46] In Syria, the young generation, in particular, uses the Internet and social networks specifically as a way of joining a dialogue about civic issues with people from different walks of life who are blogging, tweeting, facebooking, and using the Internet as a public sphere alternative. In many ways, the Internet has been the only medium for stirring debates among citizens in Syria, as all kinds of dialogue are forbidden in real life due to the enforcement of emergency law. Today, a good deal of civic discussion takes place on the Internet, not only in explicit public forums and within varieties of online journalism, but also within the vast networking of activist organizations and social movements.[47] What social networking does is allow citizens to reclaim their right/duty to be involved in civil and political issues, which in real life are out of bounds due to the repressive practices of the regime. Through this virtual engagement, citizens create a public sphere to disseminate counter-truths to official statements, thus undermining the secretive ways in which the state operates. Civil society activists in Syria have realized that knowledge is an essential step for citizens toward empowered citizenship and participatory governance; as a result, several local and international actors have been working to provide online resources for activists and individuals. Hundreds of individuals have been active on the Internet to relay information through social networks such as YouTube, Facebook, Twitter, and Flickr among others; one video on YouTube exposes a Syrian policeman receiving a bribe, which has been viewed 183,645 times and received 237 comments.[48] For some, political blogging has the potential to be the modern equivalent of subversive underground literature. Although its consequences might not immediately be visible or particularly problematic for the regime, the Internet has the power to stimulate political debate, bringing together a collection of voices that can find solace in the knowledge that they are not alone. What is more, all this can be achieved without recourse to expensive printing presses or distribution networks. Individuals in the Arab world, such as Al-Sahli,[49] are starting to take up blogging as a full-time profession that generates income and has a growing influence on society and politics.

Disrupting Online Activism

In a recent report on Egyptian bloggers, Bernardo Valli stated that "in the land of [the] pharaohs, Facebook, Twitter and blogs . . . allow internet users to bypass the imposing repressive apparatus and promote [political] ideas and projects without much caring about censorship,"[50] indicating that the state's repressive apparatus has a difficult time finding ways to disrupt, control, or influence what is on cyberspace. The empirical evidence from Syria is in line with the findings from Egypt, and demonstrates that both individual citizens and organizations have become "activated" in the cybersphere, offering an important counter-discourse to the official one. However, this does not lead for the moment to forms of political liberalization or systemic pressure for reform, and activists are mostly aware of this limitation. The emphasis in cyberspace is on daily engagement and the practice of dissent that tends to point to individual abuses by state officials or to offer a different vision of personal relationships, as in the case of women's rights. This "mass" of dissent is certainly political but not institutional, and as long as it remains confined to the cybersphere and is not translated into concrete political mobilizations through large opposition organizations, the Syrian regime can probably live with that. It is not particularly surprising to see that it is only when people take to the streets, as occurred across the country in 2011–2012, that the regime reacts through widespread violence, because it is the "masses" in the streets that regimes fear the most.

Paradoxically, the existence of a pocket of online dissent serves the regime quite well in the sense that it can show external critics that a degree of pluralism exists in Syria. The balancing act of the regime, however, has the potential for self-destruction because the presence of new technologies no longer allows for an information blackout of protests beginning in the streets of one village or town, with the consequences that contagion can spread quickly. So far, the Syrian regime has policed the Internet quite rigorously, using all sorts of technological devices to prevent and control access to certain sites, to locate problematic bloggers, and to monitor communications among dissidents. Through these means, the regime continues to promote a culture of fear, safe in the knowledge that it does not have to punish this online dissent at all times but can pick and choose its moment and target. This random forceful intervention, which can result in imprisonment, is designed to instill fear in users because at any time and for the flimsiest of reasons, they could be next. This is a strategy that other authoritarian countries have used, from China to Tunisia, in order to police what many believe to be a means of communication that does not lend itself to policing. The problem for authoritarian regimes obviously is that once dissent begins in the streets, the previous online linkages among dissidents can be mobilized to serve these new needs, making social media an important tool to counter official regime discourse, to mobilize and, importantly in the case of Syria, to spread information to the international community.

The cat-and-mouse game that dissidents and activists play in terms of developing new technologies and new software is also a testament to the perceived dangers that the Internet can pose for the regime, as it attempts to keep tabs on what is occurring online. Focussing strongly on monitoring dissent on the Internet is a crucial aspect of repression because social media are believed to be important means through which opinions can be exchanged and mobilization can occur. Some suggest that in this cat-and-mouse game the regime will always prevail because it has the resources to more effectively control the Internet, such as readily identifying dissidents through their IP address, while others argue that the heavy nature of the repressive bureaucratic apparatus means that they are always playing catch-up with innovations and innovators who are light on their feet.

Conclusion

Despite its precarious state, the Internet in Syria remains an effective tool for expressing political, cultural, and social protest. Building on this, the protests that began in 2011 have relied on social media, in particular, to facilitate further mobilization. The political opposition has used the Internet to circulate its bulletins and statements—relatively efficiently, within the limits of what is possible. For instance, petitions on a number of sensitive political and social topics have been circulated and have collected signatures online. The Damascus Spring Committee and the Committee for the Rehabilitation of Civil Society, two movements that incarnate much of the domestic anti-establishment culture, have resorted to the Web to circulate their debates, opinions, and statements. Two significant political events of the past have resonated far and wide thanks to the Internet, despite the limitations and restrictions placed on it: the Damascus Declaration for Democratic National Change in October 2005 and the Beirut-Damascus/Damascus-Beirut Declaration in April 2006. Both documents were widely circulated online and collected signatories, highlighting the significant demands for political change that existed in certain sectors of society. Virtual forums have been replacing the ones that Syrians were familiar with at the beginning of the twenty-first century, at the time of the Damascus Spring and other short-lived democratic experiments. The Internet also remains a preferred medium for the circulation of petitions and denunciations of the regime, and in the context of the uprisings, in 2012 the Internet has become a battleground for propaganda on the part of both the regime and the rebels. Information about the arrest and conviction of political activists can only be communicated by this medium since the other traditional media avoid meddling in such business. Intellectuals take advantage of this new space to escape the hold of state cultural authorities. Numerous are the poets, novelists, and essayists who use the Internet to publish their censored texts or texts that did not meet with the publishers' approval. Sites such as Jidar.com and Alawan.com publish the writings of Syrians and other Arabs, as well as translations of texts that have influenced global cultural debate. All this creates a fertile terrain that could be exploited at the right time for off-line mobilization.

Until recent demonstrations and the descent into armed chaos, the virtual life and real life of Syrians seemed to have one characteristic in common: isolation. This is no longer the case as the wall of fear has shown profound cracks. Whether this is due to online activism remains to be determined, but what is crucial in the Syrian case is that online activism prevailed over the off-line one until the spring of 2011, when protesters took to the streets to demonstrate against the regime. An "enlightened" minority of citizens sought technical solutions to access banned sites, create a blog, or simply access e-mail to exchange information and opinions. The Arab Spring has allowed this minority to connect with ordinary citizens off-line, and it is the "street," and more recently the "gun," rather than the computer that have become the protagonist of the Syrian uprising. While online dialogues did not precipitate off-line protests, the virtual networks in place before street mobilization contributed to lessen the costs of participation because they had challenged citizens' isolation. Faced with criticism about the lack of freedom of expression in Syria, the authorities first turned a deaf ear, then pretended to listen, and then turned to armed violence. Generally, they accused domestic protesters of reflecting the will of Western forces seeking to damage Syria's image at the very moment that it is confronting imperialism in its neighborhood. The penalties for dissent were and still are severe because it is supposedly still not the right time to criticize the situation even if the criticisms are justified. This pretext has been used for decades, but the moment for free public expression seems to have arrived by the spring of 2011, although the nexus between online and off-line activism can still be broken by heavy state repression. The off-line activism exposes citizens to almost unrestrained violence, which is then circulated on the Internet in order to spark even more outrage against the regime.

The growth of new media has opened up possibilities for a new type of civic engagement and activism, which allows even activated citizens in isolation to become agents of social change and, more specifically, proponents of an alternative discourse that clashes with the official one. While this per se is unlikely to lead to significant political mobilization in the absence of mass hierarchical structures of organized dissent, it still represents a modest form of activism that characterizes certain sectors of society unwilling to silently accept the dominant structures of power. When, however, such discourse connects with the demands of ordinary citizens off-line, the relevance of new technologies increases exponentially because it allows for immediate circulation of information. Thus, while the danger of democratization via the Internet is slim, what is produced in the cybersphere warrants the attention of the authorities, as the Syrian case demonstrates, because the online activism can be quickly put to the service of off-line activism. This alone should make us more positive about the influence of such technology in authoritarian settings.

Notes

The authors are grateful to the research team of the Knowledge Programme on Civil Society in West Asia for gathering some of the empirical data used in this chapter. The chapter is based on "Internet or Enter-Not: The Syrian Experience," published in 2010 by the Knowledge Programme on Civil Society in West Asia, and on the report "The Role of Social Media in Syria," compiled in 2010 for the Knowledge Programme on Civil Society in West Asia. Parts of the chapter appeared in an article by Roschanack Shaery-Eisenlohr, "From Subjects to Citizens? Civil Society and the Internet in Syria," *Middle East Critique,* Vol. 20, no. 2 (Summer 2011), pp. 127–138; reprinted by permission of *Middle East Critique.*

1. Friedman, "TV Station," p. A4.
2. Seib, *New Media,* p. 1.
3. Gladwell, "Why the Revolution Will Not Be Tweeted."
4. Ben Yahmed, "La Leçon de Tunis," p. 6.
5. Zayani, *Al Jazeera.*
6. Kalathil and Boas, *Open Networks.*
7. Haugbølle and Cavatorta, "Vive la grande famille."
8. Heydemann, "Upgrading Authoritarianism."
9. Pintak, *Reflections;* and Lynch, *Voices.*
10. Gladwell, "Why the Revolution Will Not Be Tweeted."
11. Hajnal, *Civil Society,* p. 13.
12. Hana Ashkita, speech given at the meeting of the Network for the Development of Libraries in the Arab States, Beirut, 2–4 March 2000.
13. Ibid.
14. Ibid.
15. Salem, "Syria's Cautious Embrace."
16. Salam Kawakibi, "Internet or Enter-Not: The Syrian Experience," Working Paper no. 10, Knowledge Programme on Civil Society in West Asia, University of Amsterdam, 2010, pp. 1–14.
17. "Syrian Internet Law Threatens Online Freedom," 5 November 2010, www.i-policy.org/2010/11/syria-internet-law-threatens-online-freedom.html.

18. *Thara* online magazine began in 2008, www.thara-sy.com/Thara English/modules/tinycontent/index.php?id=1.

19. Guy Taylor, "After the Damascus Spring Syrians Looking for Freedom Online," 6 March 2007, www.metransparent.com/old/texts/guy_taylor_after_the_damascus_spring_syrians_looking_for_freedom_online.htm.

20. Personal and confidential interview with a member of the Knowledge Programme research team, Damascus, Syria, 26 April 2009.

21. Ibid.

22. Personal and confidential interview with a member of the Knowledge Programme research team, Damascus, Syria, 23 April 2009.

23. Ibid.

24. Ibid.

25. Personal and confidential interview with a member of the Knowledge Programme research team, Damascus, Syria, 24 April 2009.

26. Ibid.

27. Ibid.

28. Ibid.

29. Gladwell, "Why the Revolution Will Not Be Tweeted."

30. www.alwatanonline.com/home.php; http://all4syria.info.

31. http://www.facebook.com/pages/rk-ltgyyr-lsby-fy-swry/205822696325.

32. http://alwasatmovement.com/.

33. http://www.facebook.com/profile.php?id=733202441#!/profile.php?v=info&id=632606111.

34. http://www.facebook.com/profile.php?id=100000526534351.

35. http://www.facebook.com/group.php?gid=137514459715#!/profile.php?id=100000593289317&ref=ts. Accessed 3 March 2010.

36. http://www.facebook.com/pages/Syria-Tribune-Shabab/252771563867?ref=search&sid=835465531.1985581070..1.

37. http://www.facebook.com/pages/Syria-Today/178464400722?ref=search&sid=835465531.1985581070..1.

38. http://www.facebook.com/pages/Syria-Story/130350760688?ref=search&sid=835465531.1985581070..1.

39. http://www.facebook.com/search/?q=Syria+Now&init=quick#!/pages/Damascus-Syria/syria-now/247355137984?ref=search&sid=835465531.413515464..1.

40. http://www.facebook.com/pages/Syria-News/152712952829?ref=search&sid=835465531.1985581070..1.

41. http://www.facebook.com/pages/Syria-Tribune-Culture-STC/227420049776?ref=search&sid=835465531.1985581070..1.

42. http://www.facebook.com/pages/Damascus-Syria/Syrian-News-Station/166351932892?ref=search&sid=835465531.1985581070..1.

43. Personal and confidential interview with a member of the Knowledge Programme research team, March 2010.

44. "State on the Mobile Web, January 2010," 25 February 2010, www.opera.com/media/smw/2010/pdf/smw012010.pdf.

45. Etling et al., *Mapping the Arabic Blogosphere.*

46. Van de Donk et al., *Cyberprotest.*

47. Ibid.

48. http://www.youtube.com/watch?v=yZgJWmpBgVM; Van de Donk et al., *Cyberprotest.*

49. Al-Sahli blog at http://miolog.com/about/.

50. Valli, "Egitto, la democrazia del web," 24 January 2011, www
.repubblica.it/esteri/2011/01/24/news/valli_blogger-11578175/?ref=HREC2-3.

7

From Virtual to Tangible Social Movements in Iran

Ali Honari

The emergence of Iran's Green Movement after the disputed and arguably fraudulent presidential election in June 2009 has once more generated worldwide interest in the confrontation between Iranian civil society and the authoritarian government. More specifically, much of the focus of attention in this confrontation was the role of modern media, particularly the Internet. The Internet and online activism became important not only for the local Green Movement activists who found the Internet to be a "safe haven" to operate in during the news blackout and severe repression, but also for global audiences who received massive inflows of news and information. Experts and analysts broadly agree that the Internet played a considerable role in the Green Movement, but such consensus is not unanimous in terms of the degree of impact on the movement and how this impact was brought about. Moreover, the studies to date have tended to focus on "macro-mobilization" and exploitation of the Internet by formal activists rather than on "micro-mobilization" and the mechanisms that facilitate (or impede) online collective actions of informal activists. The objective of this chapter is to shed some light on these issues, focusing on two functions of the Internet in the Green Movement: first, spreading news and information and, second, providing incentives to participate in the movement. For this purpose, the dynamics of using the Internet by the movement's activists over the two years before, during, and after the 2009 Iran presidential election will be analyzed in detail. To do so the mutual relationship between online and off-line activism and crossover between micro- and macro-mobilization is considered. A better understanding of the dynamics generated by the online and off-line linkages can provide important insights that go beyond the Iranian mobilization of 2009 and shed light on the role of online social networking during the Arab Spring.

After a short introduction, I begin the chapter by introducing the theoretical background and the methodological approach of the study. I then explain the dual role of the Internet and the dynamics of online and off-line social networks in three periods in three parts. Finally, the findings of all three parts will be combined into one larger picture.

A Twitter Revolution?

After the June 2009 election, millions of protesters took to the streets with their green banners and democratic slogans to challenge the results. Through heavy repression, the regime attempted to silence the movement by detaining political and social activists to destroy the opposition's organization and their mobilizing attempts and by suppressing or censoring newspapers and slowing down the Internet,[1] mobile phone connections, and other means of mass communications in order to block coordination among dissidents.[2] Under such repression and in the absence of organized opposition and a free press, political activists and opposition leaders believed that the considerable burden of increasing participation incentives in the Green Movement and communicating opposition opinions and news could and should be shouldered by the Internet. This idea was reinforced by the recently acquired importance of the Internet, particularly online social networks in the electoral campaign period. In addition, there was also the general belief that the decentralized structure of the Internet is conducive to democracy by allowing citizens to participate in the public discourse and by increasing media diversity.[3] Therefore, several attempts were made to shift mobilizing activities and communicating opposition opinions and news to the Internet, where the opposition had the upper hand because it was Internet-savvy and where the costs of mobilization and communication were lower than off-line or on the streets.

In the heat of the moment during the immediate postelection demonstrations, some Western media outlets explained the whole movement solely in terms of a media phenomenon related to Twitter, Facebook, and other social media—sometimes referring to the movement as "Iran's Twitter Revolution."[4] This view was so widespread that Twitter was even nominated for the Nobel Peace Prize mainly for its role in the Iranian protests, the argument being that "Twitter and other social media outlets have become the soft weapons of democracy."[5] Some experts have cast doubt on this view and have brought up counterarguments.[6] For instance, it was argued that a real concrete current of dissent was at work on the streets of Iran and explaining the whole phenomenon in terms of a media event does injustice to the reality on the ground.[7] Little by little, a discussion came into being between the two sides as to what role the Internet played in the postelection events. The role of the Internet was discussed in three areas: (1) how it helped the opposition to organize;[8] (2) how it facilitated the local circulation of the news;[9] and (3) how it disseminated news and information to the global society.[10] Next to success stories of the new media and their importance for the Green Movement stood emerging counterclaims. For instance, Ethan Zuckerman, director of the MIT Center for Civic Media, argued that "Social media are helpful in exposing what's happening to the outside world, but it's a mistake to think that these protests [in Iran] are because of social media. It's more conventional things like word-of-mouth and phone calls that really bring massive numbers of people into the streets."[11]

Nevertheless, emphasizing the coordination role of the Internet in the Green Movement and focusing on its effects has not been an exhaustive enterprise. So far, narratives of the Internet in the Green Movement tend to overlook the fact that organizing high-risk activities and mobilizing individuals to participate in social movements under severe oppression is not possible by simply spreading information or solely by endeavors of formal organizations. In other words, the fact that the Internet and online social networks can/should play a key role in providing social movement *incentives* in addition to spreading information by embedded individuals in *informal* networks has not been taken into account. Furthermore, little attention has been paid to the dynamics of the online and off-line social networks. Participation in online collective actions has two aspects: (1) the influence of online activities on the social movement and (2) the concrete reality that causes the online collective actions. From a sociological perspective, the question is to what extent—if at all—online social networks can substitute for off-line social networks in terms of not only circulating information but also providing incentives for the movement.

Theory and Methodology

To examine this question and shed some light on the role of online activism in the Green Movement by taking into account dynamics of off-line and online social networks, and the roles of informal activists, I will apply the structural-cognitive model (SCM) proposed by Karl Dieter Opp. The SCM is a synthesis of several important social movement approaches, such as resource mobilization, framing approach, political opportunities, and collective action theory.[12] The model explicitly links the macro and micro level. This approach takes into consideration the many different aspects that SCM covers at the theoretical level and, more importantly, it allows investigating the combination of off- and online social networks in a unique model.

Figure 7.1 shows the simple form of SCM. As can be seen, macro variables such as political opportunities, social contexts, and new technologies influence the outcome of cognitive processes such as changes of beliefs and attitudes, which affect individual incentives to participate in social movements. Incentives affect whether or not individuals decide to participate in a protest. Integration of individual behaviors results in the emergence of political protests or social movements at the macro level. Drawing on this simple form of the SCM, Figure 7.2 sketches a macro-micro model, which is the basis for explaining the role of online social networks in the Green Movement. According to Opp, political opportunities, social networks, new

Figure 7.1 Simplified Structural-Congnitive Model (SCM)

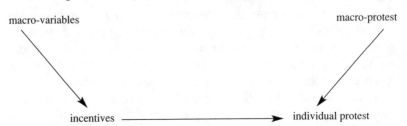

Figure 7.2 Extended Micro-Micro SCM Model

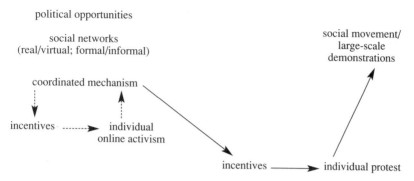

Source: Based on Opp, *Theories of Political Protest and Social Movements.*

technologies, and coordination mechanisms are macro-level variables, while incentives, including social incentives, moral incentives, and the incentives to achieve the collective good, are micro-level ones. The dependent variable is the emergence of social movements. For instance, in the Iranian context after the 2009 presidential election, the perception of fraud in the election initiated the political event. Social networks in this case study are considered to be of two types: (1) formal social networks, which were used by opposition organizations and groups, and (2) informal social networks or personal social networks. Each of the two categories is divided into two subcategories: off-line and online. It is obvious that one can be embedded in each or all of those networks. Moreover, new technologies defined in the original SCM are replaced by online social networks where circulating information generates incentives to participate in the movement. The participation in online collective/individual activities does need participation incentives. Those incentives are provided by macro variables, and, in turn, the consequences of these online activities influence movement participation incentives (this loop is shown in Figure 7.2 by dashed lines).

For the purpose of this study, the chronology of the events has been divided into three periods: the preelection campaign, postelection demonstrations (June 2009 to the end of that year), and the abeyance of the Green Movement (January 2010 to the end of that year). Each of the next sections is allocated to each period. In the first part, which covers the campaign trail, the rise of online social networks in the Green Movement will be studied. The second section is dedicated to the period of regular large-scale demonstrations when the Green Movement was present in the streets and the Internet became prominent in terms of circulation of information and news. The third section is concerned with the abeyance period when the movement exited the streets and went off-line temporarily, while the Internet was supposed to shoulder the burden of increasing participation incentives. I will analyze separately each of the variables mentioned in the three sections of this chapter. By analyzing each period, I will investigate the questions as to how and to what extent off-line and online social networks relate to one another in contributing to the creation of incentives for participation in the movement, as well as disseminating news and information.

The Campaign Trail: Emerging Out of a Website

In September 2008, the reconstruction of Mohsen Rezaei's website[13] was a strong signal that the rumors that he intended to run for the presidency were true.[14] Rezaei was not the only candidate entering the election stage by constructing a website. Abdollah Nouri, the former interior minister during Mohammad Khatami's administration, also announced the possibility of his presidential candidacy on a website constructed by some young journalists and students. Since 1999, when Nouri was sentenced to five years in prison for political and religious dissent[15] in a sensational trial, he had been on the margins of Iranian power politics and was regarded as a symbol of the structural reformist trend. Now, to become a candidate he had to first test the waters, namely, to see how the government would react to his candidacy and to what extent he could compete with other reformist candidates, particularly Khatami.[16] The website, which was named Khordaad after a newspaper Nouri had owned, soon invited its audience to a small brainstorming gathering. The audience was asked to be active on the website because Nouri did not have a physical venue of communication; after his trial he was not allowed to start another newspaper.[17]

Mehdi Karroubi, the first candidate to declare officially his bid for the presidency, had established a newspaper called *National Trust* (*Etemad-e Melli*) after the previous presidential election in 2005 when he claimed that the election was fraudulent and started preparing for the next one. Even though the high circulation of Karroubi's newspaper gave him access to a large audience, just before the election season, when radical reformists joined his campaign, Karroubi's electoral promises shifted from the center of Iranian politics toward the middle-class "progressive" interests, which were not tolerated by the regime in a physical newspaper but could only be articulated online. Thus, Karroubi's campaign set up the website Change (Tagheer .com), his campaign slogan, and an online presence, too.

Mir-Hossein Mousavi, the candidate who was to become the most significant opponent of the incumbent Mahmoud Ahmadinejad and who was heavily supported on the Internet by the youth in the country, released the first issue of his newspaper, *Kalameh Sabz*, during the period close to election day; he had recieved the permit for the paper two months earlier when the restraints on the press were loosened. Prior to that time period many websites supported his candidacy; the young campaigners were active in mowj.ir and the most prominent news website was Jomhouriat. Mousavi's campaign also ran two websites, Kalameh and Ghalamnews. His official Facebook page[18] (with more than 150,000 members in January 2011) has been administrated by a volunteer residing outside Iran since the spring of 2009.

Ironically, in January 2009 the government gave access to some previously blocked social networking sites such as Facebook and Twitter, although in the week leading to the election, those sites were filtered again. It is hard to pinpoint the causes of unblocking such popular websites. Some analysts[19] have argued that Ahmadinejad, the only candidate supported by the government and its hardliners, also used—or was tempted to use—social networking websites as well as all other Internet possibilities for his campaign. Notwithstanding negative propaganda of the government about blogging and social networking, in the Iranian blogosphere John Kelly and Bruce Etling discovered a considerable cluster of conservative/religious bloggers that support Ahmadinejad,[20] contrary to widely held expectations, and more interestingly, they report that this particular cluster expanded the more Election Day came nearer.[21]

At the start of the official campaigning period, political developments in Iran attracted global attention. To show that the country was enjoying freedom, the government opened the political sphere and extended its tolerance to some degree, thereby opening the space for more opposition voices. Moreover, during the official campaigning period, streets became a space for political discussions and face-to-face dialogues, while government pressure on newspapers decreased.

Three days before the election, Tehran witnessed an unprecedented rally, namely "the human chain" initiated by Mousavi's supporters. The number of people that held hands along 12 kilometers of the streets of Tehran to show their solidarity in large numbers is estimated to have been around 150,000. Another rally was held by Karroubi's supporters, who were mostly students and activists. Street protests proved that citizens were inspired to participate, because they never left the streets till the balloting day.

Together with the activities and the discourses on the streets, the Internet was also important for the candidates. News circulated on campaign and supporters' websites. For instance, student activists of the Office of the Stability of Unity (Daftar-e Tahkim-e Vahdat) and the youth-based party Graduates' Association (Advar-e Tahkim-e Vahdat), which supported Karroubi's promises, set up a headquarters, that was independent from Karroubi's campaign called Free Citizen (Shahrvand-e Azad). Young active members of Free Citizen worked on the streets and engaged in face-to-face interaction with people and held meetings. In addition, they launched the website shahrvandazad .com. "We intended to continue our political activities after the election," said Mohammad Sadeghi, spokesman of Shahrvandazad. "Therefore, we believe that it is impossible to function without a website." He stressed that "we use Shahrvandazad.com only as a news source and not as a means of communication with the supporters. We did it in the campaign."[22]

We can divide this period into two subperiods: (1) when the regime still restricted political activities and newspapers, so the major part of discourse took place online, which paved the way for the prominent role of the Internet; and (2) when the government loosened restraints a couple of weeks before the election, which led to the emergence of the street as a locus of participation and the revitalization of newspapers. This subperiod saw the emergence of explicit political activism and organization.

The Iranian blogosphere followed suit. Imagar, nickname of the editor of Imayan.blogsky.com, said that "before the presidential election, politics was the marginal part of the Imayan, while literature, philosophy, religion, movies, daily life were the main parts."[23] However, about eight months before the balloting day, he started writing about the election. Arash Kamangir (Abadpour), editor of Kamangir.net blog, also remembers that "one of the first posts that [he] wrote about the recent elections in Iran was on 20 February 2009. [He and] a group of Iranian bloggers decided to publish an open invitation to the blogosphere in order to encourage discussion about the election."[24] In one common post, the twelve Iranian bloggers stated that they intended to have an insightful and durable discussion in the blogosphere on the election and expected that the outcome would be a response from the politicians and candidates to those public discussions. Another blogger, Arman Amiri, the founder of the weblog Assembly of Maniacs (Majma-e Divanegan; divanesara2.blogspot.com), stated that months before the campaigning in the streets began, many hot discussions were under way in the blogosphere. However, with the approach of the election this changed. Amiri adds:

> We all had the experience of the 2005 election, when the connection between the intellectual elites and the masses of the society was cut out. For this reason our analysis was that if we were to operate only in the cyberspace, we would be dealing with an audience belonging to the upper classes of the society. Therefore, we spent most of our time on the streets in the south of Tehran for the purpose of political advertisements.[25]

The period can be explained by the proposed SCM model. In the presence of organizations and formal activists, formal and informal social networks play a key role in increasing incentives for political participation. Openness was a political opportunity that allowed organizations to be active. To increase incentives, off-line social networks played a more significant role than that of the online networks, with both formal and informal ones operating at full capacity. Although informal and formal online social networks were present at that time, they were mainly functioning as sources of news and information dissemination rather than providing participation incentives. The election environment that politicized the society provides incentives for people to participate in online cooperation, too. The emergence of mass street rallies is also an indication that individual incentives were also at a high level in this period.

Mass Calendar Demonstrations: Interaction Between the Streets and the Internet

The night before the balloting, the text messaging service of mobile phones was cut off. Later that day security forces attacked the main office of Mousavi's campaign. After the shocking results of the election were announced on Saturday afternoon, people spontaneously took to the streets. The results showed that the incumbent, Ahmadinejad, won some 63 percent of the votes cast, while the oppositionist candidate, Mousavi, received some 34 percent. On Saturday night the arrests of political activists began. Monday afternoon was the beginning of four consecutive days of "silent demonstrations," in which protesters stayed quiet.[26] That evening police and *bassij* militias attacked the headquarters of Mousavi's paper *Kalameh Sabz* and the office of Kalameh, the official website of Mousavi's campaign. After the election for a number of weeks, security forces were present at the publishing centers of newspapers and magazines of dissidents to monitor what could and what could not be published. At the time, the regime's top priorities were the shutting down of newspapers and suppressing and monitoring the circulation of news and information. The regime first suppressed official news sources before moving on to individual journalists and political activists. According to Reporters Without Borders, six months after the election, more than 100 journalists were arrested and 50 others were expelled from the country (the real number is certainly higher than this), and 12 newspapers and journals were shut down in this period. It added that

> several newspapers have been censored after publishing articles contradicting the official line, while others, including more than 10 national dailies, have been closed down altogether. They include *Kalameh Sabz* (13 June), *Etemad-e Melli* (17 August) and the business newspaper *Sarmayeh* (2 November). The last one to be closed was the daily *Hayat-e no* on 8 December after carrying reports about the crackdown on the previous day's National Student Day protests.[27]

Next the regime arrested the administrators of the websites that had supported the two opposition candidates.[28]

At this juncture, the Internet became the venue of collective discourse and opposition. The transfer to the Internet was almost natural because it had already taken root in the political culture of the country and had played a significant role circulating information in the preelection period. Since it was no longer possible to operate via official media, which were totally suppressed, the Internet came to the rescue. Mousavi once more stressed his campaign slogan, "Each Iranian is a [campaign] headquarter." In the previous campaign trail, this meant face-to-face and off-line communication, campaigning, and mobilization. Now, however, he was referring to the oppositional discourse and activism in online social networks and online interactions. He stated, "Today, a cyber-network has popped up that in the absence of [standard] media is performing very effectively and the social cores that are active behind this cyber-network are less vulnerable and members of these cores have given the movement a dynamic nature which has made us more hopeful to the effectiveness of this network."[29]

Soon after the severe repression of the press, news circulation moved fully onto the Internet, and the opposition made several attempts to counter the suppressive measures of the government. The opposition upgraded the websites that were launched before the election and were operating only moderately to a very active level (e.g., mowj.ir), while some websites came into being during the suppressive postelection days, mainly outside the country, to give opposition journalists a forum in which to express themselves (e.g., Jaras, rahesabz.net). Thus, a professional space in the Internet for information dissemination was created. Opposition groups experimented with different ways to relay information, including an attempt to circulate e-mail newsletters. One of the groups that started this process was the Student Information Centre (SIC), which ventured onto the scene from outside the country with the following self-introduction: "[SIC] was created by a group of Iranian students on 16 June 2009, four days after Iran's presidential elections, to help bypass filtering of websites and news resources." SIC sent three bilingual (Persian/English) e-mails to its subscribers. Their aim is "to break through the censorship and Internet filtering, send news to those who don't have time to read various news websites and those with limited familiarity or access to the Internet." Another such group, which operated inside the country with a different political view, was Green Freedom Wave (Mowjcamp.com), previously the Green Movement's news website that took up the trend of sending newsletters to its subscribers.

A different sort of oppositional experiment was the production of video media. Mohsen Sazegara, an opposition activist and former politician residing outside the country, was one of the first to resort to this medium. Immediately after the election he began to put ten-minute video clips on YouTube, which included news, analysis, and recommendations as to how opposition activists should proceed with their agendas. The number of viewers of these daily shows has a slight downward trend from July 2009 to December 2009 and then again from February 2010 onward, with fluctuations on calendar days (see Figure 7.3). A similar experiment was carried out by an academic from Columbia University, Hamid Dabashi, who began to issue weekly videos of fifteen minutes' length, called "The Week in Green," in which he provides brief news items, analysis, and interviews with intellectuals.[30]

The activities on the Web related to the Green Movement during this period were not exclusively by formal activists who have selective incentives to participate, but by informal activists and ordinary citizens as well. Balatarin.com, a social news aggregator website similar to Digg.com and considered one of the most active and influential websites in the Green Movement,[31] is regularly updated through the cooperation of a huge number of its users. The dramatic increase in June 2009 in the number of political and societal posts

Figure 7.3 Viewership of Sazegara's Daily Show on YouTube, 6 June 2009–13 November 2010

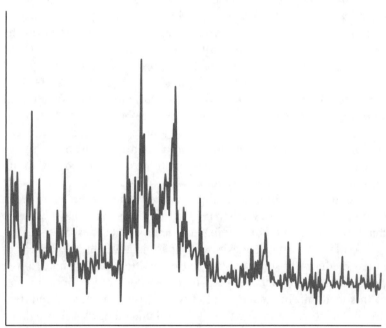

Source: YouTube, http://www.youtube.com/user/adminsazegara.

submitted by Balatarin users and the number of active users during the mass demonstrations period demonstrates that off-line upheavals and political salience positively affect online activism incentives.[32] Interestingly, the number of users with more than 200 submissions to Balatarin—in eight months—is relatively the same in the three same-length periods in 2008, 2009, and 2010, whereas the numbers of users with less than 30 submissions in 2009 remarkably were greater than ones in 2008 and 2010 (see Figure 7.4).[33] Not only did real off-line factors inspire the users to online activism but also informal and emergent online activists played a considerable role in Iran's Green Movement.

After the election, in addition to the banning of all official oppositional channels of communications, information, and news, hundreds

**Figure 7.4 Number of Participants Categorized
by the Range of Submissions in Balatarin**

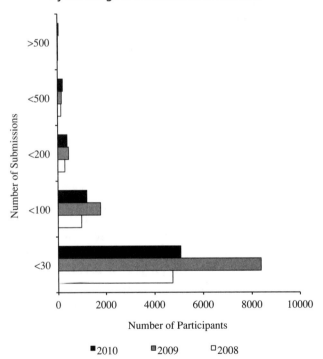

Source: Honari, "The Consequences of Iran's Green Movement for an On-line Network Structure: The Case of Balatarin.com," IAMCR conference, Istanbul, 2011, http://alihonari.com/slides/IAMCR_2011[5].pdf.

of political activists, journalists, students, academics, and human rights activists were detained.[34] On top of that, many ordinary dissidents, those who did not have any official or strong ties with oppositional organizations and parties,[35] were jailed by the government in order to paralyze the movement. In spite of the absence of oppositional organization and the clamping down on all official channels of news and information, ordinary citizens undertook various kinds of collective action, such as collectively shouting "Allahu akbar" from rooftops, boycotting state TV channels, and, most importantly, participating in massive demonstrations on important calendar days. Thus, in the absence of formal social networks and with the regular flow of information disrupted, the incentives for participating in the Green Movement not only existed but were potent and translated into well-organized events. The questions that arise in relation to this are: What are the sources of such incentives? Where to and how do news and information spread? Which means facilitate coordination?

Annabelle Sreberny and Gholam Khiabany concluded that social networking sites such as Facebook and Twitter did not play a major role in organizing postelection demonstrations.[36] Information about the date and place of demonstrations easily spread among people by face-to-face interactions, satellite TVs, and text messaging, even during the four days of silent demonstrations, when people informed each other about the next demonstrations in the streets. However, after the demonstrations took place, video clips and photos were disseminated through the Internet, and those clips, in addition to social communication between Internet users, increased the incentives of participation by demonstrating that a significant number of fellow citizens was taking part in the protests. Figures 7.3 and 7.5 illustrate, respectively, the number of viewers of a daily show about the Green Movement, and Google search numbers for four influential online news websites, which all have relatively similar profiles in that they experienced substantial rapid growth in June 2009, then declined steadily but without falling as low as before election, with fluctuations on the Green Movement's events. Figures 7.3 and 7.5 reveal that demands for information and news were considerable in the demonstrations period, with the Internet playing a major role in supplying this demand. On the other hand, ordinary people had enough incentives to contribute to online actions.

When analyzing how incentives are generated in these types of settings, the literature relies on the work of Karl Dieter Opp and

Figure 7.5 Volume of Google Searches for the Words *Balatarin, Fars News, BBC,* and *Jaras* in Iran

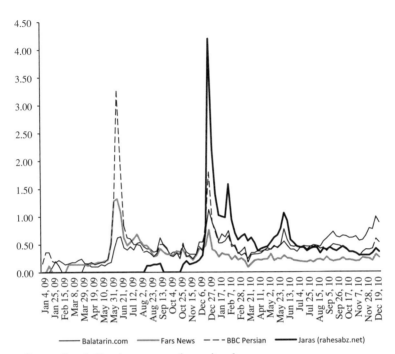

———— Balatarin.com　━━━━ Fars News　— — — BBC Persian　━━━━ Jaras (rahesabz.net)

Source: Google Trends, www.google.com/trends.

Note: Volume reflects how many searches have been done for a particular term, relative to the total number of searches done on Google over time. The data is normalized and presented on a scale from 0–100. Each point on the graph is divided by the highest point, or 100; 0 is shown when Gooogle does not have enough data.

Christiane Gern. They explain the emergence of large-scale Monday demonstrations in Leipzig in 1989 by using the basic SCM model.[37] In former East Germany, as an authoritarian system, there were no opportunities for forming opposition groups and organizations to mobilize members or personal networks. To investigate how the demonstrations could emerge without any organization, Opp and Gern collected huge datasets in 1990 examining the situation in 1989. Their findings show that political events such as the liberalization of the neighboring countries increased the dissatisfaction of former East German citizens and roused collective incentives through demands for more freedom. Personal networks among friends who criticize and those who were politically active boosted social incentives. Finally, Monday peace services decreased the perception of risk of participation by getting many people together at a certain time at a certain place (Karl Marx Square). This mechanism, which is called "spontaneous coordination," relaxed the start-up problem of collective action: when the cost of individual participation is more than the probability of success.

Comparing the Iranian context to Opp and Gern's study, the model explains the Iranian postelection period, leading to the conclusion that the political events, spontaneous coordination, and informal social networks (online and/or off-line) at the macro level increase incentives at the micro level. The way the election was engineered and carried out as a political event created the perception of a "big sham" among people. Additionally, brutal repression in combination with, paradoxically, the considerable circulation of information before and after the election increased the collective incentive for democracy. These influences were manifested in the opposition's major slogans "Where is my vote?" and "Down with the dictator." Those changes in the political scene and off-line social contexts also provided incentives to participate in online activities, which in turn strengthened participation in the Green Movement. What facilitated the spontaneous coordination in the movement was the fact that people were aware that on some calendar days many more people would participate in demonstrations.

However, in the absence of organizations and formal social networks, the most important reasons for the increase of incentives were the informal social networks, which, after this period, became the center of attention for opposition elites and leaders. Mousavi described this situation in a meeting on 30 September 2009: "For instance, although there was no official announcement made for the Qods Day,[38] we witnessed this massive presence in the Qods Day's rallies and this was despite the fact that many families were concerned and had prevented their children from taking to the streets due to the threats and the events that had happened in the past three months, so this was only a result of the effectiveness of this network." He added: "Forming a new party cannot add to the country's existing capacities, while strengthening the cores of the social movement will create new capacities and improve the movement."[39] In his statement number 13, Mousavi elaborated on his purpose in strengthening the social networks: "When we speak of enhancing social networks or living the Green Path, we are immediately asked how. The same way that you are. This is not to form social networks that do not exist and then strengthen them; the point is that people's power lies in the social networks that have formed naturally and by the guidance in their nature. We have to understand their importance."[40] He emphasized personal networks because at that time it was accepted that working through formal social networks was not possible. The postelection period and events proved the major importance of informal social networks.

Abeyance Period: Coming Back to the Internet

On 11 February 2010, the first unsuccessful demonstration took place. The Green Movement's plan to highjack the official rally which was called the "Trojan Horse" tactic, did not work. They could not reveal their signs during the progovernment mass rally because either they were relatively few compared to progovernment participants or they were scared to expose their green banners among a dense population of police and security agents.[41] Afterwards no more mass demonstrations occurred. On the anniversary of the uprising of the Green Movement, in June 2010, when people expected that another massive demonstration would be organized, opposition leaders believed that the scale of repression on the part of the authorities would be high and participation would be therefore relatively low. Thus, they demanded that no one take to the streets. Mehdi Karroubi described the situation thus: "The Movement has moved beyond the point of being present on the streets every day, and we are now in the phase in which it is stabilizing."[42] Ardashir Amir Arjomand, Mousavi's adviser, also pointed out that this phase is one of "stability and expansion through democratic dialogue and the creation of unity."[43] He considers it necessary at this juncture for the opposition to be in possession of different forms of media.[44]

In a meeting, Mousavi stated that he saw no bright prospects in the future for freedom of expression and freedom of the press in Iran and called on everyone to contribute to the expansion of information and strengthening of the independent media through the Internet. He asked dissidents to be politically active in their homes and workplaces, which indicates the importance of employing all forms of informal social networking in this phase of the movement. He famously said that:

> Every opening that is shutdown another window should be opened immediately. When a newspaper is closed down, the legal means to open another one must be sought. When a weblog is closed down, tens of other weblogs must be initiated in order to defend people's rights. This is the only way and we are countless and we can do this.[45]

The YouTube channel "Stands with Fist"[46] was one of the success-ful attempts to acknowledge and respond to Mousavi's call, carried out by an informal art group. The members of this group have never been members of any political organization, although they describe their po-litical roles as Mousavi campaigners. The director of the group[47] made his first video clip about the Mousavi-Ahmad election debate[48] a few weeks prior to the 2009 election. He believes the only way he is able to contribute "voluntarily" and "anonymously" to the Green Move-ment is by making these video clips. In this period the group is mainly focusing on making and distributing their own video clips, which are informative about the demands and views of the movement and aim to spread hope among people. However, they also submitted video clips of street demonstrations in the heat of the movement in order to spread information. According to the director, "We are now in the mainte-nance phase of the Green Movement. In all video clips we deliberately use the slogan of 'Where is my vote?' to demonstrate that our move-ment along with its demands is still very much alive."[49]

This period can be described as the absence of organizations and formal social networks, the suppression of formal media, silence in the streets, the necessity of providing participation incentives in the movement, and the desire to have new media available. The new sit-uation required new strategies that Mousavi highlighted in statement number 18; one such strategy was the expansion of social networks (both online and off-line).[50] In the absence of political events, spon-taneous coordination, and formal social networks, informal off- and online social networks should have played a role in increasing incen-tives of participation in the Green Movement. Moreover, they should have facilitated the flow of information.

The area of news and information underwent a transformation during this period. The distribution of newsletters via e-mail (e.g., mowjcamp, Neda Newsletter, and SIC) almost came to an end be-cause it did not seem useful anymore. Other forms of online ac-tivism were taken up, as the situation and its constraints differed from those of the other periods. New attempts and experiments with online social networks differed in one obvious way from the previ-ous ones: along with the dissemination of news and information, they aspired to create new hopes and incentives for the opposition. Sabzlink.com, a social news aggregator website, came into being to strengthen Green online social networks. IranGreenVoice.com, which replaced mowjcamp.com, declared at the beginning that it came on the scene to disseminate accurate information and also to create "hope" and "thought" for the movement.[51] In January 2010 two websites (Divarnevis[52] and Khabarnameh-Kaghazi[53]) launched their initiatives. Divarnevis announced that it wrote to stay hopeful and to instill hope in others. Blogger Amiri explained the reason behind his introduction of a podcast on his weblog, which is a half-hour weekly overview of Green Movement news: "A tide of dejection is apparent in the stagnant stage of the movement [the abeyance period]. With this, I would like to keep my friends' hopes alive and tell the world that there are still people who are concerned with the fate of the movement."[54]

Given the circumstances at this stage, the expectations people had of cyberspace were more than obtaining news and information. There is the aspiration that it could affect participation incentives in all forms of protests (street demonstrations as well as online protests). In practice, this strategy did not immediately fulfill the promise of hope, and incentives did not increase. In this period, although some political elites and leaders emphasized strengthening and expanding informal social networks, what they focused on is the online social networks, because they have no hopes for the off-line informal social networks to undergo a radical change. The movement is trying to work on those drawbacks to make itself more vibrant and for this purpose has attempted to publish online newspapers designed exclusively for printing so that they can be distributed off-line.

In this period one macro change affecting online activism is that the diaspora's activism on the Internet is becoming more effective and more attuned to the reality on the ground. During the two decades from the first half of the 1980s, when a wave of political opposition activists emigrated from Iran because of severe repression, the gap in terms of political view between Iranians inside and outside widened.[55] However, the recent wave of migrants who began to leave in the wake of Ahmadinejad's first term in 2005 included many activists who were young and Internet-savvy and who changed the characteristics of political activism outside Iran.[56] The majority of the recent emigrants emerged from the Reformist Movement (1997–2005), the Green Movement, and electoral campaigns. These characteristics, which are different from those of previous Iranian migrants, created an opportunity for the Internet to be used in accordance with the real and practical needs of the Green Movement.

One of the successful experiences of the Iranian diaspora was the campaign "We Are All Majid" (men in veil). On 7 December 2009,

"student day" in Iran,[57] Majid Tavakoli, one of the leaders of the student movement, was arrested after delivering a speech. One of the
media outlets associated with the Iranian state published photos of
him while he was forced to wear a hijab, which is traditionally associated with women, in order to "humiliate" him. The official claim
was that he was arrested trying to escape from the university in such
clothing. No more than a night later, a small group of young Iranians
in the diaspora (all recently had left Iran) responded to the published
photo. They made a Facebook page and asked men "to take a picture
[of] themselves while wearing 'women's clothes' and send it . . . so
that [they] can publish the photos in mass, in order to express solidarity with Majid, subvert the Iranian government's intentions, and
mock the regime's ideology on gender binaries."[58] This idea became
rapidly popular, and in less than twenty-four hours many Iranian
men, mostly young, joined this campaign. Following this, video
clips were made about the Facebook event, and support for Tavakoli
gained momentum.[59] Ali Abdi, one of the campaign organizers,
highlights the achievements of the campaign: it "attracted a diverse
group of participants and audiences. Not only the well-known activists but also academics and ordinary people get engaged in the
campaign. Moreover, it passed the 'language barrier' and 'media
prejudice.' It was one of the first few times that the non-Persian
mainstream media in the West, such as CNN, the *New York Times,*
France 24, etc. covered the story."[60] This only could be done by
Iranian youth who live outside Iran, because they could reveal their
faces and be familiar with non-Persian language. A change in the
way of using the Internet for the formation of online campaigns that
effectively coupled with protests and events was another feature of
this period. This resulted from the unintended change in the characteristics of the Iranian diaspora.

Conclusion

In this chapter, I investigated the role of the Internet and online social
networks in the Green Movement in the period between the electoral
campaign and the seemingly petering out of mass demonstrations in
the fall of 2010. The aim was to assess to what extent the Internet
played a role in Iran's Green Movement, specifically relating to the
dissemination of news and information and to increasing incentives

for active participation. The following conclusions can be drawn from this study.

In the first period, the preelection campaign, freedom of participation sprang from the nature of the election atmosphere as a political opportunity accompanied by activities within and between formal and informal social networks, which led to increased participation in the election. Information and news circulated by means of formal/informal and online/off-line social networks/media. The online political activities of the younger, better-educated generation of the country and the widespread use of new media by presidential candidates in this period paved the way for the increased reliance on the Internet after the election. In the second period, the postelection demonstrations, both the "big sham" and the brutality of the repression, which were exposed by citizen journalism and modern media, increased incentives to participate in the protests. At this time, streets and off-line social networks were a source of incentives, with spontaneous coordination playing a major role in the emergence of large-scale calendar demonstrations and silent demonstrations. When severe repression heavily weakened the formal social networks, the Internet began to shoulder the burden of circulating information locally and globally. In the third period, the abeyance of the Green Movement, there were no political opportunities for the formal movement activities. When the lack of incentives became evident, only informal social networks functioned as a source of incentives and as a means to spread information and news.

This study shows that placing the considerable burden of increasing participation incentives and communicating oppositional opinions and news on the shoulders of online social networks was not entirely successful and created a number of difficulties. A possible explanation for this finding might be a result of the mistrust of online social networks. Social trust positively correlates with participation in a collective action or civic participation.[61] Therefore, an online social network, on the one hand, is a safe environment for distributing critical news and opinions, but, on the other hand, might not be an effective arena for increasing participation in a social movement. Another factor contributing to the lack of trust in the Internet is the systematic monitoring of online networks by a so-called cyberarmy, that is, a government agency specifically for the Internet and cyberspace, and interference by the regime through the spreading of misleading rumors and other manipulative tactics.

Another possible explanation for this might be the limitations of online social networks in connecting to all social groups. Demographic surveys of Iranian Internet users reveal that the overwhelming majority of users are young, highly educated city dwellers. This implies that to mobilize the potential participants of the movement among economically lower classes, ethnic minorities, blue-collar workers, and people with low education and limited economic resources, the movement should consider other ways of gaining sympathy, recruiting members, and stimulating participation incentives.[62] A remedy would be for online activists to pay attention to "the strength of weak ties" and bridge the information gap between highly educated city dwellers and young people and other social classes and groups on the streets. Mark Granovetter argues that in social networks *weak ties* link separate clusters with *strong ties*. It implies that weak ties also play a key role in transferring information, opinions, and behavior. Another solution to avoid the narrow homogeneity of online social networks is to link the online discussions, information, and activities to off-line ones in different ways, such as through graffiti, distributing leaflets, and hard-copy newsletters and newspapers. Some attempts in such direction have already been made: *Kalameh,* the banned newspaper of Mousavi's campaign, has started to put the newspaper online using a pdf file, which can be easily printed and distributed. Other opposition groups such as student activists and the National Trust Party have started following the same strategy.

The Green Movement's attempts to employ the Internet more effectively and influentially are still being carried out successfully. However, it should not be expected that the Internet per se will lead the Green Movement to victory and make Iran more democratic. Nor is it expected that online social networks will function as real social networks that could provide enough incentive to lead to high-risk mass demonstrations. However, the Internet in the long term provides opportunities for ordinary people to exercise "the art of presence," as Asef Bayat defines it in real space (i.e., streets).[63] In order to popularize even further the Green Movement, these attempts can go toward creating bridges between clusters that have access to the Internet and those who do not. Furthermore, these efforts provide suitable ground on which to intensify the incentives for participation in demonstrations by finding and implementing the successful strategies that increase the likelihood of cooperation in online collective behavior whose goals relate to the off-line reality. Such collective virtual activities manifest themselves in the outcome of a tangible social movement.

Notes

1. For the detailed report, see Labovitz, "Iranian Traffic Engineering."
2. See Agence France-Presse report from Tehran on 13 June 2009: "The main mobile telephone network in Iran was cut in the capital Tehran Saturday evening while popular Internet websites Facebook and YouTube also appeared to be blocked."
3. This position has been questioned from several perspectives. For instance, see Shapiro, "The Internet."
4. For instance, see Quirk, "Iran's Twitter Revolution."
5. Pfeifle, "A Nobel Peace Prize for Twitter?"
6. See Gladwell, "Why the Revolution Will Not Be Tweeted"; and Morozov, "Iran: Downside to the 'Twitter Revolution.'"
7. Esfandyari, "The Twitter Devolution."
8. See the interview with Hamid Dabashi in Layne, "How Iran's Political Battle Is Fought in Cyberspace."
9. Ashraf, "The Digital Media Response."
10. "Twitter didn't start the protests in Iran, nor did it make them possible. But there's no question that it has emboldened the protesters, reinforced their conviction that they are not alone and engaged populations outside Iran in an emotional, immediate way that was never possible before." Grossman, "Iran Protests."
11. Schectman, "Iran's Twitter Revolution?"
12. Opp, *Theories of Political Protest and Social Movements.*
13. www.rezaee.ir/.
14. Yazdanpanah, "Namzadi-e Mohsen Rezali Jeddi Shod," *Kargozaran,* 21 shahrivar 1387 (12 September 2008).
15. Saba, "Profile of Abdollah Nouri."
16. At that time Khatami was the reformists' candidate. Later, when Mousavi announced his candidacy, Khatami withdrew and gave his full support to Mousavi.
17. Abdollah Nouri later withdrew his candidacy.
18. See http://www.facebook.com/mousavi.
19. See Sreberny and Khiabany, *Blogistan: The Internet and Politics in Iran,* pp. 170–171; Yahyanejad, "The Effectiveness of Internet," p. 9; and Esfandyari, "Why Did Iran Unblock Facebook?"
20. Kelly and Etling, *Mapping Iran's On-line Public.*
21. See Kelly and Etling, "Mapping Change in Iranian Blogosphere."
22. Personal communication, 15 November 2010.
23. Personal communication, 21 November 2010.
24. Personal communication, 27 November 2010.
25. Personal communication, 18 November 2010.
26. Four so-called silent demonstrations took place in Tehran streets in the week after the 2009 Iranian election.
27. Reporters Without Borders, "Iran's Six-month-old Crackdown."
28. They included Mohammad Davari, editor of Sahamnews.org, the National Trust party's formal website; and Hamzeh Karami, administrator, and Masoud Bastani, editor of Jomhouriat.com.

29. Mousavi's lecture in a meeting with the members of the Imam Path Fraction (Reformists) in the Parliament on 30 September 2009; retrieved from www.facebook.com/note.php?note_id=146750392605.

30. The first video was released on 24 October 2009. The official website is www.weekingreen.org/.

31. See Yahyanejad, "The Effectiveness of Internet"; and Sreberny and Khiabany, *Blogistan.*

32. See Honari, "The Consequences of Iran's Green Movement for an On-line Network Structure"; and Yahyanejad, "The Effectiveness of Internet."

33. Honari, "The Consequences of Iran's Green Movement."

34. For a report on the postelection arrests, see Amnesty International, *From Protest to Prison.*

35. Up to 5,000, according to the regime's estimates.

36. Sreberny and Khiabany, *Blogistan.*

37. Opp and Gern, "Dissident Groups."

38. "Qod's Day" is an annual event on the last Friday of Ramadan, for which the Iranian government holds rallies of its supporters to express solidarity with the Palestinian people.

39. Mousavi's lecture in a meeting with the members of the Imam Path Fraction (Reformists) in the parliament on 30 September 2009.

40. Mousavi, *Nurturing the Seed of Hope,* 83.

41. Abedi, "Iran, Facebook, and the Limits of Online Activism."

42. See an exclusive interview with Karroubi by alarabiya.net, 9 June 2010, www.alarabiya.net/articles/2010/06/09/110877.html.

43. Arjomand, "Green Media Outlet Vital to Informing People."

44. Ibid.

45. Mousavi in a meeting with the members of the student branch of Mojahedin of the Islamic Revolution Organization, www.facebook.com/note.php?note_id=383898487605.

46. www.youtube.com/user/standswithfist60.

47. The director wished to remain anonymous.

48. In Front of History's Mirror, http://youtube.com/watch?feature=plpp&v=wlDxtfsOo14.

49. Personal communication, 10 January 2011.

50. Mousavi, *Nurturing the Seed of Hope.*

51. www.irangreenvoice.com/content/489.

52. In English graffiti, http://www.divarnevis.com/.

53. http://khabarnameh88.blogspot.com/.

54. Personal communication, 18 November 2010.

55. "On the one hand, the diaspora's memory of the repressive situation in Iran made them suspicious of any kind of activism from within the country. . . . On the other hand, Iranian activists inside the country felt ignored and distrusted the judgment of those living in the diaspora, believing that this group had been gone too long and was too far away to know the true situation." Ghorashi and Boersma, "The 'Iranian Diaspora' and the New Media."

56. There was also an emigration wave in the beginning of 2010 when the first round of prisoners who were set free began to flee the country, particularly after the last popular demonstrations, which led to attempts by the police to identify the protesters.

57. Iran's student day commemorates the anniversary of the Shah's military attack on the students of Tehran University on 7 December 1953, which resulted in the death of three students.

58. http://i-anima.blogspot.com/2010/12/queering-life.html.

59. The reader can see one of the clips that belongs to this campaign at www.youtube.com/watch?v=xNgN1rbXjLc&list=UUrxtqcKsV83kKKlaTS epeQ&index=14&feature=plcp.

60. Personal communication, 9 January 2011.

61. Putnam, Leonardi, and Nanetti, *Making Democracy Work.*

62. Klandermans, *The Social Psychology of Protest.*

63. Bayat, *Life as Politics.*

8

The Paradox of Government-Organized Civil Activism in Syria

Salam Kawakibi

During the first decade of the new millennium, Syria underwent a number of significant social and economic changes that profoundly affected its social structures, as other contributors to this volume have highlighted. These changes have been particularly evident in the economic realm and took place with the leadership's stated intention to transfer large parts of the state-controlled economy to the market, in a radical ideological shift from previous decades of economic management. According to Bashar al-Assad and his team of advisers, economic reforms were to be the building block for the gradual process of political liberalization that would see Syria slowly move away from its strict brand of political authoritarianism. Over the last decade significant legislative changes have been introduced to improve the climate for private investment through both Arab and other foreign investors. These reforms, which Bassam Haddad discusses in great detail in Chapter 4, have had a considerable impact on Syrian social structures, with new spheres of activity opening for the Syrian private sector, leading to hybrid economic patterns that mixed private enterprise with state intervention. Despite the continued presence of the state in the sphere of economic activities, ten years of market-oriented reforms led to state structures being progressively weakened in the economic arena, with the role of the state as direct producer declining significantly.

Early hopes that the progressive withdrawal of the state from direct economic activities would spill over to the political and social

169

domain have been shattered however, as state structures continued to maintain complete control of the public sphere and of social and political action. The violent repression of the antiregime demonstrations that started in the spring of 2011 indicates clearly that the regime is not ready to relinquish control of the state and weaken its authoritarian nature. The descent of the country into chaos due to the increasingly violent confrontation between rebels and regime loyalists is a powerful signal of the unwillingness of the ruling elites to give up power. This suggests that the spate of economic reforms and the relaxation of some of the more severe restrictions that had characterized Hafez al-Assad's rule were part of a larger process of authoritarian upgrading.[1] Together with the introduction of market-oriented reforms, the incumbent regime espoused the notion that Syrian civil society should have a prominent role in transforming the state, without altering its nature and challenging the pillars of the political system.

The emphasis on civil society activism and development was due to two factors. First, as a result of its withdrawal from the economy and the decline in the standard of living of low-wage earners and even of many members of the free professions, the Syrian government was unable to fully pursue its declared liberal economic policy. As a result, economic reforms remained piecemeal and selective, leading the regime to hesitantly at first allow greater room to maneuver to civil society organizations that would substitute the state for the delivery of services involving health, social affairs, and culture. Second, President Bashar al-Assad, in order to consolidate his position, needed to move away from his reliance on Baath Party structures and corporatism. To begin relying on different social constituencies from the ones that supported his father, he used the device of civil society. He stripped the concept of civil society activism of its liberal significance and made it fit his political project whereby civil society should serve the state's latest modernization project without challenging its political structures. Thus, permits to operate legally and in the open have been mainly granted to nonprofit organizations engaged in development, health, and social affairs, but not to associations engaged in advancing citizens' political and civil rights. This is also made clear in Line Khatib's Chapter 2 of this volume, where she argues that the religious nongovernmental associations benefited from not getting involved directly in political matters and could organize their charitable activities free from state interference.

The state went as far as setting up nongovernmental organizations (NGOs) in order to stimulate civil activism, and this chapter analyzes in detail one of these government-organized NGOs (GON-GOs). This is a relatively new phenomenon that blurs both the theoretical and empirical boundaries of what it means to be a civil society and where to look for it on the ground. In this chapter, I first examine the role that GONGOs are designed to play in the context of authoritarian upgrading. Subsequently, I argue, contrary to the extremely negative normative assumptions of the literature on GONGOs, that the creation of such organizations might have unintended consequences, which create semiautonomous dynamics within society that can have political repercussions. I explore in detail the case of the Syria Trust for Development. I offer readers a detailed analysis of this important organization, highlighting how it operates and what influence it has and might have on Syrian society and politics. In the extremely repressive climate within which the country finds itself after the early demonstrations of the spring of 2011, it might seem redundant to focus on the role of a GONGO since an armed struggle has broken out between rebels and regime loyalists, but the way in which civil society operates in Syria could make an important contribution to a more general understanding of how such organizations function in authoritarian contexts.

GONGOs and Civil Society Activism in the Arab World

As pointed out by Francesco Cavatorta and Vincent Durac,[2] there are three broad traditional understandings of civil society activism in the Arab world. First, it is perceived to be the realm of a limited number of organizations operating according to the traditional canons of liberal-democratic thinking and interested in promoting the democratization of the regime. Second, civil activism is simply seen as the space within which all sorts of different groups and associations operate and enter into a dynamic relation with the state; this sphere of activism is not necessarily concerned with liberal-democratic rights but can include apolitical groups as well. Finally, the third view convincingly argues that civil society, understood as a value-neutral concept, has grown significantly in the Arab world since the beginning of the 1990s, but this does not indicate that ruling elites are losing control of their own society, because both Islamist and secular groups are beholden to the state.

The main argument of the third approach is that the galaxy of civil society is largely composed of two types of associations. On the

one hand, we find groups that are autonomous from the state but realize that in order to operate they have to come to terms with the authoritarian structures in place; through this process of accommodation, they strengthen authoritarian practices.[3] On the other hand, we
have a large number of associations that are directly or indirectly set
up by high-ranking officials and members of the ruling elites and can
be considered GONGOs. For example, in Jordan two of the largest
development NGOs, the Jordanian Hashemite Fund for Human Development (JOHUD) and the Noor al-Hussein Foundation (NHF), are
effectively run by the royal family. These associations are perceived
to lack significant autonomy, to be part of new corporatist arrangements that serve regimes' aims to control rather than liberate society,
and to implement activities that attempt to relegitimize discredited
ruling elites.[4] The creation of this artificial civil society is therefore
part of authoritarian upgrading.

It is in the context of this third approach to the study of civil society that the analysis of GONGOs in Syria is placed. There is certainly more than a degree of truth to the argument that the explosion
of civil society activism and the considerable increase in the number
of associations across the Arab world is the product of the regimes'
intention to design new means of social control. In fact, a significant
number of civil society associations are a direct or indirect emanation
of the state itself or of people linked to the state's apparatus, as numerous empirical studies demonstrate.[5] This problematic linkage
with the regime meant that many of these organizations have been
overlooked in the academic scholarship on civil activism and their
activities have not been taken seriously because they are believed to
be simply an arm of the regime rather than a genuine form of social
expression. However, it would be a mistake to ignore them because,
in a restrictive environment, they offer insights on how the regime
thinks about its relations to society, how society views such organizations and makes use of them and, finally, how they can have unintended consequences once they have been set up.

For the regime, the direct setting up of GONGOs generally responded to three types of needs. First, economic reforms across the
region have diminished the state's capacity to deliver essential services, and the service-providing associations were perceived to be a
perfect vacuum filler. It is no coincidence that prominent members of
the ruling families of the Arab world are involved in such activism,
as the cases of Queen Rania in Jordan[6] or Leila Trabelsi in Tunisia[7]

demonstrate. Victorian-style charity work is the substitute for state intervention, whereby selected philanthropic and developmental projects that are run by members of the ruling elite for the benefit of disadvantaged groups replace effective wealth redistribution and equality of access to services.

Second, most Arab rulers have had to move away from traditional supportive constituencies and design new corporatist structures to satisfy emerging social groups that were favored by economic changes. The creation of GONGOs constituted an opportunity to tie members of these emerging social groups to the regime by offering both material (employment) and moral (doing good) benefits.

Third, GONGOs could attract significant sources of foreign funding, through their capacity as organic links to the regime, to deliver quickly and implement projects without much hindrance from the authorities. This framework of GONGOs' activism has the beneficial effect of demonstrating to the international community the willingness of the regimes to reform. In short, GONGOs are perceived to be useful to the regime and detrimental to the development of a genuine civil society that would be autonomous from the state and therefore able to increase social capital and, by implication, strengthen citizenship. Syria fits this pattern well, and it was certainly the intention of the regime to achieve these objectives when it made the decision to set up GONGOs. Economic changes created the need for service-providing entities separate from the state to take over responsibility for welfare. In addition to recognizing the inability of its own institutions to meet socioeconomic development needs, the state also acknowledged the failure of the many people's organizations to play any of the roles that the government wanted, so substitutes were required. The traditional youth, workers', and women's organizations linked to the Baath Party that were used to buttress and frame support for the policies of the regime no longer fulfilled their roles, having been undermined by disenchantment and corrupt practices. A more modern framework to garner social support among new social actors that had no time for traditional associations lay on the language and practice of civil society, emptied however of its political liberal rhetoric. Finally, and importantly in the Syrian case, the state recognized that the role of service provision could not be left entirely to the resurgent Islamist movements and it needed to launch its own civil society initiatives.

As mentioned earlier, there is more than a degree of truth to this "story" about the role of GONGOs in the Arab world, which have also been dubbed "democracy's impostors."[8] In a scathing take on the GONGO phenomenon, Moisés Naim states:

> Some GONGOs are benign, others irrelevant. But many . . . are dangerous. Some act as the thuggish arm of repressive governments. Others use the practices of democracy to subtly undermine democracy at home. Abroad, the GONGOs of repressive regimes lobby the United Nations and other international institutions, often posing as representatives of citizen groups with lofty aims when, in fact, they are nothing but agents of the governments that fund them.[9]

However, one might also postulate that unintended consequences could occur when setting up GONGOs, and this assumption could be helpful in providing a different take on their role, particularly in terms of their development over time. The literature on authoritarian upgrading assumes that the upgrading is successful because liberal reforms do not have any significant impact on the nature of authoritarianism and are simply empty shells. This might indeed be the case in the short term, but in the longer term the effects of sham liberalizing policies might be quite different from the ones that were intended. It has been often demonstrated that once an institution is created to carry out a specific task, dynamics develop independently from the intention of the creators, and the institution might take on roles not designated at the beginning.[10] This has been most notable recently in studies of the European Union, whose member states have set up numerous institutions that eventually managed to transcend the task for which they were created. According to Dyonissis Dimitrakopoulos,

> Institutions are more than mere agents of their creators. They produce unintended consequences by means of their autonomous action. In the context of the European Union (EU), supranational institutions, such as the European Court of Justice (ECJ) and the European Commission produce such consequences, even in areas where no direct or overt transfer of powers has taken place, while performing the roles assigned to them by their creators.[11]

Accordingly, the creation of GONGOs might lead to similar outcomes.

GONGOs in Syria

In light of the necessity of the regime to renew its social legitimacy, and at the initiative of Syria's First Lady Asma al-Assad, a number of development programs began to sprout in 2001 and were structured around five different GONGOs. Some of these programs largely focused on providing a foundation for the concept of citizenship among young people and in the framework of an organized structure known as Massar. Other projects, under the organization Firdos, promoted the development of rural areas. Others focused on empowering young people to join the labor market and in providing tools for development of business ventures. These activities were carried out through the Shabab organization. Other associations included one dealing with culture and heritage (Rawafed), in order to exploit Syria's rich artistic talents, and the Development Research Center (DRC), which engages in civil society issues and the socioeconomic components of Syrian life. This center was an integral part of the Syria Trust for Development until 2010 and then became an autonomous entity.

In 2007, the Syria Trust for Development was established as a statutory and administrative umbrella for all these organizations and to develop new areas of activity such as fostering a culture of corporate social responsibility and aiding nonmembers through capacity building and fundraising. Before analyzing the trust's operational strategy, it is important to recognize that each of the organizations operated independently for six years, and thus their work methods were transformed and their work divided when the projects came together under one roof. This section will briefly describe the organizations before turning to the analysis of what their activities mean and what role they play in the authoritarian context of Syria.

Firdos (the Fund for Integrated Rural Development of Syria) was set up in 2001 to promote socioeconomic development in the Syrian countryside. Much of the economic development plans drawn up in Syria gave precedence to urban areas and ignored rural areas, despite the importance of the agricultural sector and the fact that most of the decisionmakers in government came from rural areas. A number of local and regional development reports noted the need for investment in the rural sector and the necessity of preventing its massive deterioration. From this arose the vision of the Firdos project: "Improving the living conditions in rural areas by empowering individuals and communities to enhance their self-reliance and create equal opportunities for its members."[12] Firdos provides a wide range of social services such as rural crèches for children, scholarships for underprivileged students, mobile libraries, and mobile information centers. Crucially, however, it also attempts to spur rural-based economic activities by providing microcredit to small businesses and entrepreneurship training. The organization is active in developing local expertise and creating work opportunities in forty villages in six different governorates. The organization receives a significant amount of donations for specific projects from private Syrian businesses, international private companies operating in Syria, the Syrian state, and international organizations such as United Nations Development Programme and UNICEF.[13]

Massar was set up in 2005 in order to create "a national learning and development programme for young people in Syria using nonformal learning techniques to inform, involve and inspire young people across the entire country to become active citizens."[14] It is very much an education-oriented project, where the focus is not simply on learning as acquiring new information but on learning how to be a more involved citizen through the improvement of education skills, by teaching critical skills.

The third organization, Shabab, also targets young people but older than the ones targeted by Massar. Aimed at people under thirty, it seeks to reach "the more open and creative young people who are self-reliant, active within their society, are aware of their abilities, and wish to achieve all that their abilities allow."[15] The association, founded in 2005, seeks, among other things, to strengthen business ventures among young people. It does this by means of programs to increase awareness and to provide participants with practical experience in public and private companies. An office was opened to provide advice to persons wanting to enter the business world and to connect supply and demand in the labor market. Project directors report limited success so far, having been able to reach only 100,000 persons within its target population of six million persons. Yet, the officials are optimistic, one reason being that the business-venture program became part of the curriculum in professional schools and academic centers in 2009.

The fourth major GONGO founded during the 2000s is Rawafed, which operates in the cultural field. For years, planning cultural politics in Syria was the responsibility of the state's Ministry of Culture and its district offices. Harsh restrictions were placed on creative works and expression, though cultural works of high quality were produced, primarily during the early 1970s. Censorship and funding difficulties left cultural centers without meaningful cultural life. Cultural matters came within the services sector and were given little attention in the development plans that were drawn up. Those in charge of cultural activity related to culture as a luxury and privilege, and not as a resource that promotes growth of local communities. Contrarily, the conception of Rawafed was that "the Syrian public should benefit from culture, which plays a vital long-term role in the country's economic, social, and human development."[16] The association began in 2007, the year that the Syria Trust for Development was founded. At first, Rawafed supported a number of musical enterprises and development of local talent. In 2009, it established frameworks to enable sustainable economic growth for the country and sought to establish a link between growth in the cultural sector and general growth. Now, Rawafed has great influence and is able to make contact with the citizenry and the media directly through its ability to organize large-scale events. Rawafed focuses on two major programs. One deals with investment in cultural activity, by mapping cultural resources in the communities. The objective is to depict the cultural resources throughout the country: museums, the music sector, oral histories, and so forth. The project's officials then work with civic organizations to invest in the resources and develop them. The second program provides support for cultural and artistic activity and for cultural institutions, creates tools and frameworks to meet the needs of the cultural sector, and supports sustainable cultural projects. Its goal and hope is that the cultural resources and cultural works will improve the quality of life and generate change in the local communities. To achieve this goal, the program encourages the cultural sector and social, economic, and human development, while convincing the leading state-development officials of the importance of culture in achieving growth.

This short description of the different organizations that are now coordinated under the umbrella of the Syria Trust for Development ticks all the boxes in the literature in terms of the nature and role of GONGOs. First, they were all established in the 2000s to accompany economic transformations that reduced the welfare provisions of the state. In order not to let Islamic charities monopolize the nonprofit service-providing sector and in order to foster values such as "entrepreneurship," the state set up government-organized associations to partly deal with this potential problem of welfare reduction. At the same time, these associations allowed the regime to begin to move away from the traditional structures of mobilization of the Baath Party, providing the new president with alternative constituencies for support in his efforts to modernize (though not democratize) Syria. These GONGOs have been able to operate freely and therefore increase social capital because they are under the patronage of First Lady Asma al-Assad, giving them the opportunity to become significant actors in a short period of time. The ability of these GONGOs to "get things done" has also attracted both domestic and international donors from the private and public sector, guaranteeing therefore a degree of legitimacy for both the al-Assad regime and for its modernization project. The rhetoric of empowerment, individual responsibility, education, and citizenship that these organizations use also contributes to legitimizing their role with the international community and potential donors. At first glance, therefore, it seems that GONGOs in Syria perform the role of "democracy impostors" that Naim highlighted in his analysis, because they "pretend" to do civil society activism, while being in fact devoid of autonomy and independence. Worse still, they become tools of increased social control, and, once past the rhetoric, this becomes more than apparent.

The following analysis, building on the idea of unintended consequences, partly challenges this extremely negative view of GONGOs. While it is indeed problematic to include them in any definition of civil society, given their suspect autonomy from the state, their activities and impacts might differ from the intentions of the agents that created them. In short, while they certainly fulfill the "political" duties they have been charged with in terms of upgrading authoritarianism, they might also do something else.

The Unintended Consequences of GONGO Activism

The Syria Trust for Development was founded to strengthen cooperation and integration between the component organizations and to benefit from common management and standard criteria for assessment, greater transparency, and in-depth examination of the projects. The trust's vision is to achieve, according to its mission statement, "a Syrian society in which its members can realize their potential for the sake of themselves and their families, their society, and their homeland."[17] Syrian society needs to build its social capacities, expand its activity in the field of activism, and develop an institutional funding infrastructure that would enable civil society associations to operate autonomously. In its statements, the trust advocates support for NGOs not operating under its umbrella. It offers aid to NGOs outside its umbrella in preparing applications for funding and for grants and loans, a task considered a weak link in civil society organizations active in the area of development in Syria. The trust's strategy reflects a desire to take positive action on behalf of NGOs not under its auspices. The trust describes itself as an information and coordination source, and as a builder of a cooperative network that assists in the advancement of Syrian society. In this context, trust officials speak of creating a communal stage for NGOs for the distribution of technical knowledge on how to obtain grants and manage them, for capacity building in how to achive the objectives that associations set out, and for providing aid in the development of Syria as whole.

In early 2011, the trust employed 190 persons, but it has encountered problems in drawing skilled personnel due to the small number of educational programs in Syrian universities in fields concerned with sustainable growth and development. Thus, it was necessary to invite Syrian experts living outside the country or offer advanced courses to train a local cadre of skilled personnel in this field. The need became critical when it sought to expand operations into new areas of the country in the mid-to-late 2000s. The trust's five-year plan calls for expanding the total number of staff, in all the projects, to 700. This ambitious goal demands great effort in building professional teams and keeping them, since many staff leave after gaining the requisite experience. Since one of the trust's major goals is to aid Syrian civil society in absorbing trained persons to help the projects succeed, and to strengthen transparency and accountability—traits acquired while they worked for the trust—trust officials are not concerned about staff leaving.

A number of aspects related to the workings of the umbrella organization and its constituent parts go beyond the rhetoric and the projects and programs. The trust hopes to prepare the terrain, at least in the longer term, for the development of a concept of citizenship that is at odds with the intentions of its creators insofar as it offers critical tools of engagement that might transfer from service provision to more politicized issues. When it comes to Firdos's work, for example, the association establishes local committees or labor committees, which it trains to build assessment and intervention programs in rural areas in order to increase the committees' autonomous decisionmaking power and make them aware of the necessity to design their own economic future. The committees are then connected to existing resources to enable them to work independently. The assumption that Syria needs to maximize its economic potential by investing in the skills of its rural labor force fits with the duty of Firdos as a GONGO, but it also leads to questioning why state structures design developments plans without taking into account local circumstances and needs. In some respects, this might seem innocent enough but the idea of challenging ministerial directives in order to follow an alternative path of development autonomously worked out within the local community is rather revolutionary in Syria.

This example is interesting for two reasons. First, it points to an underground power struggle between the president's program of modernization, based on entrepreneurship and personal initiatives, in order to strengthen Syria's integration in the global economy, and a Baath-based bureaucracy that has not entirely been convinced of this idea of liberal economic modernization. Thus, the minister of agriculture before the 2011 reshuffle was opposed to the involvement of Firdos in drawing up programs for economic growth in rural areas. The directors of the projects in the rural communities reported bureaucratic obstacles such as obtaining licenses and permits that made progress difficult, in addition to bureaucratic problems and institutional opposition of government ministries, in particular the ministry of agriculture. This is where the second interesting aspect of the example emerges. Because the association's patron is the first lady, it would be simple for the director of Firdos to "lift the phone" and use the patronage network available to him to make things happen more quickly. However, this is not done because both Firdos and the trust are attempting to break the patronage and *wasta* (cronyism) cycle that plagues Syrians' interactions with the state. This refusal to follow the traditional solutions might be detrimental to the workings of the organization in the short term, because of its inability to complete projects or have more impact, but in the longer term this "political" statement demonstrates a different approach to solving problems of this nature.

A specific Firdos project hopes to strengthen and expand training to enable implementation of local projects with, or without, state assistance. One significant indicator of the project's success is its ability to transfer responsibility to the committees and organizations whose establishment and training it funded. Monitoring and assessment are two of the project's fundamental components. In general, Firdos attempts to create confidence at the local level by means of development of civil society. It also aids in the enactment of legislation and in amending existing legislation in a way that supports its objectives. It networks with government, community, regional, and international entities engaged in the same areas of activity.

When it comes to Massar's activities, they are informed by the idea of "turning children and young people into active citizens, to enable them, through education, to acquire the understanding and ability to change the world around them, and to gain control over their present and future." According to the organization itself, 40,000 pupils a year take part in various activities. These include the opening of what the organization calls "discovery centers," the first of which was established in Latakia in 2007. Other such centers will be opened in other districts, and the main center is scheduled to be opened, in Damascus, in 2013. These centers create interactive opportunities, train teachers, and develop school curricula. They also engage in civic affairs, such as strengthening voluntarism, development, and the use of dialogue between different social actors in dealing with social issues. By means of its interactive website, Massar works with persons who are unable to take direct part in its activities. Although the central government is involved in the project, Massar officials mainly seek regional and international partners. Politically, the projects implemented are highly sensitive because they deal directly with the young generation, which is traditionally mobilized by the youth wing of the Baath Party, and address many social issues that could result in the development of civic concepts and dialogue that are liberal in nature. For decades, these civic concepts and dialogue have been lacking in Syrian society and in its political lexicon. In this case, Massar is not necessarily operating outside its mandate but is exposing younger generations to educational concepts such as individual responsibility, dialogue, and critical thinking, which run counter to what the regime actually requires from its citizens. In this case, the association has a good working relationship with primary and secondary schools across the country. Massar officials stated that the Ministry of Education opened school doors for them to expose the teachers and pupils to new pedagogic methods, such as simulation methods of role playing and interactive theater, and this cooperative effort is linked with the positive and open approach taken by the minister of education himself. This indicates that GONGOs discharge their duties and, at the same time, push boundaries that more independent organizations could not push, leaving GONGOs, paradoxically, much better placed to hold what could be termed "subversive discourse."

The DRC, funded by the trust and by other sources, provides research services for the trust and carries out other research projects—for example, analysis of state economic and social policy. The DRC's main activities are assessment, monitoring, and supervision of the projects. The DRC, which has a number of full-time researchers, seeks to turn scientific research into a major component at the building phase of projects; therefore, it encourages the project heads to research the specific sphere of activity in which they are engaged. In short, the analysis should be used for the implementation of research-based rather than ideology-based policies. The DRC is funded directly by private foundations to carry out independent research not connected to purposes for which the trust was founded, as it is intended to be fully autonomous with respect to the topics for research. As a result, its financial situation is stable. At first, the DRC gave priority to research work for the trust. After it became independent, it has balanced its time and effort between its obligations to external entities and its commitments to the trust.

The DRC has taken on a new project that will become independent: the Civil Society Organizations Forum. It should be pointed out, however, that the harsh repression of 2011 and 2012 on the part of the regime put this on hold. The DRC also nurtures researchers and develops research capabilities, the objective being to increase the success of economic development programs, and to exchange knowledge at the local and international levels. It aspires to be an authoritative reference body for local and international entities engaged in development. The DRC also is a source of knowledge and a reference body for the media. In this context, it is engaged in making its website an information center for all matters relating to development, by providing the main development indicators, analysis, and recommendations. The DRC established the Syrian Young Scholars Program in cooperation with Gulfsands Petroleum and Thomson Reuters companies. The program is intended to develop the expertise and capabilities of young Syrian researchers, in addition to dealing with the lack of scientific research to inform public policy, facilitating the exchange of information, strengthening the culture of development of scientific research, and creating opportunities for young Syrian researchers. The head of the DRC, Nader Qabbani, believes that "the existence of a center that specializes on research on the trust constitutes an important component of development work in general. The research and services that the center provides are transparent and precise with respect to the findings of the projects and the foundation's projects and programs, which contribute to their development." In addition, he stated that, "the center's activity is not limited to trust programs and projects, and it takes on external research projects and initiatives for capacity building in cooperation with local and international research centers, which provide benefit to society. Research conducted by the center provides a foundation of knowledge for economic and social development in Syria."[18]

While this might simply be "commercial and public relations speak," it points to the self-perception of those who are in charge of carrying out these tasks and the values that inform them. This research activity is designed to be connected to the development of other avenues of service provision activism in order to strengthen the way in which civil society helps the state fill a vacuum in terms of welfare provision. However, the focus on development and liberal civil activism through the provision of skills and values that are central to the process of renewing state-society relations on different bases from the traditional ones based on the primary role of the Baath Party can also have an impact on other more sensitive issues that civil society could take up. It is difficult to keep the two aspects—service provision and political engagement—neatly separated because, historically, the two have been strongly connected.

In short, the work of the GONGOs in Syria, while certainly fulfilling the role given to them by the agents that created them, is also having an influence on the type of civil activism present in the country, which does not conform to what the literature expects of them, namely that of being the arms of social control. First of all, to establish their credibility with the targeted users, the GONGOs do not necessarily rely on political patronage to get things done. While it is obviously important to be seen to be connected to the first lady, avoiding patronage in the name of credibility and professionalism demonstrate that a sense of autonomy is developing among the staff of GONGOs. Second, the professionalism with which GONGOs are run is a testimony to the critical and independent professional staff that these organizations attract, indicating that expectations of genuine service are high. Such professionalism constitutes an important side effect to how

GONGOS are set up and in the long run increases the chances that organizational loyalty and needs will prevail over political considerations. Third, interactions with foreign partners, including the UN agencies and a host of development agencies from Western countries, have by osmosis contributed not only to increased professionalism but exposed the staff and the targeted users to ideas of accountability and empowerment that might transfer to other more politicized issues.

Conclusion

The way in which GONGOs in Syria were set up and designed led analysts, following the mainstream literature on the topic, to dismiss them as irrelevant in terms of civil society activism or, worse, to see them as a new attempt by the regime to substitute the old "people's organizations" (the Young Revolutionaries Union, the Baath Pioneers Union, and so forth) with more modern forms of social control due to seeking a different path toward modernization without including political rights. The establishment of the five GONGOs that would later come under the umbrella of the Syria Trust for Development is certainly part of a process that seeks to create new, state-led social structures divorced from the conventional bureaucracy in order to build a separate power base for the younger generation in power at the moment. The regime sought more active and credible groups than the people's organizations, which tried for decades to frame and oversee community activity in the country. In many ways GONGOs reflect the same dynamics that affected previous popular organizations insofar as needing patronage networks to access the available jobs and resources, and, overall, they tend to reproduce similarly authoritarian patterns of interaction. The criticism laid at the door of GONGOs is certainly justified, and this analysis does not seek to provide normative legitimacy to such organizations, particularly in the context of the highly repressive Syrian environment and the leading role that the al-Assad family has in such repression.

Nevertheless, it should be highlighted that while their resources might still be small compared to that of more established corporatist organizations, GONGOs have come to play an important role in today's Syria, although their future development will depend on the outcome of the Syrian uprising. First, the rhetoric they employ is radically different from the past, as the mobilization of activism revolves around the ideas of individual initiative, entrepreneurship, critical thinking, empowerment, and accountability. Once the rhetoric is in place, unintended consequences can be witnessed, and it is here, looking outside traditional civil society actors, as the introduction to this volume argues, that shows the necessity of providing a clearer idea of what is occurring in society, even if this means analyzing actors such as GONGOs, whose legitimacy and "civil society" label might be highly questionable. Obviously, it is still difficult to measure precisely where and when unintended consequences have popped up, but instances of GONGOs' behavior point to their increased autonomy from their creators.

More specifically, the Syria Trust for Development has managed, as a review of its components shows, to draw and absorb many skilled professionals engaged in a variety of activities, and has trained new personnel and channeled them into civic work. Some of these people moved on to work with NGOs outside the confines of the trust after they garnered experience. Their skills and values are being channeled into activism that is more independent, which can be beneficial if a genuine civil society is to emerge in Syria.

In addition, despite the political support that patrons such as the first lady provide the trust and its stronger ability to overcome administrative and security obstacles due to this, the trust has succeeded in creating an institutional structure based on principles of civic action that, at least in appearances, correspond to Western models, relying less on patronage and clientelism and more on professionalism and engagement with public institutions. In doing so, it has potentially provided great mid- and long-term service in providing the foundation for a new, nonideological culture that can spill over from welfare-service provision—the current focus of most of the trust's work—to political issues. Undoubtedly, the trust has instilled new practices in the public sphere in Syria with respect to governance, monitoring, assessment, and accountability, which even the genuine and independent civil society organizations should recognize.

Notes

The author is grateful to the editors of the volume, Paul Aarts and Francesco Cavatorta, for their help in editing the chapter. I am also grateful to Reinoud Leenders for his helpful comments on an earlier draft.
    1. Heydemann, "Upgrading Authoritarianism."

2. Cavatorta and Durac, *Civil Society and Democratization.*

3. See Jamal, *Barriers to Democracy;* and Clark, *Islam, Charity and Activism.*

4. Wiktorowicz, "Civil Society as Social Control."

5. See, for instance, Liverani, *Civil Society in Algeria;* and Sater, *Civil Society and Political Change.*

6. Boerwinkel, "The First Lady Phenomenon."

7. Beau and Graciet, *La Reine de Carthage.*

8. Naim, "Democracy's Dangerous Impostors."

9. Ibid.

10. Cortell and Peterson, "Limiting the Unintended Consequences."

11. Dimitrakopoulos, "Unintended Consequences."

12. See Syria Trust for Development, "Draft of Five-Year Development Strategy Plan" (Damascus, 2010).

13. For a detailed overview of how Firdos originated and its activity in its first two years, see www.planning.gov.sy/SF/files/Ferdos.pdf.

14. For the mission statement of the organization, see www.massar.sy/en/about-massar.

15. Syria Trust for Development, "Draft of Five-Year Development Strategy Plan," p. 21.

16. Ibid., p. 26.

17. For the trust's mission statement see www.syriatrust.org/en/about-trust/ou.philosophy.

18. Personal interview with Mr. Qabbani in Damascus in December 2010.

9

Co-opting Civil Society
Activism in Iran

Paola Rivetti

The issue of civil society activism and its supposedly positive role in fostering political transitions to democracy is a longstanding debate in the democratization literature. It has been analyzed by scholars, as well as by politicians and international donors willing to foster civil society's democratizing activities in authoritarian states. Traditionally, civil society activism has been viewed as crucial in bringing about the democratic transformations of authoritarian regimes, but more recent studies have highlighted how civil activism may paradoxically lead to "authoritarian upgrading"[1] rather than democratic advancement.[2] Such findings run counter to the ones postulated by the democratization paradigm, and the current dichotomous debate between democratization and authoritarian resilience, highlighted in Chapter 1 of this volume, should not overlook other potential lines of inquiry, linked in particular to the other functions that civil organizations may have in a specific political system. Indeed, by examining the meanings behind the label of "civil society" and its uses,[3] it is possible to provide a clearer picture of the dynamics at work between ruling elites and civil activism in an authoritarian context such as Iran. My objective in this chapter is to capture such dynamics, going beyond the traditional representation of a country simplistically divided between civil society and the state, focusing instead on their interaction. By exploring the nature of civil activism and, in particular, the relations between state and civil organizations during the last fifteen years, I offer an account of the techniques displayed by the regime in order to set up and govern a "system of obedience" through the control of civil organizations.[4] This highlights how the Iranian regime considers violence and repression only one among the many tools of political control. Recalling Michel Foucault, the way the Iranian regime exercises power and perpetrates soft coercion will be explored. Such an "operation of alignment" can be channelled through the official bureaucracy toward any kind of organization, with little importance for its legal or supposed status—dependent or independent, governmental or non-governmental.

Following from this argument, the distinction between nongovernmental organizations (NGOs) and government-organized nongovernmental organizations (GONGOs) is not considered a useful analytical tool to explore the relations between the government and civil society groups. Although the normative difference is not questioned, even the independent and "liberal-appearing" NGOs—which, in the Iranian case, may be better labeled "reformist-oriented" and "human rights–oriented"—have at times served the government's interests, in turn protecting their interests too. In order to highlight how co-optation and closeness between civil society actors and the government take place regardless of the political orientation of the faction ruling the country, I compare a context of "authoritarian enhancement," namely Mahmoud Ahmadinejad's presidencies, with a context of political liberalization, or Mohammad Khatami's era.

In addition, I will address how those civil organizations that accepted the operational framework from the regime enjoyed significant benefits. The civil organizations' behavior will be explored, beyond the belief that the relationship between them and the government is determined by the latter. In the game of state-society relations, the regime is only one of the players, and civil organizations, even those close to the power centers, can find an independent path to raise their voices and make "unintended" and problematic demands. This means that the option for civil society groups is not simply between accepting repression and collaboration. As a matter of fact, there is a list of alternatives that could be chosen and, by analyzing both government's actions and organizations' reactions, researchers can highlight the mechanisms of consensus and mutual political strengthening.

The Mainstream Narrative of Civil Activism

For a number of years, the Islamic Republic of Iran has been depicted as being on the verge of political change and, more specifically, of a democratic transition. Khatami's election to the presidency in 1997 galvanized these expectations. His relaxed style and good-natured criticism of the harsh attitudes of the conservative establishment caused an almost universal wave of support for the "smiling mullah" among ordinary Iranians. More significantly, his political discourse, focusing on effective and forceful key words, such as "democracy," "civil society," "rule of law," and "dialogue among civilizations," appealed to the wider public. Thus, even when the "demo-crazy"[5] wave in the literature on political change in the Arab world subsided due the fact that genuine regime changes were not taking place in the Middle East,[6] the Iranian case still excited a number of scholars and policymakers who believed a radical change to democratic governance was imminent. The shared assumption was that, despite all the difficulties and the fierce conservative opposition, Khatami was ruling a dynamic country, whose active and autonomous civil society would lead to a more liberal and democratic exercise of power thanks to the strength, in particular, of young people and women's engagement.[7] Such a representation of reality became popular both in scholarly and policymaking circles, and promoted the conflation of the concepts of personal engagement, democratization, journalism, political participation, NGOs, and human rights on an all-encompassing idea of "civil society," whose activities were assumed to help such a democratic transition.[8] It has sometimes even been suggested that there is an ongoing confrontation between "modernity and tradition" in the field of social engagement,[9] where NGOs play a modernizing social and political role, educating about civility and citizenship.

The strength of this narrative, focused on people's political struggle, social resistance, and engagement, is not understandable without considering past, neo-orientalist stereotypes portraying Iranian society as submissive, politically homogeneous, and socially static. The reaction to this cliché has caused, however, a shift from representing Iran as a homogeneous society to one portraying Iran as "schizophrenic." This understanding of Iranian reality is also present in nonacademic literature. Here, the contrast is made between a public sphere dominated by a strict Islamic code of behavior and a private life characterized, on the contrary, by crazy parties and sexual libertinism.[10] Such a binary representation also molds the representation of the social and political life of the country, seen as deeply divided between a dynamic civil society and an authoritarian state system.[11] Following the logic of this comparison, Iran has often been perceived in the middle of a confrontation between modernity and tradition[12]—

which has sometimes been understood as the struggle between democracy and Islam. Claiming the existence of a civil society was thus perceived as a way to defend the idea of Iran as a diverse and tolerant country; more precisely, in this context, NGOs embodied the activists' wish of modernity and became the distinctive mark of it, distinguished from the forms of popular solidarity or informal welfare that already existed in Iran.

Civil Organization in Khatami's Era

During Khatami's two presidential terms (1997–2005), the rhetoric of civil society reached an unprecedented popularity and NGOs multiplied all over the country. A rather weak president caught between powerful opponents and an impatient electoral base, Khatami directed his efforts to establishing a diffuse and supportive base of political activism for his reform plan, a strategy that mirrored the reformists' motto: pressure from below and negotiation (*chuneh,* also translated as "bickering") at the top. This double pressure in favor of reforms coming from both the reformists' electoral base and the reformist political groups then in power, would have not only strengthened the call for political change but also defended the reformist elite from their very powerful conservative opponents. In order to build such a system, Khatami and his allies facilitated the creation of associations and civil organizations through the legislative process.

A special and dedicated bureaucratic apparatus was created to promote the establishment of NGOs because, as stated in the Third Development Plan (2000–2005), "The government, by necessity, depends on the NGOs . . . which by their sheer nature are in constant contact with the people."[13] For its part, "The government must provide necessary support, create opportunities and facilitate an empowering environment for the work of NGOs."[14] Such a governmental support for civil society was demonstrated through the establishment of a Central Supervisory Board, composed of NGO representatives in continuous contact with the Social Affairs Sector of the Ministry of Interior. The shared idea was that "an organized society is a developed society,"[15] and this should constitute the first step toward the creation of a *pasokhguy* government:[16] accountable government. Through the structuring of independent associations, according to received opinion, it would then be possible to lead the change toward democracy, even if indirectly.[17] This "organized civil society" was both independent and integrated in the state's institutions, and it is no coincidence that many positions and names on both sides overlapped.[18] For instance, many politicians and governmental officials headed NGOs or "independent" newspapers, or led governmental offices for legal initiatives while being "independent" civil society actors.

The Khatami governments did not only encourage the development of civil society, but took direct action in sponsoring the establishment of NGOs. According to some, the NGO network was established in 1998 as "a means employed by Khatami's administration to divert the attention from the crack-down of internal dissent. In this way, the government was proving that the goals stated in official statements and speeches [namely, the strengthening of civil society and organizations] had a practical application too."[19] The birth of this network of organizations was the outcome of a conference held in the same year, which saw the participation of parliamentary deputies, international organizations' representatives, and representatives of the Iranian associations sector, paradoxically headed by an influential deputy of the interior minister. The foundation of this network resulted in setting a de facto model for NGOs, justifying the government's "politics of participation,"[20] and putting forward the criteria to be followed for being a trusted and accepted organization.

The duties of this network included managing and regulating NGOs' relations with the government and with transnational channels of fundraising. From this position, the network was able to control almost all the relations of every association. The member associations were under close scrutiny from the network itself, and, furthermore, the deputy interior minister remained a key member of the NGOs' network management for many years.

The members of this network often enjoyed indirect advantages. For some, the advantage was prestige: for instance, the president of one of the most important women's organizations in Tehran was nominated as head of the presidential bureau for legal initiatives on the conditions of women. Another member, who left Iran shortly after Ahmadinejad's victory, became a leading member of the presidential bureau for NGO initiatives, an experience that allowed her to accumulate a high degree of credibility among Iranians both at home and abroad. For others, the advantage was increased political credibility. Thanks to the engagement in civil society and by being close to Khatami's administration, the activists gained a high level of social recognition and credibility—something that Daniel Gaxie called the "rewards for militancy."[21] Such a prestige followed them even outside of Iran: some activists indeed left the country after the 2009 crisis, but are viewed as important stakeholders by foreign governments and journalists who consult them when issues about Iran are raised on the international stage.[22] For others, the rewards of activism have been more direct: help from the presidency, support and protection from potential juridical harassment, and a faster administrative track to obtain permissions or documents. For instance, some organizations that received eviction notices due to their activities were taken care of by the presidency. Specifically, this was the case for a women's organization that offered shelter and legal assistance to female victims of harassment. Although the organization was told to leave its headquarters, it managed to gain informal presidential support and avoided eviction.[23]

The reformist governments of the Khatami regime also tried to improve Iran's international and diplomatic position through NGOs, because the latter can be more welcome interlocutors than the government of the Islamic Republic itself, a problematic partner for many countries. This was one of the functions of the NGOs' network and also of the Center for the Dialogue Among Religions, an NGO headed by Khatami's former vice president in the parliamentary legal affairs. The center formally helped the interreligious dialogue and informally kept contacts and fostered diplomatic ties. Another NGO headed by Khatami, the Center for the Dialogue Among Civilizations, had similar goals. Many initiatives and meetings were organized[24] with the goal of

> enhancing the cooperation between governmental and international agencies, and concerned NGOs both domestically and abroad. The most interesting thing is that the network became a tool in the reformists' hands, whilst their image abroad was the one of an independent organization, whose credibility was not questioned thanks to the political legitimacy they enjoyed domestically.[25]

The NGO network succeeded in presenting itself as a reliable representative of the democratic, independent, and good Iranian associations in the world's eyes, in particular in the Iranian diaspora. In fact, it became a tool for the recruitment of volunteer summer workers among Iranian expatriates who often are English speakers, well-educated, committed, and represented for many organizations "a considerable pool of resources"[26] to be had for free. Young people were attracted by the opportunity of going back to Iran, helping its development and democratization, while working for an NGO.[27] This shows the strength of the rhetoric of civil society and "NGOs for good" all over the world.

The construction of a coherent universe of references for social activism needed the establishment of a cultural hegemony, too. The intellectual apparatus that the reformists set up has been perceived as a sign of the independent advocacy of civil society and democratic pressure from below.[28] Yet when checking the names of those involved in the reformist intellectual circles and journalism, we find many members of the political elite, whose career is long and linked earlier to the Islamic left and to reformist political circles later—not really outsiders. Musavi Khoehinia, Sa'id Hajjarian, Mehdi Karroubi, Mohammad Reza Khatami, Hamidreza Jalaipour, Mashallah Shamsolvaezin, and Hashem Aghajari are just some of the names of those who distinguished themselves as politicians during the 1980s and later became editors, journalists, intellectuals, university professors, writers, sociologists, and members of professional associations, while maintaining an active role in the political life of the country. Thanks to this intellectual apparatus, the government and the reformist elite could thus define "reformist" and "civil society engagement." The success of this soft coercion was clear: being an activist was fashionable among young people, and, in particular, being a reformist journalist was a real status symbol, which played an important role in social reputation and self-representation.[29]

The structuring of political participation can be seen in the call for the establishment of political parties, too, considered as a mark of political modernity and part of a lively civil society participating in politics. However, the efforts for establishing political parties mirrored the fact that parties, although being many, were not independent nor a synonym to genuine political participation. In the inaugural speech of the first national congress of the Islamic Iran Participation Front (Jehbe Mosharekat-e Iran-e Islami), the reformist coalition supporting Khatami's government, Mohammad Reza Khatami, the president's younger brother and leader of the group, declared that "the constitution of an open, rational and effective political system is our goal. It must be accessible to all the activists [*bacheha fa'olliyat*], who will in this way be able to continue their work. . . . Thus we must become a real party, as this is the first step toward a broader transformation."[30] A similar position was expressed by the Islamic Labor Party (Hezb-e Kar-e Islami), which urged all the active political groups in Iran to state clearly their choices and opinions "for not creating confusion among the population."[31] In 2002, with the objective of helping and supporting the establishment of parties, the reformist administration created the House of Parties (Khane-ye Hezbha), which registered all the political formations in the country. In 2008, its list counted 168 parties,[32] while the Interior Ministry's statistics listed 240 political organizations (*tashakol-ha siasi*).[33] The organizations' names deserve attention: for instance, the registered organizations include the Islamic Association of Pathologists, the Front of Iranian Youngsters, the Islamic Medical Association of Iran, and the Azeri Graduate Association. Despite the high number of listed political groups, according to a member of one party, "We could hardly suggest that these organizations [and nominees] are independent or powerful. Instead, I would say that they are elements of a diffused network of support for well-known candidates,"[34] who are chosen in the real centers of power, namely, the Majma-e Rohanioun Mobarez (Assembly of Combatant Clerics) and the Jame-ye Rohaniat Mobarez (Association of the Combatant Clergy) at the time. More than acting as real political parties or exerting a real political agency, these organizations channel, govern, and structure political engagement. The call for participation also aimed at orienting toward moderation the requests of political change through codified "modes of participation" and acceptable models of activism. This testifies to the fact that even within the institutional political sphere, the much celebrated pressure from below was more an expression of organized consensus emanating from the top. Ziba Jalali Na'ini observed that the effort made by the then-government to protect and assist women's organizations in preparation of the 1995 Beijing conference was the embodiment of the paradox of a step toward women's empowerment but in reality a means to flatten women's requests on the government's will.[35] According to Jalali Na'ini, the support provided by the Office for Women NGOs Initiative, sponsored by the government, to women's initiatives turned into a tool for homogenizing women's activism. In particular, political requests related to rights and legal equality were downplayed in favor of developmental requests, which mirrored the government's need for economical assistantship after the end of the Iran-Iraq War (1980–1988).[36]

However, these regime techniques of "taming" or co-opting civil organizations paradoxically have sometimes engendered a desire for political independence. Indeed, civil organizations were among the most vocal critics of the government and accused Khatami of being weak and too willing to compromise with the conservative and traditionalist opposition. In some cases the reformist government reacted to this criticism by resorting to mechanisms of soft coercion, such as undermining the political credibility and trustworthiness of individual activists or organizations, and propagandizing against them through the information apparatus. This was the strategy, for instance, in the case of the student organization Tahkim-e Vahdat, which was labelled by the government a group of "hooligans" when too vocal in its criticism.[37] Before then, Khatami had extensively celebrated it as the "forerunner of democratization."[38]

Control and Interests During Ahmadinejad's Era

If Khatami's governments were associated with the expectation of a political *ouverture,* Ahmadinejad's Iran is associated with social oppression and control. Analyses on political activism in Iran under Ahmadinejad underline the governmental repression of NGOs on the one side and the rise of GONGOs on the other. Such analyses emphasize the elements of co-optation and social control, suggesting the existence of a "code of conduct," which becomes the condition to escape repression. These accounts correctly report the violent coercion enacted by Ahmadinejad's governments and the security apparatus on civil society groups. Restrictions, however, are not only imposed through violence but can be implemented through less overt means: stricter interpretations of the law or new administrative obstacles limiting social activism. Finally, new restrictions to political agency can be imposed through new definitions of "social activism." Once in office, Ahmadinejad took control of the ministries and related offices, and he proceeded swiftly to replace deputies, amend laws, and to transform the functions of official posts into duties and rights. From the beginning of his mandate, the attempt to exercise a much stricter control over civil activism was clear.

The law on civil organizations was changed in 2006 under pressure from the Information Ministry, with a new text introducing a new name for NGOs, SAMAN or community-based organizations, and allowing for a more restrictive interpretation of the organizations' legal spaces of action. A new deputy of the social sector affairs, the one dealing with NGO representatives, was nominated, and this change caused tensions within the Central Supervisory Board, where the newly elected deputy and the NGO representatives gather. In particular, a new Statute of the Board was proposed, which did not entail the presence of SAMAN representatives in the board itself. Although the proposed statute was finally amended to include one SAMAN representative, the new director ordered a general review of the permits issued to NGOs and lobbied "with individuals and institutions that previously issued permits, for centralizing all the required work at the Interior Ministry."[39] This centralization and the interference of the security apparatus into the process for issuing permits to civil organizations have caused the strengthening of the securitarian approach to SAMAN at the expense of "the spirit of voluntary service to a bigger social and humanitarian cause."[40] In 2007, a Department of Community-based Organizations within the Ministry of Interior was established,[41] which handled all the administrative and legal incumbencies concerning civil organizations. In March 2011, the law was finally amended again. Significantly, Mohammad Reza Mohseni Sani, the deputy chairman of parliament's social commission, declared that civil organizations should remain active in charitable causes, implying that social or political causes, such as women's or minorities' rights, would not be tolerated.[42] The 2011 law indeed further restricts the space of action for civil organizations, and allows easier judiciary persecution against an organization's personnel. Since the beginning, the new environment first "disoriented the NGO community,"[43] but, more significantly, later had the effect of breaking up the unity of the NGO workers and community. According to the president of a Tehranian NGO working in Bam:[44]

> There has been a strong pressure on the . . . [NGO community to abandon all political activities]. . . . There had already been cases of arrests, detentions, violent irruptions in the offices of some organizations, and people were worried. . . . Families of NGO workers were harassed. . . . Some NGO members almost enthusiastically embraced the new diktat of the government, and it was exactly what they did before, with the reformists' one. . . . They just adapted to the new course . . . so, for many the Board stopped being a trustable organ.

This account reports the strong pressure exerted on the community of civil organizations. The aim of the government was to divide the "good" from the "bad." In particular, NGOs working on political empowerment and rights were regarded with high suspicion, while a positive attitude was adopted toward charity and community development projects. Some NGOs lost their licenses, and their workers lost their work permits because they continued to carry out a more political work.[45] Many fled the country and reestablished their organizations abroad. In the regime's mind, the aim of establishing a new environment for NGOs was, however, the *normalization* of organizations' behavior, not necessarily their definitive exclusion. If the organizations were ready to correct their positions and follow the new governmental conservative line, they would be reintegrated into the social and economic life of the country. Such a difference is of great importance, as it portrays a model where the government does not aim at excluding per se but rather at gaining loyalty and affiliations.

In early 2006, a few months after Ahmadinejad started to govern the country, the name "nongovernmental organizations" was changed to *sazmanha-ye mardom-e nahad* (SAMAN), normally translated as "community-based organizations" or "people's organizations."[46] Such a change was accompanied by a shift in the institutional approach. According to the head of the economic section of a Tehranian NGO, even if "the law hasn't drastically been changed, we are under much closer scrutiny: our budget and our personal opinions are deeply scrutinized; we're under perpetual stress. Many people have passed the last few years trying to convince the government that they are not American or Israeli spies."[47] It was reported that during the first year of Ahmadinejad's presidency, almost one hundred organizations lost their permits because of "the lack of NGO functionaries' pictures in the documents or incorrect bureaucratic language in their documents."[48] The situation has even worsened after the 2009 crisis, and the current attitude of the government is characterized by a tougher securitarian outlook. The 2011 bill gives the authority of nominating the board of trustees of civil organizations to an external committee composed of regime representatives. This external committee can also revoke the work permit of the organization, while previously this happened through a court decision. Furthermore, connections with foreign partners and the possibility of funding have been severed.[49] New limitations and bans have been imposed not only through legal actions but also by exploiting the political public discourse and designing a smaller and smaller space for political agency and expression for civil organizations. Twenty days after the beginning of the 2009 protests, the Tehran judiciary prosecutor declared that NGOs are the instrument used by international imperialism to carry out coups d'état.[50] Similar remarks have been later confirmed and repeated by Alireza Afshar, former *bassij* (mobilization) commander and head of the social and cultural section of the Interior Ministry (and thus part of the apparatus controlling SAMANs), who added that the organizations do not have the right to publicly criticize the government as also stated in the 2011 law.[51]

However, the politics of participation consider different forms well beyond the divide between exclusion/inclusion and beyond violence, to normalize the organizations' behavior, which can vary from delaying the issuing of permits to undermining the credibility of activists through violence and intimidation. For example, the regime can issue permits for establishing an organization in a matter of weeks or years, thus making it possible for someone to give up on the project. In contrast to such administrative obstacles, filmed forced confessions, which are widely used, carry a significant degree of psychological or physical violence. In the case of Shirin Ebadi's husband, who talked about the couple's private life and declared that his wife abused him during episodes of domestic violence,[52] the objective was clearly to destroy her credibility as a human rights activist. What is more, soft and "testimonial" coercion are not the only ways to force organizations to obedience: arrests, detentions, arbitrary irruptions, and searches have been reported by various sources in the last years. This situation mirrors the efforts of the regime to build a sanctioned and loyal base, as associations are an important topic in the national political discourse and provide a social base for development projects.[53] Thus, rather than shut down civil society entirely, the regime gradually adopted a range of strategies to reassert state control over civil activism, getting closer to it, and following a corporative model, which has been accepted by some organizations when aligned with their interests and goals.

Among the civil society community in Iran, the change of name from NGOs to SAMANs has been perceived as a fundamental step in the effort to change the nature of civic activism, as "SAMAN does not imply, at a theoretical level, a specific relation with government. SAMAN just means popular organizations, and it has a very general meaning."[54] The government also attempted to shift the focus of NGOs toward themes, such as economic development, that the government itself wants to push. According to a representative of one of the biggest civil society organizations in Iran, which also serves as facilitator for the relationships between the SAMANs and the government, "[The government] is [more and more] interested in the topic of development. We work in this field, and our mission is to keep alive the spirit of *bassij* among the people, so that people themselves understand that we can develop."[55] The government's actions have induced a substantial change both in the shape of civil organizations, transforming their name, and in their contents, promoting development concerns over liberal matters. Undoubtedly, a shift has taken place in the symbolism and meaning that the expression "civil organizations" carries. If "NGOs" in the common sense refers to liberal matters and independent agency, "SAMAN" has no such meaning, and the regime has worked to establish another reference for this kind of association. The "politics of participation" selects certain organizations fitting the criteria of choice, such as loyalty and technical skills, thus engendering competition among the organizations, because those perceived to be more trustworthy by the regime are promoted to the detriment of others. These regime-sanctioned organizations impose their activities and views on the others by means of the legitimacy they enjoy, as demonstrated by the exacerbation of conflicts for resources, in particular in rural settings, with the so-called traditional organizations, which feel that the government imposes its presence through the "modern" ones. The government's positive estimation of technical skills is another element strengthening the soft coercion toward the abandonment of a model of human rights–concerned organization. It should be noted, however, that the emphasis placed on technocratic issues is not only due to the fear of human rights–related activities, but is also a way of reallocating resources through development projects to constituencies close to the regime. As a manager of an organization involved in a rural project in the province of Southern Khorasan, close to the Afghan border, declared: "These projects always see the participation of economic actors close to the regime."[56] SAMANs are "considered to be the strategic partners for the government in carrying out the activities in which they are specifically experts . . . without imposing astronomical expenditures upon it [the government],"[57] but also have another important function that goes beyond the management of the distribution of resources. Together with professional associations, they increasingly are the channel of communication between the different sectors of the elites, indicating the importance of the politics of connections. In a country like Iran, where political parties exist in a contested and ambiguous legislative terrain and where even former legal (and governmental) political groups can become illegal very quickly—as happened to the Mosharekat Party and Mujaheddin of the Islamic Revolution— SAMANs are one of the vehicles that select the elites of tomorrow and reinforce the partnerships of today. According to a member of one of the biggest organizations working in the field of development in the country, "In the last few years, one of the most evident changes is the unprecedented involvement of public and semiprivate sector managers in our field."[58] According to him, it becomes "mandatory to establish a collaborative relation between the government and skilled people, in order to become active and carry out the projects."[59]

One of the most effective means to enhance this connection is the organization of large conferences and workshops. These conferences have seen the increasing attendance of managers and professional associations, entrepreneurs and businessmen. "The reason is to make the notion of development more concrete thanks to the participation of people potentially interested in investments, whilst before we were used to deal with ministerial functionaries and politicians."[60] The presence of semipublic managers reinforces the symbolic private-public connection, which benefits civil organizations, too. Engaged in the field of development, SAMANs might be interested in the construction of infrastructures and in being included in development projects. And, of course, in this case personal connections are of great help.

"Unintended" Consequences of Being Close to the Government

Khatami and Ahmadinejad had different aims in promoting a corporatist model of state-society interactions. Khatami set up an administrative and bureaucratic apparatus for promoting the establishment of a network of loyal political support, which was composed of numerous civil society organizations. When Ahmadinejad gained power, he had to deal with these social networks and civil organizations in some way and shape them according to his interests, which fundamentally diverged from Khatami's. In some ways, however, Ahmadinejad followed Khatami's example, as he had offered new meanings and intellectual elaboration to the concept of civil society. Ahmadinejad also strongly relied on administrative and legal devices to shape social activism, targeting both its form and its essence. He changed the organizations' objectives by targeting their names, their topics of interest, and the space where they would be politically relevant. Ahmadinejad's efforts have been directed to the creation of a homogeneous society of *khodi* (insiders, meaning loyal people), while Khatami wanted to create a supportive, organized society to carry out his reform plans and channel the protest potential his reforms would have caused.

However, for the politics of participation to work, all the actors have to be involved and not only the government. Civil organizations therefore are not merely victims but actively participate in this system of incentives and disincentives. It is clear that the standard for being included is the acceptance of a corporatist model of state-society relations. It should be pointed out, however, that such collaboration does not always reinforce the government, as it also provides civil organizations with a certain bargaining power and with the possibility of achieving independent dynamics. If the regime doesn't rule out the idea of full-scale disappearance of civil society activism, then margins for negotiations exist, and it is within these margins that some civil society groups can become more autonomous, even if formally linked to and accepting the framework the regime has put in place to regulate their activities.

This is what happened, for instance, in the case of the student association Tahkim-e Vahdat, which has historically been close to leftist and reformist political circles. Shortly after the 1999 unrest,[61] it decided to follow an independent path from the reformist government but paid the price for its desired autonomy with political marginalization. After the adoption of the *gozar az Khatami* ("transition from Khatami," the expression used to indicate that the student movement had to become more independent from the Khatami government), the organization was increasingly marginalized but was still the most important student organization in the country and a prominent critic of Khatami's administration. After Ahmadinejad's electoral victory, the organization encountered further difficulties, yet was able to survive and show its strength during the 2009 electoral crisis. In the complex game of state-society relations, civil organizations can at certain stages achieve their own dynamic, and bargain with the government from a position of quasi-parity, thanks to the political relevance, popular support, or closeness with the government they previously enjoyed.

This is what happened in the case of professional organizations, as well. A small-businessman, who works as consultant for foreign companies willing to invest in Iran, said that "professional associations are today, more than ever, full of 'compliant' people and split over government pressure."[62] They may not be "the right means for channeling the diffused discontent existing in Iran," he continued, reflecting on the situation of his professional milieu. However businessmen whose discontentment is caused by Ahmadinejad's economic policies and UN sanctions have succeeded in imposing some of their requests as well. "The UN sanctions, together with the sanctions of the United States and the European Union, have had a real impact on trade and investment in Iran. A number of Iranian banks are blacklisted which prevents the allocation of . . . services to Iranian businessmen. This situation results in growing stress among the new Islamic capitalism . . . in Iran and in Dubai, Malaysia, and Europe, where Iranian businessmen are particularly active."[63] In July 2010, the grand bazaar of Tehran organized a huge strike after the government announced a hike in the income tax for merchants, already hit by the sanctions and macroeconomic difficulties. According to Becky Lee Katz and Ramin Mostaghim, "Local merchants don't trust the government,"[64] a situation that could result in independent and more confrontational dynamics against the government. For the moment, the associations of merchants succeeded in obtaining the abolition of the tax hike.

Conclusion

Moving away from a narrow definition of civil activism as synonymous for formal organizations focused on human rights and prodemocracy issues solely, activism has proved to be a fundamental force within Iranian society. It has exploded in the context of the 2009 events, going well beyond reformist parties and other formal organizations. A broader definition of civil activism is indeed needed in order to make sense of the wide participation in the 2009–2010 protests and of the general discontent with the political system that the protesters conveyed. In some way, the presence of unusual actors voicing their claims against the regime is a consequence of Ahmadinejad's determination in reshaping the more usual civil activism, notably devoted to human rights and similar issues. The entrance of new actors within the realm of civil society, as was set by Khatami some years before, has strengthened this trend and confirms the arrival of nontraditional actors on the social and political scene, which in turn reconfigures the role and objectives of activism, as Chapter 1 underscores. The "domination thesis," which considers the overwhelming power of authoritarian states in dominating the society, indeed explains the strength of the limits posed by the regime in shaping and setting the rules of the game, but does not prevent nontraditional civil society organizations from acquiring capacity, prestige, and bargaining power for negotiating almost *au pair* with the regime.

In this perspective, the government is not the only master, deciding the sorts of civil organizations it creates and directing their actions. Rather, the government becomes one of the actors in the political economy of state-society interaction. This is the crucial similarity between Ahmadinejad's and Khatami's management of civil activism. Their efforts for control, structuring, and coercion resulted in an effective mastering of organizations on the one side, while, on the other side, they engendered dynamics of independent advocacy, which have often taken their strength from the closeness to the government the organizations enjoyed.

Notes

1. Heydemann, "Upgrading Authoritarianism."
2. See, for instance, Jamal, *Barriers to Democracy.*
3. In his contribution to the debate on postdemocratization studies, Andrea Teti has also suggested this approach (Teti, "Beyond Lies the *Wub,*" pp. 7–8).
4. Wiktorowicz, "Civil Society"; and Hibou, "Domination and Control in Tunisia."
5. Valbjørn and Bank, "Examining the 'Post' in Post-Democratization."
6. Albrecht and Schlumberger, "Waiting for Godot."
7. See, for example, Butel, "L'individu post-islamiste"; Yaghmaian, *Social Change in Iran;* Paivandi, *Religion et éducation en Iran;* Paivandi, "Vers un système éducatif advantage islamisé?"; Khosrokhavar, "Towards an Anthropology of Democratization"; Khosrokhavar and Nikpey, *Avoir vingt ans au pays des Ayatollahs.*
8. Camau, "Sociétés civiles réelles et téléologie de la démocratisation."
9. Amirahmadi, "Emerging Civil Society in Iran."
10. Zolghadr, *Softcore;* Moaveni, *Lipstick Jihad.*
11. Kamali, "Civil Society in Islam," p. 460; Abootalebi, "The Struggle for Democracy"; and Mahdavi, *Passionate Uprisings.*

12. Shayegan, *Cultural Schizophrenia;* and Jahanbegloo, *Iran: Between Tradition and Modernity.*

13. Namazi, "Iranian NGOs: Situation Analysis," p. 47.

14. Ibid. See also, Katirai, "NGOs Regulation in Iran."

15. On this, see the editorial article by Mohammad Soltanifar, former director of the newspaper *Iran News,* who on 11 December 1999 called for the establishment of political parties in order to promote an integrated, more efficient, and democratic political system. The lack of such "facilities," in Soltanifar's opinion, leads the country to intolerance.

16. Jehbe Mosharekat Iran-e Islami, "Bianeh be monasebat salgard-e qatlha-ye zangurey va elham-e tashkil-e dadgah motehman-e in parvandeh."

17. Saghafi, "Aqaz va paian-e jáme madani," p. 86.

18. Similar findings are presented in Liverani, *Civil Society in Algeria.*

19. Personal interview with one member and worker of the NGO network, Tehran, August 2008.

20. Bank and Richter, *Neo-patrimonialism in the Middle East and North Africa,* p. 7.

21. Gaxie, "Economie des partis et rétributions du militantisme," p. 123.

22. There are many examples. Many of those who left Iran are now research fellows or consultants at US foundations such as the Washington Institute for Near East Policy or the National Endowment for Democracy, or received support from foreign governmental institutions (two examples are Akbar Ganji and Hasan Yousefi-Eshekevari, who both received support and hospitality from the Italian Regional Government of Tuscany, and continued their political and social activism). For many who resisted Ahmadinejad's oppression, emigration is the sole alternative, as staying in Iran would have caused denial of the work permit and being put in jail—or worse.

23. Personal interview and visit, Tehran, August 2005. This NGO, funded by a European NGO, does not exist anymore, and many of its members are outside of the country because of personal security reasons.

24. For example, the conferences held at the Wilson Woodrow Center in November 2003 and in Tehran at the Ministry of Foreign Affairs in 2002 and in 2005.

25. Personal interview with one member and worker of the NGO network, Tehran, August 2008.

26. Personal interview with a worker of the NGO network, Tehran, July 2008.

27. Personal interview with two volunteers from the United States, July–August 2005, Tehran and Bam. They came to work for the Iranian organizations through one of the biggest US youth organizations of Iranian Americans, which offered summer stage and volunteering opportunities in Iran.

28. Samii, "Sisyphus Newsstand."

29. This consideration is an outcome of my fieldwork in Iran. For instance, many young people I met defined their occupation as "journalist," even if they only intermittently had published articles in unofficially recognized reviews or journals.

30. *Iran News,* "Iran's Reformers Seek to Forge Political Parties," 22 July 2000.

31. *Iran News,* "Parties Must Adopt Clear-cut Strategies," 8 April 2001.

32. House of Parties, *Tashakolha-ye eslami,* Tehran 2007.

33. Ministry of Interior, *Moshakhsat-e Tashakolha-ye siasi,* Tehran 2008.

34. Personal interview with a representative of the Jehbe Mosharekat-e Iran-e Islami at the House of Parties, Tehran, September 2008.

35. Jalali Na'ini, "Doulati ia gheir-e doulati?" pp. 106–108.

36. Ibid., pp. 98–99.

37. On 16 and 12 June 2003, the Islamic Republic News Agency reported two declarations on the issue of the student protests. Mehdi Karroubi, one of the two reformists candidates in the 2009 presidential election, charged that the rallies were full of foreign spies, while Abdolvahed Mussavi-Lari, the interior minister and leading member of the League of Militant Clerics, accused the students of being "hooligans" and holding "illegal gatherings."

38. Rivetti, "Student Movements in the Islamic Republic."

39. Personal interview with the president of a Tehranian NGO working in Bam. Tehran, June 2007.

40. Ibid.

41. Alamooti, "Progress Report: The First Round of Representation."

42. Arash Aramesh, "New Bill Restricts NGO Activities,'" *Inside Iran,* 11 April 2011, www.insideiran.org/media-analysis/new-bill-restricts-ngo-activities/.

43. Personal interview with the president of a Tehranian NGO working in Bam. Tehran, June 2007.

44. Ibid.

45. Alamooti, "Progress Report: The First Round of Representation," p. 49.

46. See Ministry of Interior, Islamic Republic of Iran, "Disposals for the Establishment and Activities of SAMAN."

47. Personal interview with the head of the economic section of a Tehranian NGO, Tehran, September 2008. For the current law, see Ministry of Interior website, http://portal2.moi.ir/portal/Home/Default.aspx?Category ID=a39fcad9-06e6-4eb3-973e-5226d70bd350.

48. Personal interview with the head of the public relations office of a Tehranian NGO, Tehran, July 2008. This account has been referred to by many people and many reports dealing with this subject.

49. For an English translation of the bill, see http://iranrooyan.org/wp-content/uploads/2011/12/IR-Trans-NGO-Bill2.pdf.

50. Niki Mahjob, *Sazmanha-ye gheir-e doulati dar mezan-e eteham,* 2 August 2009, www.bbc.co.uk/persian/iran/2009/08/090802_nm_iran_ngo .shtml. See also Muhammad Sahimi, "Show Trials Get Underway," Tehran Bureau, 1 August 2009, www.pbs.org/wgbh/pages/frontline/tehranbureau/ 2009/08/show-trials-get-under-way.html.

51. Radio Zamaneh, "NGOs Barred from Political Activity in Iran," 16 October 2010, http://www.radiozamaneh.com.

52. Some excerpts from Ebadi's husband's forced confession are available at www.youtube.com/watch?v=oOESPRSrhfk&feature=endscreen, in

particular from minute 05:40 to 06:30. The displayed video is a program dated June 2010 from the Iranian State TV that in itself aims at discrediting Shirin Ebadi. The film has been commented on by Shirin Ebadi in Paris in July 2010 during a conference, www.youtube.com/watch?v=wFECIeUQkPs &feature=related (accessed 7 November 2010).

53. See, for example, the dedicated page on the Interior Ministry website, http://nezarat.moi.ir/default.aspx.

54. Personal interview with a SAMAN worker, Tehran, August 2008.

55. Personal interview with a SAMAN worker, Tehran, August 2008.

56. Personal interview with a SAMAN worker, Tehran, July 2008.

57. Alamooti, "Progress Report," p. 50.

58. Personal interview with a worker of a developmental organization, Tehran, August 2008.

59. Ibid.

60. Personal interview with the head of the economic section of a Tehranian NGO, September 2008.

61. In July 1999, students protested against the closure of the newspaper *Salam,* which resulted in days of urban guerrilla activism in Tehran and other big cities. Tahkim was one of the protagonists of the unrest. Although the students protested in support of Khatami's reform plan, Khatami's reaction was not supportive of the students.

62. Personal interview with the head of a medium-size business counseling firm based in Tehran, September 2008. The man, who is in his middle forties, had gone abroad and came back to Iran, persuaded by the expectations for democratization and liberalization suggested by Khatami and reformist governments.

63. Mozaffari, *The Iranian Green Movement,* p. 2.

64. Katz and Mostaghim, "Bazar strike triumphs as government retreats from tax hikes," *Los Angeles Times,* July 7, 2010.

10

Civil Society Activism in Authoritarian Regimes

Mustapha Kamel Al-Sayyid

There is no doubt that the concept of political change implies much more than simply the transition from authoritarian to democratic regimes. However, a major drawback of transitology studies is that they narrow the study of political change, particularly in countries of the South, to change *of* regimes, while overlooking change *in* regimes. In fact, all regimes, democratic or authoritarian, are subject to change, and one of the major findings of several chapters of this book is the vivid demonstration of political change in the two authoritarian regimes of Iran and Syria.

In fact, in his famous critique of the modernization school, the late Samuel Huntington pointed out that it is possible to formulate a value-free concept of political change that liberates the study of political change from the normative assumptions of theories of modernization and political development.[1] One may argue along the same lines that this concept would be a better way of looking at the reality of what is happening in countries that have not gone through the journey of "transition," but without using the transitology prism. In this way, the scholar or the political analyst would be more concerned with the content of change, rather than its direction, meaning that the change in these political systems is rather *about* than *where* these systems are heading.

Huntington defined political change as a change in the value or the content of any of the components of the political system. He proceeded to identify five of these components: leadership, policies, groups, structures, and culture. He formulated also some of the possibly interesting questions within this perspective. Some of these relate to the relationship between the power of one component and its content: Does the change in the content of major political groups in a political system mean an increase in their power, too? A relevant question in the case of Syria or Iran would be whether the increasing presence of technocrats within their ruling elite means also an increase in their power over decisionmaking compared to party politicians in one case and members of the clergy in the other.

Another interesting question he suggested is the impact of change in one component on the content or power of other components. Does the change of leadership entail necessarily a change of policies or structures? A third question would be to identify the most powerful component of the political system and to assess the credibility of political change in light of the relative stability of this component. If we agree that culture is the most powerful component of the Iranian system, then a change in any of the other components, while the substance of political culture remains the same, would be considered a case of political decay rather than political change. Only when this most important component undergoes change would it lead to credible political change, because most probably the change in this component would entail changes in the other components.

Within this perspective, there is no doubt that the two political systems of the Islamic Republic of Iran and Baathist Syria have experienced political change. The durability of the political system in the two countries does not mean that all features of the political system are completely stagnant. Chapters 4 and 5, by Bassam Haddad and Peyman Jafari, respectively, on business groups in Syria and Iran, dwelt on the changes in the economic policies of the two governments, which have effected a shift in their economic policies, abandoning many features of a "statist" economic model. They adopted measures offering increased freedom for the private sector; liberalized policies of foreign trade, foreign exchange, and entry into certain lines of production; and accepted the principle of privatization of state-owned enterprises. Chapters 2, 4, and 5, by Line Khatib, Haddad, and Jafari, respectively, suggest a rise in the power of business groups and Sunni clergy in Syria and private sector executives in Iran. Moreover there are indications of decline of secularist culture in Syria, as indicated in Chapter 2.

One may add that the political leadership in the two countries has experienced change—with one major succession in Syria from Hafez al-Assad to his son Bashar, and from Ali-Akbar Hashemi Rafsanjani to Muhammad Khatami to Mahmoud Ahmadinejad in Iran. Thus, no less than three components of the political system have undergone change in their content in the two countries: leadership, groups, and culture. But if we agree that businesspeople in the two countries are junior partners within the ruling elite, that the clergy and the Assad family are the most powerful groups within this elite, and that the group composition of the ruling elite is the most powerful component of the political system in the two countries, then it would be safe to conclude that what happened in the two countries amounts only to a change within the system and not by any means a change of the system. These efforts were aimed at upgrading authoritarianism rather than moving away from authoritarian rule.

Interestingly, the change of economic policies in the two countries coincides with declared hostility to international financial institutions and to the United States. While the adoption of neoliberal economic policies is definitely one indicator of the triumph of economic globalization, media in the two countries continue to denounce the process of globalization in general, viewing it as a manifestation of the imperialist design of capitalist countries. Unlike other countries in the Middle East, such as Egypt, Tunisia, or Algeria, which had introduced these policies on the advice of the International Monetary Fund (IMF) or the World Bank following agreements signed with the two institutions, neither Iran nor Syria has signed a stabilization agreement with the IMF or a structural adjustment program with the World Bank. Nor was the shift in economic policies of the two countries a product of any pressures exerted by their entrepreneurial groups. The most powerful entrepreneurial groups in Syria consist of members of the ruling elite, if not the ruling family. Although they benefited from the shift of economic policy, they did not by any means push for its adoption. The private sector in Iran was too weak to take the initiative of calling for this fundamental change of economic policy and revision of Article 44 of the Constitution, which had banned privatization. The real agent for this kind of change was, in fact, the hegemony of capitalism worldwide. The two countries were faced by serious economic difficulties in the late 1980s and early 1990s—the period of the fall of Communist regimes in Eastern Europe and the subsequent fall from grace of the socialist model of development. This model was attractive to the leaders of the Baath Party in Syria and exerted influence over the economic policymakers in the early years of the Islamic Republic.

Faced therefore by economic difficulties, the governments of the two countries, particularly under Rafsanjani in Iran and Bashar al-Assad in Syria, adopted what seemed to them realistic and pragmatic economic policies. Despite the radical rhetoric of Ahmadinejad's administration, these neoliberal policies continued. It is therefore ironic that hostility to globalization by the governments of the two countries did not prove too much of an obstacle when practical considerations persuaded them to conform to some economic globalization trends. They continued, however, to view political liberalization as surrendering to the diktat of international imperialist powers.

Civil Society and Democracy

Another controversial issue in transitology writings is the optimistic expectations of the role of civil society under authoritarian regimes. These writings expect civil society to become an agent of democratization in all authoritarian regimes, including the two under consideration. This proposition was derived from the experience of countries in Latin America and Eastern Europe where civil society organizations such as trade unions, human rights groups, and churches supposedly led the struggle for democracy in the last phase of authoritarian regimes, particularly in Argentina, Poland, Brazil, and Chile, to cite only few examples.[2] Some of these civil society groups had existed for years under authoritarian and Communist regimes, such as churches in Poland and trade unions in Argentina, with some of them even acquiescing to repressive policies at earlier points of time. Other groups, such as trade unions in Poland and human rights groups in Brazil, struggled to get their regimes to legally recognize them. In the 1980s they took advantage of the weaknesses of these regimes to push demands for democratization. Enthusiasm for civil society in the writings of the transitology school was predicated on the assumption that repressive regimes that remained in other parts of the world, particularly those of the Middle East, would move from the phase of "harsh" to a phase of "soft" authoritarianism during which they would hesitantly allow a margin of freedom for civil society organizations. These organizations would eventually seize the proper moment to mobilize people to turn against these regimes and promote democratization. However, the durability of authoritarian regimes in the Middle East, the Arab Spring notwithstanding, cast doubt on this narrative, particularly because most of these regimes did allow some presence of civil society organizations yet survived for decades. The recent experience of the Green Movement in Iran and massive protests in Syria since March 2011 have shown the extent to which the two regimes are willing to use violence against civil society groups and unorganized citizens when they start protest actions to demand accountability and more freedom.

In fact, the optimistic narrative of the role of civil society in the democratization process has many problems. First, the transitology school was not the first to use the concept of civil society. The major pioneers of the use of this concept assumed a necessary association between civil society and the presence of some form of political democracy. Georg Wilhelm Friedrich Hegel, with his denunciation of the rivalry among civil society organizations, assumed that they would be free to set up their structures and operate in such a way as to require a "state" to confer a sense of unity and coherence on society. Both Karl Marx and Antonio Gramsci assumed that no major constraints on civil society would exist under a bourgeois democracy. For these authors, the presence of a civil society is a product of the evolution of a capitalist economy.[3] If this reading of the writings of these founding fathers of the civil society concept is correct, two interpretations of the persistence of authoritarianism in Iran and Syria are possible. One is that because neither of the two countries is a fully developed capitalist state, the necessary conditions for the presence of both democracy and civil society are not met yet. The second interpretation, derived from Chapters 4 and 5, suggests that capitalist classes could accommodate themselves easily to the presence of an authoritarian regime, with its restrictions on civil society organizations, so long as they could operate reasonably well. One may refer here to Marx's famous understanding that capitalist classes sometimes are more than willing to trade political power for the capacity to make money.

The second problem revolves around the rationale for the expectation in transitology studies that all civil society organizations are concerned with the struggle for democracy. While a full-fledged civil society does include a wide variety of associations, the demand for democracy is not normally a major concern for many of them. Not only entrepreneurial groups could accommodate themselves to the presence of an authoritarian regime so long as it allows their members to operate their enterprises but also trade unions and some professional associations as well as nongovernmental organizations (NGOs) oriented toward economic and social development. These latter organizations care more about other issues than establishing democracy, which several chapters of this book have suggested. An NGO interested in eliminating illiteracy, a trade union demanding improved work conditions, or an engineers' or medical doctors' syndicate in charge of, respectively, defining construction requirements or improving health services would all find no difficulty operating under an authoritarian regime so long as they can attain the goals they have been set up to achieve. In this sense, there is no problem whatsoever with the presence of these civil society organizations under an authoritarian regime. Definitely these organizations would be interested in acquiring a larger degree of freedom of association, but if the authoritarian regime is not threatened by a greater margin of freedom in the organization's specific area of activity, the regime would not oppose granting it this freedom. In fact, the regime would find it more advantageous to do precisely that, because these organizations could relieve it from the burden of responsibility of development in areas that the organizations are active. It is for this reason that authoritarian regimes in the Middle East welcome development-oriented NGOs but are wary of advocacy organizations.

The third issue relates to the identification of civil society organizations that struggle for democracy. How to identify these organizations when so many business groups, trade unions, and development-oriented NGOs accommodate themselves to the presence of authoritarian regimes? The distinction made by Gramsci between political society and civil society makes it difficult to conceive of civil society organizations that are interested in political matters. In fact, it would be difficult to identify civil groups involved in democratic struggles in the Middle East if this distinction is maintained. In both Iran and Syria, these groups include political parties but also professional associations such as the Iranian Sociological Association as well as journalists, writers, and university professors. In Syria in the early 1980s, these groups included the professional associations of lawyers, journalists, and medical doctors. At present in the two countries, they include Internet activists, mainly using the social communication media of Facebook and Twitter. The Western definition of civil society, which separates political society and civil society, would not be useful in analyzing the struggle for democracy in the Middle East. This struggle brings together organizations and groups belonging to both categories. Most definitions of civil society in the Middle East include opposition political parties, professional associations, and independent trade unions. The rationale for excluding political parties from the civil society category, namely that they are close to centers of power and may be part of the government at some point, does not hold under authoritarian regimes, because these regimes confine the exercise of politics only to leaders of the ruling party. In fact, they even ban the exercise of politics by members of the ruling party, who are expected to obey instructions of their leaders. In this sense, most members of the ruling elite, such as technocrats who occupy leading posts in government departments and state enterprises but who do not speak on political matters—which remains the territory of the innermost circle of the regimes—are no different from civil society people. Neither has influence over politics.

Why Iran and Syria?

The choice of the two cases of Iran and Syria allow the contributors to this volume to test these important questions about political change under authoritarian regimes and possibilities of action by civic society groups therein. Most authoritarian regimes in the Middle East have been for decades on good terms with Western countries, particularly the United States. This was definitely the case of Egypt under Hosni Mubarak, Tunisia under Zine El Abidine Ben Ali, and Yemen under Ali Abdallah Saleh, although the regimes were suspicious that some civil society organizations and even types of civil activism were inspired and assisted by foreign aid donors who offered them funding and were even setting their agendas. Even the small degree of freedom of association that governments of these countries tolerated could be seen as the outcome of the combination of stick-and-carrot approach used by Western aid donors. Civil society activism in Iran and Syria, both confrontational states, is more purely of the home-grown kind. Several chapters of the book have illustrated how business groups, religious orders, Internet networks, and even government-organized nongovernmental organizations (GONGOs) adapted to this situation and succeeded in engaging in various types of civic action that enabled them to exert some influence over their governments. This type of civic engagement was carried out despite the official rhetoric that was quite hostile to the political liberalization project, perceived to be encouraged and promoted by Western governments, especially at the time of President George W. Bush.

The two regimes have also faced major challenges by their masses. This was the case in Iran in the summer of 2009 following the announcement of the results of the presidential elections of June of that year. This is the case in Syria, too, since March 2011 with the uprising against Bashar al-Assad's regime, which has turned into a violent confrontation despite the initially peaceful character of the protest. How could those associations and groups that chose to work, and are even seen as "collaborating," with an authoritarian regime maintain their credibility, particularly following the onset of collective protest actions? The chapters on these groups in Iran suggest that their credibility was not impaired much by the relationships they had with Ahmadinejad's regime. It might be too early to come to conclusions about Syrian groups, given the harsh repression that the regime has used against the opposition since the beginning of the uprising. It is perhaps a different matter with GONGOs in Syria, which are affiliated with the Syria Trust for Development headed by Asma al-Assad, wife of the Syrian president. Undoubtedly, the credibility of their civic engagement came seriously into question in the aftermath of the Syrian uprising.

Moreover, both authoritarian regimes and civil society organizations of Middle East countries learn from each other, irrespective of the foreign policy positions of their governments. For example, protest movements in the region engage in identical practices. Social communication media, particularly Twitter and Facebook, were used extensively in Iran, before and during the days of the Green Movement. The Ahmadinejad government suspended Internet service in order to stop its use by the opposition in the June 2009 presidential election. The Egyptian government did the same in the early days of the January 2011 Tahrir Revolution. Iranian militants established a Facebook group called "We Are All Majid" in solidarity with a young Iranian who was the victim of a character assassination campaign by the Iranian regime. (The account of this campaign is given in Ali Honari's Chapter 7.) Wael Ghoniem, former Google sales manager in Dubai at the time of the Iranian presidential elections, established the Facebook group "We Are All Khaled Said," in honor of the young Egyptian who was tortured to death by Egyptian police officers in Alexandria in June 2010 for his attempt to publicize their corrupt practices through the Internet. It is unlikely that it is accidental that both the Egyptian government and protesters engaged a year later in the same practices as their Iranian counterparts. Obviously, a degree of learning took place.

State-Society Relations in Iran and Syria

A major feature of all authoritarian regimes is the absence of an over-all framework for the organization of state-society relations. Communist regimes, termed totalitarian in the past, together with fascist ones, all had elaborate schemes of controlling society, mostly through the presence of a single party in almost all areas of social action. Authoritarian regimes, on the other hand, are more pragmatic, do not necessarily aim at controlling all social activities, and limit their attention to those activities that might threaten their survival. Any method of regulating state-society relations is good so long as it stops such threats. Whenever one of these methods fails, another could replace it with no difficulty whatsoever.

The two cases of the Islamic Republic of Iran and Baathist Syria illustrate this approach, as state-society relations have gone through several phases in the two countries. The general trend in Iran has been tightening of state control over society with the shift from political liberalization under Rafsanjani and particularly Khatami to a system of obedience under Ahmadinejad, well explained by Paola Rivetti in Chapter 9. An opposite trend was observed in Syria until the outbreak of the uprising in March 2011, moving from repression of professional associations in the early 1980s to selective political liberalization under Bashar al-Assad, as argued in Chapter 2. What emerged in Iran after all these years are clear signs of what amounts to a state-corporatist structure. Syria, on the other hand, offered a misleading image of the growing importance of an increasingly autonomous modern private sector and active Sunni religious associations. But the curious question in this case is the identity of those who represent the state and those who represent society. The demarcation lines between state and society are blurred as the new emerging private sector is dominated by members of the ruling elite and their families. There is no need for state corporatism in all sectors because the state bourgeoisie leaves little space in the economy for other actors.

Those other actors, namely the authentic private entrepreneurs who are not part of the state bourgeoisie, would normally benefit from the economic liberalization policies of the two regimes. Although they do perhaps find a better business climate, their civic action is constrained by a host of other conditions. In Syria, the old-time organizations of businessmen, namely the Syrian Chambers of Commerce and Industry, are forced to accept government appointees in their national councils. Important decisions are mostly informally made with the participation of government representatives. The so-called Guidance Committee defines rules of operation of these entities. Moreover, the major influence over business is exerted by two holding companies that operate in the modern lucrative branches of the economy, such as informatics and telecommunications. These branches are dominated by both the Shams Holding and the Syria Holding, both owned by relatives of prominent figures of the ruling elite. In Iran, the private sector is weakened by its relatively small share of the gross domestic product that does not exceed 30 percent. The major part of the economy is in the hands of state-owned enterprises and the semiprivate sector composed mostly of institutions established under the Islamic Republic. In Chapter 5, Jafari pointed out other features that limit the effectiveness of the private sector's civic engagement. He argued that this sector is structurally weak because most of its establishments are small, employing only a small number of workers, mostly less than ten. It is organizationally divided among a number of organizations, including the Iran Chamber of Commerce, Industry and Mines; the Confederation of Iranian Industry; the Society of Producers; and the Association of Industrial Managers. The bazaar merchants also founded their own bodies, the most important of which are the Society of Islamic Coalition and the Society of Islamic Association of Guilds and Bazaars of Tehran. They are highly dependent on the state for different kinds of licenses and import permits. Moreover, they are crippled by a psychology of fear of what may happen as a result of the economic sanctions imposed on Iran by the UN Security Council, which is extensively covered in Ali Fathollah-Nejad's Chapter 3, and of the consequences of political instability brought about by massive protest actions against the government.

Under these conditions, the will and determination to engage in civil action within this section of the private entrepreneurs would be quite feeble unless their direct interests are at stake. An example of such civic action was mentioned in Chapter 9, which described a successful strike by the merchants in Tehran's bazaar to protest against the tax hike decreed by the Ahmadinejad government, which relented on this decree.

Besides these pluralist features in the organization of business groups in the two countries, one finds features of corporatism in the regime governing citizens' associations or NGOs, but again more clearly in Iran than in Syria. Even under the political reforms of Khatami and his discourse glorifying civil society, the regime set up a framework to manage NGOs, which consisted of a network of NGOs led by a committee that included the deputy interior minister. In addition, NGOs had to be registered with the Social Affairs Department at the Ministry of Interior. In Chapter 9, Rivetti argued that NGOs presumably had more freedom of action under Khatami than under Ahmadinejad, particularly because several leaders of NGOs were themselves members of Khatami's ruling elite. The situation was reversed under Ahmadinejad, who tried to put NGOs firmly under his control. He used a variety of methods, not all of the harsh type, although he did not hesitate to use the stick by rescinding the permit of operation for over one hundred NGOs. One major ploy he used was to change the NGO law and to label them community organizations (SAMANs), thus dropping any suggestion that they operate outside of the governmental sphere. His administration adopted a strict interpretation of the law and strove to centralize control over these organizations in the hands of the Department of Community-Based Organizations in the Ministry of Interior. In this way, only citizens' societies recognized by the state would be allowed to operate in Iran. Other organizations did not get legal recognition and were harassed by authorities. Also the state defined legitimate fields of activities for SAMANs, emphasizing involvement in the implementation of development programs rather than concerns about human rights and democracy, which were a major focus for NGOs under Khatami. In return, the state would offer technical assistance to NGOs in terms of training and advice about how to manage their programs.

The Syrian approach to the management of relations between NGOs and the state was less straightforward. It strove to integrate state-sponsored institutions into the field of civic action in the form of GONGOs, with the president's wife leading these new entities. Thus a number of organizations operating in different fields were established since 2002. In 2007, all these activities were brought under the umbrella of a new entity called the Syria Trust for Development. In Chapter 8, Salam Kawakibi argued that these organizations are expected to promote a true understanding of what citizenship means and encourage participation in development efforts.

Groups out of Control: Virtual Networks

The two governments in Iran and Syria have managed to muzzle entrepreneurial groups and NGOs as well as traditional civil society organizations. They succeeded in limiting the groups' activities to those areas the governments favored and to focus their efforts either on development defined in narrow terms, excluding promotion of human rights and political participation. But the two governments failed to discipline other groups that operated in cyberspace, using the modern media of social communication. The two chapters (6 and 7) on the use of the Internet in Syria and Iran demonstrate the success of young people who used this media so effectively that the governments of the two countries could only counter their activity by cutting off the Internet or imprisoning administrators of Facebook and Twitter groups. The new media offered young people several ways to escape their governments' hold over the minds of their fellow citizens. They used text messages, electronic mail, Facebook, and Twitter to fulfill four related functions. The first is using an alternative source of information beyond official censorship to provide information that the government wants to conceal, particularly its lies about perceived government achievements and the truth about its violations of fundamental human rights. The second is access to a means of mobilization that does not require authorization from the government. Using the Internet, supporters could be called upon to gather in certain places in order to demonstrate, march in protest to government offices, or engage in strike or sit-in actions. The third is coordinating collective action among activists with no need to be physically present in one place, in order to reduce security risks. Finally, this medium of social communication is also useful in informing international public opinion and therefore building external support that could exert pressure on the activists' governments when they proceed to persecute the activists. The authors in both chapters find that this new communication medium has been used well in the two countries but are skeptical that virtual communication could be sufficient in establishing social movements and bringing radical social change in either country. The question is important as international media reports suggested that the success of the Tunisian and Egyptian revolutions in the early weeks of the winter of 2011 was due largely to the use of these means of communications by young people in the two countries. The authors argue rightly that such methods of social communication are useful mainly when combined with other methods in real situations and not limited to cyberspace. In Chapter 7, the author added three other conditions to be met before social movements can succeed and enjoy a good measure of support among the population.

Much still depends on the astuteness of leaders of protest movements and the reactions of government leaders. The two cases of the Tunisian and Egyptian revolutions of the winter of 2011 illustrate that use of social communication media alone does not guarantee success of social movements. In the case of Egypt, in particular, political opportunities for revolt were met following the rigging of elections of the People's Assembly in the autumn of 2010 and the expectation that President Mubarak was preparing to hand over power to his son in a mock election sometime in the summer of 2011. A network of activists already existed among militants of both virtual groups, as well as real political movements. Coordination was carried out through the Internet. Masses of people were motivated to participate in protest actions to declare their discontent at the deteriorating conditions of life, brutal violations of human dignity by police forces, and erosion of Egypt's regional and international influence. Young leaders of the revolution were clever in misleading security forces through the use of the Internet about their movements and in devising techniques to penetrate the large numbers of police forces that were massed against them. Mubarak's and Ben Ali's loss of touch with the people and the real situation in the two countries, including the depth of discontent against incumbent regimes, was also an important factor contributing to the success of the two revolutions. In fact, the suspension of all Internet services as well as the use of mobile phones did nothing to stop revolutionary activities, as militants found other ways to continue communicating with each other and with the masses.

Finally, the lesson that could be drawn from the nine chapters of this book is that authoritarian regimes can buy time by limiting civil society freedom of action and by confining civil activism to the groups they favor and over the issues they like. However, if they do not manage to acquire legitimacy in the eyes of their citizens, some of the educated people in their societies can take advantage of the new communication technologies in order to mobilize citizens against the continuation of their rule. When other favorable conditions are met, those authoritarian leaders are bound to face the destiny of Ben Ali of Tunisia and Mubarak of Egypt.

Notes

1. Huntington, "The Change to Change."
2. Keane, *Civil Society: Old Images, New Visions.*
3. Seligman, *The Idea of Civil Society.*

Bibliography

Aarts, Paul, "The Longevity of the House of Saud: Looking Outside the Box," in Oliver Schlumberger (ed.), *Debating Arab Authoritarianism,* Palo Alto, CA: Stanford University Press, 2007, pp. 251–270.

Ababsa, Myriam, "Contre-réforme agraire et conflits fonciers en Jazîra syrienne (2000–2005)," *Revue des mondes musulmans et de la Méditerranée,* No. 115–116, 2006, pp. 211–230.

Abdolvand, Behrooz, and Heinrich Schulz, "Elitenkampf um Ressourcen" (Elite struggle for resources), *WeltTrends Zeitschrift für internationale Politik,* Vol. 18, No. 70, January/February 2010, Potsdam, pp. 55–64.

Abedi, Cameron, "Iran, Facebook, and the Limits of Online Activism," *Foreign Policy* (online), 12 February 2010, http://www. foreignpolicy.com/articles/2010/02/12/irans_failed_facebook_revolution.

Abootalebi, Ali, "The Struggle for Democracy in the Islamic Republic of Iran," *Middle East Review of International Affairs,* Vol. 4, No. 3, 2000 (online version), http://meria.idc.ac.il/journal/2000/issue3/jv4n3a4.html.

Adib-Moghaddam, Arshin, "Iran's Nuclear File and Human Dignity," *openDemocracy,* 8 August 2012, http://www.opendemocracy.net/arshin-adib-moghaddam/irans-nuclear-file-and-human-dignity.

Agha, Hussein, and Robert Malley, "The Arab Counterrevolution," *New York Review of Books,* 29 September 2011.

Aita, Samir, "Abattre le pouvoir pour libérer l'Etat," *Le Monde Diplomatique,* No. 685, April 2011.

Al-Ali, Nadje, "A Feminist Perspective on the Iraq War," *Works and Days,* Vol. 29, Nos. 1 and 2, 2011, pp. 99–114.

———, "Gendering Reconstruction: Iraqi Women Between Dictatorship, Wars, Sanctions and Occupation," *Third World Quarterly,* Vol. 26, Nos. 4–5, 2005, pp. 7–47.

———, "Women, Gender Relations, and Sanctions in Iraq," in Shams Inati (ed.), *Iraq: Its History, People and Politics,* Amherst, NY: Humanity Books, 2003, pp. 233–250.

221

Alamooti, Mohammad, "Progress Report: The First Round of Representation of the Community-based Organisation at the Central Supervisory Board," in Tori Egherman, Sohrab Razzaghi, and Kamran Ashtary (eds.), *Attack on Civil Society in Iran,* Arseh Sevom Report 2005–2010, pp. 47–52.

Alizadeh, Parvin, "Iran's Quandary: Economic Reforms and the 'Structural Trap,'" *Brown Journal of World Affairs,* Vol. 9, No. 2, 2003, pp. 267–281.

Albrecht, Holger, and Oliver Schlumberger, "'Waiting for Gotot': Regime Change Without Democratization in the Middle East," *International Political Science Review,* Vol. 25, No. 4, 2004, pp. 371–392.

Amid, Javad, and Amjad Hadjkhani, *Trade, Industrialization and the Firm in Iran. The Impact of Government Policies on Business,* London and New York: I. B. Tauris, 2005.

Amirahmadi, Hooshang, "Emerging Civil Society in Iran," *SAIS Review,* Vol. 16, No. 2, 1996, pp. 87–107.

Amnesty International, *From Protest to Prison: Iran One Year After the Election,* London, 2010.

Amuzegar, Jahangir, "Iran's Third Development Plan: An Appraisal," *Middle East Policy,* Vol. 12, No. 3, 2005, pp. 46–64.

Anderson, Lisa, "Demystifying the Arab Spring: Parsing the Differences Between Tunisia, Egypt, and Libya," *Foreign Affairs,* May–June 2011, pp. 320–327.

———, "Searching Where the Light Shines: Studying Democratization in the Middle East," *Annual Review of Political Science,* Vol. 9, 2006, pp. 189–214.

Arjomand, Ardashir Amir, *After Khomeini: Iran Under His Successors,* Oxford, UK: Oxford University Press, 2009.

———, "Green Media Outlet Vital to Informing People of the Truth," www.facebook.com/note.php?note_id=405113002605.

Ashraf, A., "Chamber of Commerce, Industries and Mines in Persia," *Encyclopedia Iranica,* Vol. V, Berkeley, CA: Mazda Press, 1992, pp. 354–358.

Ashraf, Cameran, "The Digital Media Response to the 2009 Iranian Elections," *Berkman Centre for Internet and Society,* 2009, http://cyber.law.harvard.edu/events/luncheon/2009/11/iranelection.

Azimi, Fakhreddin, *The Quest for Democracy in Iran: A Century of Struggle Against Authoritarian Rule,* Cambridge, MA, and London: Harvard University Press, 2008.

Azimi, Negar, "Hard Realities of Soft Power," *New York Times,* 24 June 2007.

Bahrami, Natasha, and Trita Parsi, "Blunt Instrument: Sanctions Don't Promote Democratic Change," *Boston Review* (online), 6 February 2012, http://www.bostonreview.net/BR37.1/trita_parsi_natasha_bahrami_ira_sanctions.php.

Bank, André, and Thomas Richter, *Neo-patrimonialism in the Middle East and North Africa: Overview, Critique and Alternative Conceptualization,* Hamburg: German Institute for Global and Area Studies, 2010.

Batatu, Hanna, *Syria's Peasantry, the Descendants of Its Rural Notables, and Their Politics,* Princeton, NJ: Princeton University Press, 1999.

————, "The Syrian Muslim Brethren," *MERIP Reports,* No. 110, pp. 12–20, 34, 36.

Bayat, Asef, *Life as Politics: How Ordinary People Change the Middle East,* Amsterdam: Amsterdam University Press, 2010.

————, *Street Politics: Poor People's Movements in Iran,* New York: Columbia University Press, 1997.

Beau, Nicolas, and Catherine Graciet, *Quand le Maroc sera Islamiste,* Paris: La Découverte, 2006.

————, *La Reine de Carthage,* Paris: La Découverte, 2009.

Behdad, Sorhab, "From Populism to Liberalism: The Iranian Predicament," in Parvin Alizadeh (ed.), *The Economy of Iran: Dilemmas of an Islamic State,* London: I. B. Tauris, 2000, pp. 100–145.

Behdad, Sorhab, and Farhad Nomani, "What a Revolution! Thirty Years of Social Class Reshuffling in Iran," *Comparative Studies of South Asia, Africa and the Middle East,* Vol. 29, No. 1, 2009, pp. 84–104.

Bellin, Eva, "Contingent Democrats: Industrialists, Labor, and Democratization in Late-Developing Countries," *World Politics,* Vol. 52, No. 2, 2000, pp. 175–205.

————, "Reconsidering the Robustness of Authoritarianism in the Middle East," *Comparative Politics,* Vol. 44, No. 2, 2012, pp. 127–149.

Ben-David, Alon, "Jordanian Indictment Reveals Operations of Jund al-Sham Terror Network," *Jane's Intelligence Review,* 16 June 2003.

Ben Nefissa, Sarah, "L'Egypte saisie par la fièvre régionale" (Egypt seized by the regional fever), *Le Monde Diplomatique,* No. 683, February 2011, pp. 12–13.

Ben Yahmed, Marwane, "La Leçon de Tunis," *La Jeune Afrique,* 16–22 January 2011.

Berman, Sheri, "Islamism, Revolution and Civil Society," *Perspectives on Politics,* Vol. 1, No. 2, 2003, pp. 257–272.

Bjorvatn, Kjetil, and Kjetil Selvik, "Destructive Competition: Factionalism and Rent-Seeking in Iran," *World Development,* Vol. 36, No. 11, November 2008, pp. 2314–2324.

Boerwinkel, Felia, "The First Lady Phenomenon," HIVOS Knowledge Programme, Working Paper, No. 19, 2011, pp. 1–31.

Brehmer, Marian, "'We Should Hate Each Other': The Iranian-Israeli Circle," translated from German by J. Tayler, *Qantara.de,* 21 August 2012, http://en.qantara.de/We-Should-Hate-Each-Other/19676c20951i1p500/.

Browers, Michaelle, *Democracy and Civil Society in Arab Political Thought: Transcultural Possibilities,* Syracuse, NY: Syracuse University Press, 2006.

Brown, Nathan, and Amr Hamzawy, *Between Religion and Politics,* Washington, DC: Carnegie Endowment for International Peace, 2010.

Brumberg, Daniel, "The Trap of Liberalized Autocracy," *Journal of Democracy,* Vol. 13, No. 4, 2002, pp. 56–68.

————, "Authoritarian Legacies and Reform Strategies in the Arab World," in Rex Brynen et al. (eds.), *Political Liberalization and Democratization in the Arab World, Vol. 1, Theoretical Perspectives,* Boulder, CO: Lynne Rienner, 1995, pp. 229–259.

Brynen, Rex, Bahgat Korany, and Paul Noble, "Introduction: Theoretical

Perspectives on Arab Liberalization and Democratization," in Rex Brynen et al. (eds.), *Political Liberalization and Democratization in the Arab World, Vol. 1, Theoretical Perspectives,* Boulder, CO: Lynne Rienner, 1995, pp. 3–27.

Butel, Eric, "L'individu post-islamiste: la nouvelle jeunesse," CEMOTI, No. 26, 1998 (online version), http://cemoti.revues.org/37?lang=en.

Camau, Michel, "Sociétés civiles réelles et téléologie de la démocratisation," *Revue Internationale de Politique Comparée,* Vol. 9, No. 2, 2002, pp. 213–232.

Campaign Against Sanctions on Iraq, *Sanctions on Iraq: Background, Consequences, Strategies,* Proceedings of the conference hosted by the Campaign Against Sanctions on Iraq, 13–14 November 1999, Cambridge, UK, 2000.

Canterbury, Dennis, *Neoliberal Democratization and New Authoritarianism,* Aldershot, UK: Ashgate, 2005.

Carothers, Thomas, "The End of the Transition Paradigm," *Journal of Democracy,* Vol. 13, No. 1, 2002, pp. 5–21.

———, "The Backlash Against Democracy Promotion," *Foreign Affairs,* Vol. 85, No. 2, 2006, pp. 55–68.

———, "Think Again: Arab Democracy," *Foreign Policy,* 10 March 2011.

CASMII (Campaign Against Sanctions and Military Intervention in Iran), "Iranian Academicians Call for Long-Lasting Peace," press release, 3 July 2008, http://www.campaigniran.org/casmii/index.php?q=node/5486.

———, "Iran's Civil Society Movement Sets Up 'National Peace Council,'" 10 July 2008, http://www.campaigniran.org/casmii/?q=node/5573.

Cavatorta, Francesco, "The Convergence of Governance: Upgrading Authoritarianism in the Arab World and Downgrading Democracy Elsewhere?," *Middle East Critique,* Vol. 19, No. 3, 2010, pp. 217–232.

———, *The International Dimension of the Failed Algerian Transition,* Manchester, UK: Manchester University Press, 2009.

Cavatorta, Francesco, and Vincent Durac, *Civil Society and Democratization in the Arab World: The Dynamics of Activism,* London: Routledge, 2010.

Chaichian, Mohammad, "Structural Impediments of the Civil Society Project in Iran," *International Journal of Comparative Sociology,* Vol. 44, 2003, pp. 19–50.

Challand, Benoit, "The Counter-power of Civil Society in the Middle East," http://www.deliberatelyconsidered.com/2011/03/the-counter-power-of-civil-society-in-the-middle-east-2.

Chomiak, Laryssa, and John P. Entelis, "The Making of North Africa's Intifadas," *Middle East Report,* No. 259, Summer 2011, pp. 8–15.

Clark, Janine, *Islam, Charity and Activism,* Bloomington: Indiana University Press, 2004.

Clawson, Patrick, "The Continuing Logic of Dual Containment," *Survival,* Vol. 40, No. 1, 1998, pp. 33–47.

Collinson, Stephen, "Obama Signs New Iran Sanctions into Law," *AFP,* 1 January 2012.

Cook, Steven, "The Right Way to Promote Arab Reform," *Foreign Affairs,* Vol. 84, No. 2, 2005, pp. 91–102.

Cortell, Andrew, and Susan Peterson, "Limiting the Unintended Consequences of Institutional Change," *Comparative Political Studies*, Vol. 34, No. 7, 2001, pp. 768–799.

Council of the European Union, "Council Conclusions on Iran," press release, 3142th Foreign Affairs Council meeting, Brussels, 23 January 2012, http://www.consilium.europa.eu/uedocs/cms_data/docs/pressdata/EN/foraff/127446.pdf.

Courpasson, David, "'Managerial Strategies of Domination: Power in Soft Bureaucracy,'" *Organization Studies*, Vol. 21, No. 1, 2000, pp. 141–161.

Dabashi, Hamid, "Iran: The Garrison State Conducts a Parliamentary Election," Al Jazeera English, 20 February 2012.

———, "U.S. Dollars Could Kill Iran's Protest Movement," CNN.com, 30 June 2009, http://articles.cnn.com/2009-06-30/world/dabashi.us.iran_1_iranian-presidential-election-islamic-republic-green-movement?_s=PM:WORLD.

———, *Iran: A People Interrupted*, New York: New Press, 2007.

Dahi, Omar S., "Understanding the Political Economy of the Arab Revolts," *Middle East Report*, No. 259, Summer 2011, pp. 2–6.

Daraghi, Borzou, and Ramin Mostaghim, "Iran Hard-Liners Skirt Sanctions," *Los Angeles Times*, 23 August 2010.

Darinejad, S., "Fifteen Thousand Industrial Units Will Be Subsidized," *Donya-ye Eghtesad* (19 October 2010).

Davidson, Neil, "From Uneven to Combined Development," in Bill Dunn and Hugo Radice (eds.), *100 Years of Permanent Revolution: Results and Prospects*, London: Pluto, 2006, pp. 10–26.

Day, R.B., and D. F. Gaido (eds.), *Witnesses to Permanent Revolution: The Documentary Record*, Chicago: Haymarket Books, 2011.

de Vries, Stephan, "United States Policy on 'Democratizing' Iran: Effects and Consequences," *Democracy & Society*, Vol. 8, No. 1, Winter 2011, pp. 7–10, 18.

Diamond, Larry, "Rethinking Civil Society: Toward Democratic Consolidation," *Journal of Democracy*, Vol. 5, No. 3, 1994, pp. 4–18.

Dimitrakopoulos, Dyonissis, "Unintended Consequences: Institutional Autonomy and Executive Discretion in the European Union," *Journal of Public Policy*, Vol. 21, No. 2, 2001, pp. 107–131.

"Dolat pedarkhande-ye otagh-e bazargani" (The state, the godfather of the Chamber of Commerce), *Hamshahri*, 14/09/91 (12 May 2002).

Donya-ye Eghtesad, "Asman-e abi-ye Nahavandian va khaterat-e khakestari-ye Khamoushi" (Nahavandian's blue sky and Khamoushi's grey memories), 24/03/1386 (14 June 2007).

———, "Nemigozarim otagh-e Iran dolati shavad" (We will not allow the Iran Chamber to become governmental), 26/03/1386 (16 June 2007).

———, "Doran'e eghtesad-e dolat mehvar be payan reside ast" (The period of statist economy has ended), 13/04/1386 (4 July 2007).

Doorenspleet, Renske, *Democratic Transitions: Exploring the Structural Sources During the Fourth Wave*, Boulder, CO: Lynne Rienner, 2005.

Dreazen, Yochi J., "The U.S. and Iran Are Already Locked in Economic War: Bombs May Not Be Falling, But Sanctions and Markets Are the New, Hard-Hitting Tools of This Escalating Conflict," *The Atlantic* (on-

line), 5 January 2012, http://www.theatlantic.com/international/archive
/2012/01/the-us-and-iran-are-already-locked-in-economic-war/250872/.

Economic Sciences Association, Tuesday Lectures on topic of economic reform, Damascus: Economic Sciences Association, 1991–2008.

Ehsani, Kaveh, "Survival Through Dispossession: Privatization of Public
Goods in the Islamic Republic," *Middle East Report,* No. 250, Spring
2009, pp. 26–33.

Ehteshami, Anoush, and Emma Murphy, "Transformation of the Corporatist
State in the Middle East," *Third World Quarterly,* Vol. 17, No. 4, 1996,
pp. 753–772.

Ehteshami, Anoush, and Mahjoob Zweiri, *Iran and the Rise of Its Neoconservatives: The Politics of Tehran's Silent Revolution,* London and New
York: I. B. Tauris, 2007.

Eisenstadt, Shmuel Noah, *Traditional Patrimonialism and Modern Neopat-
rimonialism,* Thousand Oaks, CA: Sage Publications, 1973.

El Alaoui, Hicham, and Ben Abdallah, "Tunisie, les éclaireurs," *Le Monde
Diplomatique,* No. 683, February 2011, pp. 1 and 10–11.

Encarnacion, Omar, "Civil Society Reconsidered," *Comparative Politics,*
Vol. 38, No. 3, 2006, pp. 357–376.

Esfandyari, Golnaz, "In Iran, Talk of Military Strikes from Above Raises
Fears Below," Radio Free Europe/Radio Liberty, 9 November 2012.

———, "Iranian Women's Rights Activists Say No to War," Radio Free Eu-
rope/Radio Liberty, 9 March 2012.

———, "The Twitter Devolution," *Foreign Policy* (online), 7 June 2010.
http://www.foreignpolicy.com/articles/2010/06/07/the_twitter_revolution
_that_wasnt.

———, "Why Did Iran Unblock Facebook?" Radio Free Europe, 14 March
2009, http://www.rferl.org/content/Why_Did_Iran_Unblock_Facebook
/1510005.html.

Etling, Bruce, John Kelly, Robert Faris, and John Palfrey, *Mapping the Arabic
Blogosphere: Politics, Culture and Dissent,* Berkman Center Research
Publication, No. 2009–06, 2009, http://cyber.law.harvard.edu/sites/cyber
.law.harvard.edu/files/Mapping_the_Arabic_Blogosphere_0.pdf.

Evans, Peter, "State Structures, Government-Business Relations and Economic Transformation," in Sylvia Maxwell and Ben Ross Schneider
(eds.), *Business and the State in Developing Countries,* Ithaca, NY: Cornell University Press, 1997, pp. 63–87.

Farag, Iman, *Croyance et intérêt: Réflexions sur deux associations isla-
miques* (Belief and interest: Reflections on two Islamic associations),
Cairo: CEDEJ, 1992.

Farhadian, M., "Beyond Khatami's Reform Era: Economic Talibanization or
Liberalization?" *Iran Analysis Quarterly,* Vol. 1, No. 3, 2004, pp. 7–10.

Farhi, Farideh, "Religious Intellectuals, the 'Women Question,' and the
Struggle for the Creation of a Democratic Public Sphere in Iran," *International Journal of Politics, Culture, and Society,* Vol. 15, No. 2, Winter 2001, pp. 315–339.

Fathollah-Nejad, Ali, "Iran: Die falsche Medizin" (Iran: The wrong medicine), *Blätter für deutsche und internationale Politik,* Berlin, Vol. 57,
No. 4, April 2012, pp. 9–13.

————, "Auf Kollisionskurs mit dem Iran: Von Spektakeln, lähmenden Sanktionen und der Vorbereitung eines Krieges" (On collision course with Iran: On spectacles, crippling sanctions, and the preparation of a war), *Hintergrund: Das Nachrichtenmagazin* (Germany), No. 2, 2012, pp. 15–19.

————, "Salient Sanctions and Regime Resilience: The Case of Iran," paper presented on the panel, "The Crisis of Legitimacy: Transformations in Governance and Civil Society in the Contemporary Islamic Republic of Iran," British Society for Middle Eastern Studies (BRISMES) Annual Conference 2012, "Revolution and Revolt: Understanding the Forms and Causes of Change," in association with the European Association for Middle Eastern Studies (EURAMES) and the Asian Federation of Middle East Associations (AFMA), London School of Economics and Political Science (LSE), London, 26–28 March 2012.

————, "Security and Cooperation in the Middle East: Searching for a Solution," *openDemocracy,* 1 December 2011, http://www.opendemocracy.net/ali-fathollah-nejad/security-and-cooperation-in-middle-east-searching-for-solution.

————, *Der Iran-Konflikt und die Obama-Regierung: Alter Wein in neuen Schläuchen?* (The Iran conflict and the Obama administration: Old wine in new skins?), Potsdam, Germany: Potsdam University Press, 2010 and 2011.

————, "Collateral Damage of Iran Sanctions," *The ColdType Reader,* No. 46, May 2010, pp. 56–57.

————, "Sanktionsregime gegen den Iran: Entstehung und Auswirkungen" (The sanctions regime on Iran: Its formation and impacts), *inamo: Berichte und Analysen zu Politik und Gesellschaft des Nahen und Mittleren Ostens* (Berlin), Vol. 16, No. 63, Fall 2010, pp. 33–39.

Fathollah-Nejad, Ali, and Kaveh Yazdani, "Das Verhältnis von Religion und Staat in Iran: Von den Safaviden bis heute" (The relationship between religion and state in Iran: From the Safavids until today), *Zeitschrift für Religion und Gesellschaft* (Cologne), Vol. 1, No. 2 Fall 2011, pp. 298–312.

Freedom House, Radio Free Europe/Radio Liberty, and Radio Free Asia, *Undermining Democracy: 21st Century Authoritarians,* Washington, DC: Freedom House, June 2009.

Friedman, George, "Egypt: The Distance Between Enthusiasm and Reality," 13 February 2011, http://www.stratfor.com/weekly/20110213-egypt-distance-between-enthusiasm-and-reality.

————, "Re-Examining the Arab Spring," 15 April 2011, http://www.stratfor.com/weekly/20110815-re-examining-arab-spring.

Friedman, Thomas, "TV Station a Beacon of Freedom in Mideast," *Gadsden Times* (Alabama), 1 March 2001.

Fukuyama, Francis, *The Origins of Political Order: From Prehuman Times to the French Revolution,* London: Profile Books, 2011.

Gambill, Gary, "Syria Rearms Iraq," *Middle East Intelligence Bulletin,* Vol. 4, No. 9, 2002, http://www.meforum.org/meib/articles/0209_s2.htm.

Ganji, Akbar, *Republican Manifesto* (Manifeste Jomhourikhahi), available in Persian at http://www.ketabfarsi.org//ketabkhaneh/ketabkhani/ketab489/ketab.pdf.

Gause, F. Gregory III, "Saudi Arabia in the New Middle East," US Council on Foreign Relations, Special Report No. 63, December 2011.

Gaxie, Daniel, "Economie des partis et rétributions du militantisme" (The economy of parties and rewards for militancy), *Revue française de science politique,* Vol. 27, No. 1, 1977, pp. 123–154.

Gengler, Justin, Mark Tessler, Darwish Al-Emadi, and Abdoulaye Diop, "Civil Society and Democratization in the Arab Gulf," 25 July 2011, http://mideast.foreignpolicy.com/posts/2011/07/25/civil_society_and_democratization_in_the_arab_gulf.

Gharib, Ali, "Do Neoconservatives Really Care About the Iranian Opposition?" *ForeignPolicy.com,* 16 November 2010, http://mideast.foreign policy.com/posts/2010/11/16/do_neoconservatives_really_care_about_the_iranian_opposition.

Ghorashi, Halleh, and Kees Boersma, "The 'Iranian Diaspora' and the New Media: From Political Action to Humanitarian Help," *Development and Change,* Vol. 40, No. 4, 2009, pp. 667–691.

Gladwell, Malcolm, "Why the Revolution Will Not Be Tweeted," *New Yorker,* 4 October 2010, pp. 42–49.

Gordon, Joy, *Invisible War: The United States and the Iraq Sanctions,* Cambridge, MA: Harvard University Press, 2010.

———, "'Smart Sanctions' on Iran Are Dumb," *Foreign Policy In Focus,* 9 September 2010.

Granovetter, Mark, "The Strength of Weak Ties," *American Journal of Sociology,* Vol. 78, 1973, pp. 1360–1380.

Grossman, Lev, "Iran Protests: Twitter the Medium of the Movement," *Time,* 17 June 2009, http://www.time.com/time/world/article/0,8599,1905125,00.html.

Haddad, Bassam, "The Formation and Development of Economic Networks," in *Business Networks: The Political Economy of Authoritarian Resilience,* Palo Alto, CA: Stanford University Press, 2012.

———, "The Syrian Regime's Business Backbone," *Middle East Report,* No. 262, Spring 2012, pp. 26–27, http://www.merip.org/mer/mer262/syrian-regimes-business-backbone.

Haghighi, Alireza, and Victoria Tahmasebi, "The 'Velvet Revolution' of Iranian Puritan Hardliners: Mahmoud Ahmadinejad's Rise to Power," *International Journal,* Vol. 61, No. 4, Fall 2006, pp. 959–970.

Hajnal, Peter (ed.), *Civil Society in the Information Age,* Surrey, UK: Ashgate, 2002.

Hakimian, Hassan, "Institutional Change, Policy Challenges, and Macroeconomic Performance: Case Study of the Islamic Republic of Iran (1979–2004)," *Working Paper* 26, Washington, DC: World Bank, 2008.

Hamid, Shadi, "Arab Islamist Parties: Losing on Purpose?" *Journal of Democracy,* Vol. 22, No. 1, January 2011, pp. 68–80.

Hamidi, Ibrahim, "Damascus Rises Economically and Establishes 68 Business Associations," *Al-Hayat,* 9 February 2010.

Harris, Kevan, "Pseudo-Privatization in the Islamic Republic: Beyond the Headlines of Iran's Economic Transformation," 15 October 2010, http://muftah.org/?p=326&page=2.

Hassan Nia, A., "Othagi baraye tose-e va democracy siyasi" (A chamber for development and political democracy), *Hamshahri,* 24/3/82 (14 June 2003).

Hatina, Meir, "Restoring a Lost Identity: Models of Education in Modern Islamic Thought," *British Journal of Middle Eastern Studies,* Vol. 33, No. 2, 2006, pp. 179–197.

Haugbølle, Rikke, and Francesco Cavatorta, "Will the Real Tunisian Opposition Please Stand Up?" *British Journal of Middle Eastern Studies,* Vol. 39, No. 3, 2011, pp. 323–341.

———, "Vive la grande famille des media tunisiens! Media reform and authoritarian resilience in Tunisia," *Journal of North African Studies,* Vol. 17, No. 1, 2012, pp. 97–112.

Havaar, "Iranians and Allies Demonstrate Against Tightening Sanctions," 1 July 2012, http://havaar.org/2012/07/iranians-allies-demonstrate-against-tightening-sanctions.

Hen-Tov, Elliot, and Nathan Gonzalez, "The Militarization of Post-Khomeini Iran: Praetorianism 2.0," *Washington Quarterly,* Vol. 34, No. 1, Winter 2011, pp. 45–59.

Hersh, Seymour, "The Iran Plans: Would President Bush Go to War to Stop Tehran from Getting the Bomb?" *New Yorker,* 17 April 2006.

———, "Preparing the Battlefield," *New Yorker,* 7 July 2008.

Heshmati Mola'i, H., "Asib shenasi-ye jaygah va amalkard–e othagh–e bazargani dar tose–eye naghsh–e bakhshe khosusi dar tejarat–e khareji" (The pathology of the position and function of the Chamber of Commerce in the development of the private sector in trade), *Padjuhesh va Majlis,* Vol. 61, 2010, pp. 235–261.

Heydemann, Steven, *Authoritarianism in Syria: Institutions and Social Conflict,* Ithaca, NY: Cornell University Press, 1999.

———, "The Political Logic of Economic Rationality: Selective Stabilization in Syria," in Henri Barkey (ed.), *The Politics of Economic Reform in the Midde East,* New York: St. Martin's Press, 1992.

———, "Upgrading Authoritarianism in the Arab World," Washington, DC: Brookings Institution, Analysis Paper, No. 13, 2007, pp. 1–37.

——— (ed.), *Networks of Privilege in the Middle East,* London: Palgrave Macmillan, 2004.

Heydemann, Steven, and Reinoud Leenders, "Authoritarian Learning and Authoritarian Resilience: Regime Responses to the 'Arab Awakening,'" *Globalizations,* Vol. 8, No. 5, October 2011, pp. 647–653.

Hibou, Béatrice, "Domination and Control in Tunisia: Economic Levers for the Exercise of Authoritarian Power," *Review of African Political Economy,* Vol. 33, No. 108, 2006, pp. 185–206.

——— (ed.), *Privatising the State,* London: Hurst, 2004.

Hinnebusch, Raymond, "Calculated Decompression as a Substitute for Democratization: Syria," in Rex Brynen et al. (eds.), *Political Liberalization & Democratization in the Arab World,* Vol. 2, *Comparative Experiences,* Boulder, CO: Lynne Rienner, 1998, pp. 223–240.

———, "The Islamic Movement in Syria: Sectarian Conflict and Urban Rebellion in an Authoritarian-Populist Regime," in Ali Hillal Dessouki (ed.), *Islamic Resurgence in the Arab World,* New York: Praeger, 1982.

————, "The Political Economy of Economic Liberalization in Syria," *International Journal of Middle East Studies,* Vol. 27, No. 3, 1995, pp. 305–310.

————, "State and Islamism in Syria," in Abdel Salam Sidahmed and Anoushirivan Ehteshami (eds.), *Islamic Fundamentalism,* Boulder, CO: Westview Press, 1996, pp. 199–214.

————, "Syria: The Politics of Economic Liberalization," *Third World Quarterly,* Vol. 18, No. 2, 1997, pp. 249–265.

————, *Syria: Revolution from Above,* New York and London: Routledge, 2001.

Honari, Ali, "The Consequences of Iran's Green Movement for an On-line Network Structure: The Case of Balatarin.com," International Association for Media and Communication Research (IAMCR) conference, Istanbul, 13–17 July 2011, PowerPoint slides retrieved from http://alihonari.com/slides/IAMCR_2011[5].pdf.

Huntington, Samuel, "The Change to Change, Modernization, Development, and Politics," in Norman Provizer (ed.), *Analyzing the Third World: Essays from Comparative Politics,* Cambridge, MA: Schenkman, 1978, pp. 30–69.

ICCIM, *Two-Years Report on the Activities of the Iran Chamber, March 2007–March 2009,* October–November 2010, http://127.iccim.ir/index.php?option=com_content&view=article&id=177:1389-07-26-20-50-01&catid=1&Itemid=206.

Ilias, S., "Iran's Economic Conditions: US Policy Issues," Congressional Research Service, 22 April 2010, http://www.fas.org/sgp/crs/mideast/RL34525.pdf.

International Campaign for Human Rights in Iran, *Raising Their Voices: Iranian Civil Society Reflections on the Military Option,* New York, July 2011.

International Civil Society Action Network, "Killing Them Softly: The Stark Impact of Sanctions on the Lives of Ordinary Iranians," *What the Women Say Brief,* No. 3, July 2012, Washington, DC: International Civil Society Action Network (ICAN), in association with the MIT Center for International Studies; the Center for Women's Global Leadership, Rutgers, the State University of New Jersey; Global Network of Women Peacebuilders; Institute for Inclusive Security; Association for Women's Rights in Development (AWID); and Women for Women's Human Rights (WWHR)–New Ways.

International Monetary Fund (2006), "Staff Report for the 2006 Article IV Consultation," Prepared by staff representatives for the 2006 Consultation with the Syrian Arab Republic, IMF Country Report No. 06/294, 13 July 2006, p. 38, http://www.imf.org/external/pubs/ft/scr/2006/cr06294.pdf.

"Iran and Sanctions: When Will It Ever End?" *The Economist,* 18–24 August 2012.

Iran Human Rights Documentation Center, *Silencing the Women's Rights Movement in Iran,* New Haven, CT, August 2010.

Iran Labor Report, "New Year Begins with Fresh Layoffs, Protests," 15 April 2012, http://iranlaborreport.com/?p=1828.

———, "Radio Interview," translation of *Deutsche Welle* interview with Jafar Azimzadeh (Free Union of Iranian Workers), 30 April 2011, http://iranlaborreport.com/?p=1516.

Jafari, Peyman, *Der andere Iran: Geschichte und Kultur von 1900 bis zur Gegenwart* (The other Iran: History and culture from 1900 until today), trans. from Dutch to German by W. Hüsmert, Munich: C. H. Beck, 2010.

Jahanbegloo, Ramin (ed.), *Iran: Between Tradition and Modernity,* Lanham, MD: Lexington Books, 2004.

Jalali Na'ini, Ziba, "Doulati ia gheir-e doulati? Negah be tajrobe-ye daftar-e hamhangi sazmanha-ye gheir-e doulati zanan dar Iran" (Governmental or non-governmental? A glance at the experience of the Office for Women NGOs Initiative), *Goftogu,* No. 10, 1374/1996, pp. 97–108.

Jamal, Amaney, *Barriers to Democracy: The Other Side of Social Capital in Palestine and the Arab World,* Princeton, NJ: Princeton University Press, 2007.

Al-Jawaheri, Yasmin Husein, *Women in Iraq: The Gender Impact of International Sanctions,* Boulder, CO: Lynne Rienner, and London: I. B. Tauris, 2008.

Jehbe Mosharekat Iran-e Islami, "Bianeh be monasebat salgard-e qatlha-ye zangurey va elham-e tashkil-e dadgah motehman-e in parvandeh" (Message about the anniversary of the chained murders and announcement of the establishment of a special tribunal for the defendant), in Jehbe Mosharekat Iran-e Islami, *Ta Kongre Dovvom: Bianieha-ye va movazah-e jehbe Mosharekat Iran Eslami* (Toward the second congress: Messages and communications of the Front for the Participation of the Islamic Iran), Tehran: Jehbe Mosharekat Iran-e Islami Publications, 2001, pp. 44–47.

"Jours de Victoire," 17 January 2011, http://bechir-ben-yahmed.blog.jeune afrique.com/index.php/2011/01/17/772-jours-de-victoire.

Kalathil, Shanthi, and Taylor Boas, *Open Networks, Closed Regimes: The Impact of the Internet on Authoritarian Rule,* Washington, DC: Carnegie Endowment for International Peace, 2003.

Kamali Dehghan, Saeed, "Sanctions on Iran: 'Ordinary People Are the Target,'" *The Guardian* (online), 10 August 2012, www.guardian.co.uk.

———, "Iran Sanctions Strengthen Ahmadinejad Regime—Karroubi," *The Guardian,* 12 August 2010, p. 13.

Kamali, Masoud, "Civil Society in Islam: A Sociological Perspective," *European Journal of Sociology,* Vol. 42, No. 3, 2001, pp. 457–482.

Kamrava, M., "The Civil Society Discourse in Iran," *British Journal of Middle Eastern Studies,* Vol. 28, No. 2, 2001, pp. 165–185.

Karbassian, A., "Islamic Revolution and the Management of the Iranian Economy," *Social Research,* Vol. 67, No. 2, 2000, pp. 621–640.

Kargozaran, "Entekhabat-e sarmayedaran-e Iran bargozar shod" (The elections of Iran's capitalists took place), 3/12/1385 (22 February 2007).

Katirai, Negar, "'NGOs Regulation in Iran,'" *International Journal of Not-for-Profit Law,* Vol. 7, No. 4, 2005 (online version), www.icnl.org/research/journal/.

Katz, Mark N., "The United States and Iran: Ready for Rapprochement?" *SAIS Review* (Paul H. Nitze School of Advanced International Studies, Johns Hopkins University), Vol. 18, No. 2, 1998, pp. 169–183.

Katzman, Kenneth, "Iran Sanctions," *CRS Report for Congress,* Washington, DC: Congressional Research Service (CRS), 6 January 2012.

Keane, John, *Civil Society: Old Images, New Visions.* Palo Alto, CA: Stanford University Press, 1998.

Kelly, John, and Bruce Etling, "Mapping Change in Iranian Blogosphere," *Internet & Democracy Blog,* 12 February 2009, http://blogs.law.harvard.edu/idblog/2009/02/12/mapping-change-in-the-iranian-blogosphere/.

———, *Mapping Iran's On-line Public: Politics and Culture in the Persian Blogosphere,* Cambridge, MA: Berkman Center for Internet and Society, Harvard University, 2008.

Keshavarzian, A., *Bazaar and State in Iran: The Politics of the Tehran Marketplace,* Cambridge, UK: Cambridge University Press, 2007.

———, "Regime Loyalty and Bazari Representation Under the Islamic Republic of Iran: Dilemmas of the Society of Islamic Coalition," *International Journal of Middle East Studies,* Vol. 41, No. 2, 2009, pp. 225–246.

Khajehpour, B., "Domestic Political Reforms and Private Sector Activity in Iran," *Social Research,* Vol. 67, No. 2, 2000, pp. 577–598.

Khanlarzadeh, Mina, "Iranian Women and Economic Sanctions: The Threat of War and Economic Sanctions Contribute to a Patriarchal Culture," *Z Magazine,* Vol. 22, No. 2, February 2009, pp. 38–40.

Khatib, Line, *Islamic Revivalism in Syria: The Rise and Fall of Ba'thist Secularism,* New York and London: Routledge, 2011.

Khojasteh Rahimi, Reza, and Maryam Sheibani, "Gerdhamai roshanfekran bara-ye democracy" (Gathering of intellectuals for democracy), *Shargh,* 18 May 2005.

Khosrokhavar, Farhad, "Towards an Anthropology of Democratization," *Middle East Critique,* Vol. 9, No. 16, 2000, pp. 3–29.

Khosrokhavar, Farhad, and Amir Nikpey, *Avoir vingt ans au pays des Ayatollahs,* Paris: Laffont, 2009.

Kian, Azadeh, *L'Iran—Un mouvement sans révolution? La vague verte face au pouvoir mercanto–militariste* (Iran—A movement without revolution? The Green Wave facing mercanto–militarist power), Paris: Michalon, 2011.

Kinninmont, Jane, "Bread and Dignity," *The World Today,* August–September 2011, pp. 31–33.

Klandermans, Bert, *The Social Psychology of Protest,* Oxford, UK: Blackwell Publishers, 1997.

Klebnikov, P., "Millionaire Mullahs," *Forbes,* July 2003, http://www.forbes.com/forbes/2003/0721/056_print.html.

Kleinberg, R. B., and J. Clark (eds.), *Economic Liberalization, Democrati-*

zation and Civil Society in the Developing World, London: Macmillan Press, 2000.

Kubba, Laith, "The Awakening of Civil Society," *Journal of Democracy,* Vol. 11, No. 3, 2000, pp. 84–90.

Labovitz, C., "Iranian Traffic Engineering," Arbor Networks security blogs, 17 June 2009, http://asert.arbornetworks.com/2009/06/iranian-traffic-engineering/.

Lacroix, Stéphane, "Is Saudi Arabia Immune?" *Journal of Democracy,* Vol. 22, No. 4, October 2011, pp. 48–59.

Laithy, Heba, "Poverty in Syria: 1996–2004," UN Development Programme Report, New York, June 2005, www.planning.gov.sy/SD08/MSF /povertyinsyria.englishversion.pdf.

Landis, Joshua, "The Syrian Opposition," *Washington Quarterly,* Vol. 30, No. 1, 2006/2007, pp. 45–68.

Layne, Jon, "How Iran's Political Battle Is Fought in Cyberspace," interview with Hamid Dabashi, 11 February 2010, *BBC News,* http://news.bbc.co .uk/2/hi/8505645.stm.

Leenders, Reinoud, "Rethinking the Promotion of Democracy After the Syrian Uprising," Norwegian Peacebuilding Resource Centre, 29 February 2012, http://www.peacebuilding.no/Regions/Middle-East-and-North-Africa/Publications/Rethinking-the-promotion-of-democracy-after-the-Syrian-uprising.

Lefebvre, Henri, *The Production of Space,* trans. D. Nicholson-Smith, Malden, MA, Oxford, UK, and Carlton, Victoria (Australia): Blackwell, 1991 (1974, 1984).

Leverett, Flynt, *Inheriting Syria: Bashar's Trial by Fire,* Washington, DC: Brookings Institute Press, 2005.

Levitsky, Steven, and Lucan Way, *Competitive Authoritarianism: Hybrid Regimes After the Cold War,* Cambridge, UK: Cambridge University Press, 2010.

Licht, Amanda A., "Falling Out of Favor: Economic Sanctions and the Tenure of Leaders," paper presented at the 2011 Midwest Political Science Association, 31 March–3 April 2011, Chicago, IL, http://polisci .osu.edu/conferences/vim/LichtMPSA2011FallingOutOfFavor.pdf (14 March 2012).

Liodakis, G., *Totalitarian Capitalism and Beyond,* Aldershot, UK: Ashgate, 2010.

Lipset, Seymour Martin, "Some Social Requisites of Democracy: Economic Development and Political Legitimacy," *American Political Science Review,* Vol. 53, No. 1, 1959, pp. 69–105.

LiPuma, E., and T. A. Koelbe, "Social Capital in Emerging Democracies," *Voluntas,* Vol. 20, No. 1, 2009, pp. 1–14.

Liverani, Andrea, *Civil Society in Algeria: The Political Functions of Associational Life,* London: Routledge, 2008.

Lust, Ellen, "Why Now? Micro Transitions and the Arab Uprisings," *APSA Comparative Democratization,* Vol. 9, No. 3, October 2011, pp. 1, 3–8.

Lynch, Marc, *Voices of the New Arab Public,* New York: Columbia University Press, 2006.

Mahdavi, Pardis, *Passionate Uprisings: Iran's Sexual Revolution*, Palo Alto, CA: Stanford University Press, 2008.

Malm, Andreas, and Shora Esmailian, *Iran on the Brink: Rising Workers and Threats of War*, London: Pluto Press, 2007.

Maloney, S., "Agents or Obstacles? Parastatal Foundations and Challenges for Iranian Development," in P. Alizadeh (ed.), *The Economy of Iran: Dilemmas of an Islamic State*, London: I. B. Tauris, 2000, pp. 145–177.

Mansour, Muhammad Firaz, and Muhammad al-Tawashi, "Business Associations: Concessionary Prizes or a Fundamental Base for Economic Development?" *All for Syria*, 17 July 2010, http://all4syria.info/index2 .php?option=com_content&task=view&id=29394&pop=1&.

Mehrabi, Ehsan, "Report from Tehran: How Sanctions Hurt the Lives of Ordinary Iranians," *InsideIRAN*, 26 July 2012, http://www.insideiran.org/ featured/report-from-iran-how-sanctions-hurt-the-lives-of-the-ordinary-iranians/.

Mehrjoo, B., "Otagh bazargani az sal 1358 ta 1386 dar goftogoo ba Alla Aldin Mir Mohammad Sadeghi" (The Chamber of Commerce from 1980 to 2008 in an interview with Alla Aldin Mir Mohammad Sadeghi), in *Shargh*, 12 July 2007, http://www.tccim.ir/spconv.aspx?id=209.

———, "Piruzi-ye eslahtalabane" (A reformist victory), *Etemad*, 5/12/1381 (24 February 2007).

Mercer, C., "NGOs, Civil Society and Democratization: A Critical Review of the Literature," *Progress in Development Studies*, Vol. 2, No. 1, 2002, pp. 5–22.

Milani, Abbas, *The Myth of the Great Satan: A New Look at America's Relations with Iran*, Stanford, CA: Hoover Institution Press, 2010.

———, "Transition to Democracy in Iran: Observations on International Influences on Democratization in Iran," CDDRL (Center on Democracy, Development, and the Rule of Law) Working Papers, Freeman Spogli Institute for International Studies, Stanford University, No. 109, March 2009, pp. 1–40.

Ministry of Interior, Islamic Republic of Iran, "Disposals for the Establishment and Activities of SAMAN" redacted by the Ministry of Interior, 2006, http://portal2.moi.ir/portal/Home/Default.aspx?CategoryID=af44a651 -6ea4-4518-8052-9f58402b351a.

Moaveni, Azadeh, *Lipstick Jihad: A Memoir of Growing Up Iranian in America and American in Iran*, New York: Public Affairs, 2005.

Moghissi, Haideh, and Saeed Rahnema, "The Working Class and the Islamic State in Iran," *Socialist Register*, 2001, pp. 197–218.

Mohab'ali, N., "Saf ara'i-ye dolat dar barabar-e bakhsh-e khosusi: Shora-ye ali-ye nezarat sharayet-e kandidaha-ye entekhabat-e otagh-e bazargani ra taghir dad" (The state confronts the private sector: The Supervisory Council changes the requirements for the candidates of the Chamber of Commerce), *Etemad Melli*, 20/10/1385 (10 January 2007).

Molavi, R., and H. Salimi, *Privatise to Democratise?* Policy Brief No. 5, Durham, UK: Durham University Centre for Iranian Studies, June 2008, http://www.dur.ac.uk/resources/iranian.studies/privatise-democratise final.pdf.

Moore, B., *Social Origins of Dictatorship and Democracy,* London: Allen Lane and Penguin Press, 1966.

Morgan, T. Clifton, and Navin A. Bapat, "Multilateral Versus Unilateral Sanctions Reconsidered: A Test Using New Data," *International Studies Quarterly,* Vol. 53, No. 4, December 2009, pp. 1075–1094.

Morozov, Evgeny, "Iran: Downside to the 'Twitter Revolution,'" *Dissent,* Fall 2009, http://www.evgenymorozov.com/morozov_twitter_dissent.pdf.

———, *The Net Delusion: How Not to Liberate the World,* London: Allen Lane, 2011.

Moslem, M., *Factional Politics in Post-Khomeini Iran,* New York: Syracuse University Press, 2002.

Moubayed, Sami, "Islamic Revival in Syria," *The Mideast Monitor,* Vol. 1, No. 3, 2006, http://www.mideastmonitor.org/issues/0609/0609_4.htm.

Mousavi, Mir-Hossein, "Statement No. 13," trans. http://khordaad88.com, 28 September 2009, www.campaigniran.org/casmii/index.php?q=node/8700 (14 March 2012).

———, *Nurturing the Seed of Hope: A Green Strategy of Liberation,* trans. Daryoush Mohammad Poor, London: H&S, 2012.

Mozaffari, Mehdi, *The Iranian Green Movement, One Year After,* Aarhus, Denmark: CIR-Aarhus University, 2010.

Naim, Moisés, "Democracy's Dangerous Impostors," *Washington Post,* 21 April 2007, http://www.washingtonpost.com/wp-dyn/content/article/2007/04/20/AR2007042001594.html.

Namazi, Baqer, "Iranian NGOs: Situation Analysis," Tehran: N.p., 2000.

Nasr, Vali, *The Rise of Islamic Capitalism. Why the New Muslim Middle Class Is the Key to Defeating Extremism,* New York: Free Press, 2009.

Nasrabadi, Manijeh, "Iran and the US Anti-War Movement," based on a talk given in the workshop, "Solidarity Not Intervention," organized by Raha Iranian Feminist Collective, at the United National Antiwar Coalition (UNAC) Conference, 24 March 2012, Stamford, CT.

National Public Radio, "Iranians Would Unite Against War, Says Writer," Hooman Majd and Sussan Tahmasebi interviewed by "Tell Me More" host Michel Martin, 16 February 2012, http://www.npr.org/2012/02/16/146987523/iranians-would-unite-against-war-says-writer.

Nebehay, Stephanie, "Nobel Laureate Ebadi Calls for Sanctions on Iran," Reuters, 12 February 2010, http://www.reuters.com/article/2010/02/12/us-iran-ebadi-idUSTRE61B3JY20100212.

Nomani, Farhad, and Sohrab Behdad, *Class and Labor in Iran: Did the Revolution Matter?* Syracuse, NY: Syracuse University Press, 2006.

Norton, Augustus Richard, "Associational Life: Civil Society in Authoritarian Political Systems," in Mark Tessler (ed.), *Area Studies and Social Science: Strategies for Understanding Middle East Politics,* Bloomington and Indianapolis: Indiana University Press, 1999, pp. 30–47.

Ong, Carah, "Iranians Speak Out on Regime Change Slush Fund," *Iran Nu-*

clear Watch, Washington, DC: Center for Arms Control and Nonproliferation, 15 July 2008.

Opp, Karl Dieter, *Theories of Political Protest and Social Movements: A Multidisciplinary Introduction, Critique, and Synthesis,* New York: Routledge, 2009.

Opp, Karl Dieter, and Christiane Gern, "Dissident Groups, Personal Networks, and Spontaneous Cooperation: The East German Revolution of 1989," *American Sociological Review,* Vol. 58, No. 5, 1993, pp. 659–680.

Ottaway, Marina, "The Presidents Left, the Regimes Are Still There," 14 February 2011, http://carnegieendowment.org/publications/?fa=42627.

Ottolenghi, Emanuele, "Setting the Sanctions Agenda," *The Journal of International Security Affairs* (Washington: The Jewish Institute for National Security Affairs), No. 18, Spring 2010, pp. 19–30.

Owen, Roger, "Military Presidents in Arab States," *International Journal of Middle East Studies,* Vol. 43, No. 3, August 2011, pp. 395–396.

Paciello, Maria Cristina, "Egypt: Changes and Challenges of Political Transition," Mediterranean Prospects Technical Report, No. 4, May 2011.

Paivandi, Said, *Religion et éducation en Iran: L'échec de l'islamisation* (Religion and education in Iran: The failure of Islamization), Paris: L'Harmattan, 2006.

———, "Vers un système éducatif advantage islamisé?" (Toward an Islamized-oriented educational system?), *Les cahiers de l'orient,* No. 100, 2010, pp. 77–85.

Parsi, Trita, "Denying Iran's Democrats," *Huffington Post,* 19 December 2007.

———, "Sanctions Making War More Likely," *Daily Beast,* 23 March 2012.

Peksen, Dursun, "Better or Worse? The Effect of Economic Sanctions on Human Rights," *Journal of Peace Research,* Vol. 46, No. 1, January 2009, pp. 59–77.

———, "Coercive Diplomacy and Press Freedom: An Empirical Assessment of the Impact of Economic Sanctions on Media Openness," *International Political Science Review,* Vol. 31, No. 4, September 2010, pp. 449–469.

Peksen, Dursun, and A. Cooper Drury, "Economic Sanctions and Political Repression: Assessing the Impact of Coercive Diplomacy on Political Freedoms," *Human Rights Review,* Vol. 10, No. 3, September 2009, pp. 393–411.

Perthes, Volke, *Syria Under Bashar al-Asad: Modernisation and the Limits of Change,* London and New York: Routledge, 2004.

Pfeifle, M., "A Nobel Peace Prize for Twitter?" *Christian Science Monitor,* 6 July 2009, http://www.csmonitor.com/Commentary/Opinion/2009/0706/p09s02–coop.html.

Pierret, Thomas, and Kjetil Selvik, "Limits of 'Authoritarian Upgrading' in Syria: Private Welfare, Islamic Charities, and the Rise of the Zayd Movement," *International Journal of Middle East Studies,* Vol. 41, No. 4, 2009, pp. 595–614.

Pintak, Lawrence, *Reflections in a Bloodshot Lens,* London: Pluto Press, 2006.

Pipes, Daniel, "Dealing with Middle Eastern Conspiracy Theories," *Orbis,* Vol. 36, No. 1, 1992, pp. 41–56.

Posch, Walter, "Die Sanktionsspirale dreht sich: Europäische Iranpolitik auf dem Prüfstand" (The spiral of sanctions is swinging: European Iran policy put to the test), *SWP-Aktuell,* No. 26, March 2010 (German Institute for International and Security Affairs of the Stiftung Wissenschaft und Politik [SWP], Berlin), p. 2.

Przeworski, Adam, "Some Problems in the Study of the Transition Towards Democracy," in Guillermo O'Donnell, Philippe C. Schmitter, and Laurence Whitehead (eds.), *Transition from Authoritarian Rule: Comparative Perspectives,* Baltimore: Johns Hopkins University Press, 1986, pp. 47–63.

Putnam, Robert, Robert Leonardi, and Raffaella Y. Nanetti, *Making Democracy Work: Civic Traditions in Modern Italy,* Princeton, NJ: Princeton University Press, 1993.

Quirk, P. W., "Iran's Twitter Revolution," *Foreign Policy in Focus,* 17 June 2009, http://www.fpif.org/articles/irans_twitter_revolution.

Radio Zamaneh, "Sanctions Against Iran Reviewed by European Parliament," 9 March 2012, http://www.radiozamaneh.com/english/content/sanctions-against-iran-reviewed-european-parliament.

Raha Iranian Feminist Collective, "Solidarity and Its Discontents," *Jadaliyya,* 19 February 2011, http://www.jadaliyya.com/pages/index/683/solidarity-and-its-discontents.

———, "Sanctions Against Iran: A Duplicitous 'Alternative' to War," *Jadaliyya,* 14 May 2012, http://www.jadaliyya.com/pages/index/5518/sanctions-against-iran_a-duplicitous-alternative-t.

Ravand Institute for Economic and International Studies, "Sanctions," *Economic Trends,* Tehran: Ravand Institute for Economic and International Studies, March 2008, pp. 16–18.

Reed, Stanley, and Babak Pirouz, "Election Aftershock in Corporate Iran," *Business Week,* 11 July 2005.

Reporters Without Borders, "Iran's Six-month-old Crackdown on Media and Internet," 12 December 2009, http://en.rsf.org/iran-iran-s-six-month-old-crackdown-on-12-12-2009,35324.html.

Rivetti, Paola, "Student Movements in the Islamic Republic: Shaping the Country's Politics Through the Campus," Chaillot Paper 128, EUISS Paris, 2012, pp. 81–101.

Rostami-Povey, Elaheh, *Iran's Influence: A Religious-Political State and Society in Its Region,* London and New York: Zed Books, 2010.

———, "Political-Social Movements, Unions and Workers' Movements: Iran," in Suad Joseph (ed.), *Encyclopedia of Women & Islamic Cultures, Volume II—Family, Law and Politics,* Leiden, Netherlands, and Boston: Brill Academic Publishers, 2005, pp. 669–670.

Rueschemeyer, D., E. H. Stephens, and J. D. Stephens, *Capitalist Development and Democracy,* Chicago: University of Chicago Press, 1992.

Saba, Sadegh, "Profile of Abdollah Nouri," *BBC News,* 27 November 1999, http://news.bbc.co.uk/2/hi/middle_east/539470.stm.

Sadeqi, Fatemeh, "'Siasat zoday az jame' madani: tajrobe-ye sazmanha-ye gheir-e doulati dar eslahat" (Politics against civil society: The experience of NGOs during the reformist era), *Goftogu,* No. 47, 1385/2007, pp. 45–60.

Saeidi, A. A., and F. Shirinkam, *Moghe'iyat-e tojjar va saheban-e sanaye dar Iran-e dore-ye Pahlavi: Sarmayedari-ye khanevadegi-ye khandan-e Lajevardi* (The position of Iranian merchants and industrialists in the Pahlavi period: The family capital of the Lajevardis), Tehran: Gam-e No, 1384/2005.

Saghafi, Morad, "Aqaz va paian-e jame madani" (The beginning and the end of civil society), *Goftogu,* No. 47, 1385/2007, pp. 85–98.

Salak, S., and J. Hosseinzadeh, "Otagh-e Iran arse'i baraye jedal-e do negah" (Iran Chamber: A stage where two visions collide), *Etemad,* 9/8/83 (29 November 2004).

Salehi-Isfahani, Djavad, "The Oil Wealth and Economic Growth in Iran," in A. Gheissari (ed.), *Contemporary Iran: Economy, Society, Politics,* Oxford, UK: Oxford University Press, 2009, pp. 3–37.

——, "Iran Sanctions: Who Really Wins?" Washington, DC: Brookings Institution, 30 September 2009, http://www.brookings.edu/opinions/2009/0930_iran_sanctions_salehi_isfahani.aspx.

——, "Iran's Youth, the Unintended Victims of Sanctions," *Dubai Initiative—Policy Brief,* Belfer Center for Science and International Affairs, Harvard University, August 2010.

Salehi-Esfahani, Hadi, and M. Hashem Pesaran, "The Iranian Economy in the Twentieth Century: A Global Perspective," *Iranian Studies,* Vol. 42, No. 2, 2009, pp. 177–211.

Salem, Amr, "Syria's Cautious Embrace," *Middle East Insight,* March–April 1999, pp. 49–50.

Salloukh, Bassel, "Organising Politics in the Arab World: State-Society Relations and Foreign Policy Choices in Jordan and Syria," McGill University, PhD diss., 2000.

Samad, Ziad Abdel, and Kinda Mohamadieh, "The Revolutions of the Arab Region: Socio-economic Questions at the Heart of Successful Ways Forward," *Perspectives,* No. 2, pp. 112–118.

Samii, William, "Sisyphus Newsstand: The Iranian Press Under Khatami," *Middle East Review of International Affairs,* Vol. 5, No. 3, 1999 (online version), http://meria.idc.ac.il/journal/2001/issue3/jv5n3a1.html.

San'at va tose-e, "The Bazaar Under the Threat of the New Principalists" (Bazaar zire tighe osulgarayan-e jadid), July/August 2010, p. 16.

——, "The Medicine Mafia Is in the Hands of the State," July/August 2010, p. 10.

Sanger, David E., "The Larger Game in the Middle East: Iran," *New York Times,* 2 April 2011, http://www.nytimes.com/2011/04/03/weekin review/03sanger.html?_r=1&pagewanted=all.

Sater, James, *Civil Society and Political Change in Morocco,* London: Routledge, 2007.

Satoof al-Shaykh Husseyn, *al-batala fi suriya 1994–2004* (Unemployment in Syria 1994–2004), Damascus: Syrian Central Bureau of Statistics, July 2007.

Sauer, Tom, "Coercive Diplomacy by the EU: The Case of Iran," *Discussion Papers in Diplomacy,* No. 106, The Hague: Netherlands Institute of International Relations (Clingendael), 2007.

Sayigh, Yezid, "Hurting Stalemate in Syria," Beirut: Carnegie Middle East Centre, 24 January 2012.

Schectman, Joel, "Iran's Twitter Revolution? Maybe Not Yet," *Bloomberg Businessweek,* 17 June 2009, http://www.businessweek.com/technology/content/jun2009/tc20090617_803990.htm.

Schedler, Andreas, "Authoritarianism's Last Line of Defense," *Journal of Democracy,* Vol. 21, No. 1, 2010, pp. 69–80.

Schlumberger, Oliver (ed.), *Debating Arab Authoritarianism: Dynamics and Durability in Nondemocratic Regimes,* Palo Alto, CA: Stanford University Press, 2007.

Schwedler, Jillian, *Faith in Moderation,* Cambridge, UK: Cambridge University Press, 2006.

Secor, Laura, "Protest Vote," *New Yorker,* 29 June 2009.

Seeberg, Peter, "Union for the Mediterranean: Pragmatic Multilateralism and the Depoliticization of EU–Middle Eastern Relations," *Middle East Critique,* Vol. 19, No. 3, 2010, pp. 287–302.

Seib, Philip (ed.), *New Media and the New Middle East,* London: Palgrave, 2007.

Seligman, Adam B., *The Idea of Civil Society,* New York: Simon & Schuster, 1992.

Shapiro, A. L., "The Internet," *Foreign Policy,* No. 115, Summer 1999, pp. 14–27.

Shargh, "Otagh bashgah-e siyasat nist" (The Chamber is not a political arena), 24/02/86 (14 April 2007).

Sharif Institute for Economic and Industrial Studies, *Evaluation of the Consequences of the Energy Subsidy Reforms* (Arzyabi-ye peyamadha-ye eslah-e nezam-e yarane energy), Tehran: TCCIM, June–July 2010.

Shayegan, Dariush, *Cultural Schizophrenia: Islamic Societies Confronting the West,* Syracuse, NY: Syracuse University Press, 1997.

Sikkar, Nabil, *al-Islah al-Iqtisadi fi Suriya* (Economic reform in Syria), Damascus: al-Rayes Books, 2000.

——, "Hatmiyat al-Islah al-Iqtisadi fi Suriya" (The inevitability of economic reform in Syria), *Al-Iktissad Wal-Aamal,* 247 (July) 2000.

Slavin, Barbara, "U.S. Warns Syria; Next Step Uncertain," *USA Today,* 17 September 2003, p. 2.

Springborg, Robert, "The Political Economy of the Arab Spring," *Mediterranean Politics,* Vol. 16, No. 3, 2011, pp. 427–433.

Sreberny, Annabelle, and Gholam Khiabany, *Blogistan: The Internet and Politics in Iran,* London and New York: I. B. Tauris, 2010.

Stenberg, Leif, "Young, Male and Sufi Muslims in the City of Damascus," in Jorgen Baek Simonsen (ed.), *Youth and Youth Culture in the Contemporary Middle East,* Aarhus, Denmark: Aarhus University Press, 2005.

Syrian Central Bureau of Statistics and UNICEF, *al-Maseh al-'Unqudi Muta'aded al-Mu'ashirat,* 2006, http://www.cbssyr.org/people%20statistics/Final_Report_Syria_ARB.pdf.

Syria Trust for Development, http://www.syriatrust.org.

Teti, Andrea, "Beyond Lies the *Wub:* The Challenges of (Post)Democratization," *Middle East Critique,* Vol. 21, No. 1, 2012, pp. 5–24.

Tétreault, Mary Ann, "The Winter of the Arab Spring in the Gulf Monarchies," *Globalizations,* Vol. 8, No. 5, 2011, pp. 629–637.

Therborn, Göran, "The Role of Capital and the Rise of Democracy," *New Left Review,* No. 103, May–June 1977, pp. 3–41.

Tignor, Robert L., "Can a New Generation Bring About Regime Change?" *International Journal of Middle East Studies,* Vol. 43, No. 3, 2011, p. 384.

Torbat, Akbar E., "Impacts of US Trade and Financial Sanctions on Iran," *World Economy,* Vol. 28, No. 3, March 2005, pp. 407–434.

Torfeh, Massoumeh, "Sanctions Against Iran May Boost the Protest Movement," *The Guardian* (online), 11 June 2010, http://www.guardian.co .uk/commentisfree/2010/jun/11/iran-sanctions-may-spur-protest.

Tripp, Charles, "State, Elites and the 'Management of Change,'" in Hassan Hakimian and Ziba Moshaver (eds.), *The State and Global Change: The Political Economy of Transition in the Middle East and North Africa,* London: Curzon, 2001, pp. 211–231.

Trotsky, L., *Permanent Revolution and Results and Prospects,* New York: Path Finder, 1969.

United Nations Development Programme (UNDP), Syria Report, *The Impact of Subsidization of Agricultural Production on Development,* October 2006, http://www.undp.org.sy/files/psia.pdf.

US Department of State, "Update on Iran Democracy Promotion Funding," Media Note by the Office of the Spokesman, 4 June 2007.

US Labor Against War (USLAW) Steering Committee, "USLAW Calls for More Diplomacy, Not the Military in Dealing with Iran," Washington, DC, 12 March 2012, http://www.uslaboragainstwar.org/article.php?id =25519.

Valbjørn, Morten, and André Bank, "Examining the 'Post' in Post-Democratization: The Future of Middle Eastern Political Rule Through Lenses of the Past," *Middle East Critique,* Vol. 19, No. 3, 2010, pp. 183–200.

Van de Donk, Wim, Brian Loader, Paul Nixon, and Dieter Rucht (eds.), *Cyberprotest: New Media, Citizens and Social Media,* London: Routledge, 2004.

Vigual, Leïla, "La 'nouvelle consommation' et les transformations des paysages urbains à la lumière de l'ouverture économique: l'exemple de Damas" (New consumption patterns and the transformation of urban landscapes at a time of economic opening), *Revue des Mondes Musulmans et de la Méditerranée,* 115–116, December 2006, http://remmm .revues.org/3011.

Voice of America, "Obama: Iran Facing 'Unprecedented, Crippling Sanctions,'" 6 March 2012, http://blogs.voanews.com/breaking-news/2012/ 03/06/obama-iran-facing-unprecedented-crippling-sanctions/.

Warnaar, Maaike, "So Many Similarities: Linking Domestic Dissent to Foreign Threat in Iran," Working Paper No. 20 (March 2011), Amsterdam: Hivos.

Wehrey, Frederic, Jerrold D. Green, Brian Nichiporuk, Alireza Nader, Lydia Hansell, Rasool Nafisi, and S. R. Bohandy, *The Rise of the Pasdaran: Assessing the Domestic Roles of Iran's Islamic Revolutionary Guards Corps,* Santa Monica, Arlington, Pittsburgh: Rand Corporation, 2009.

Weisman, Itzchak, "Sa'id Hawwa and Islamic Revivalism in Ba'thist Syria," *Studia Islamica,* Vol. 85, 1997, pp. 131–154.

——, "Sa'id Hawwa: The Making of a Radical Muslim Thinker in Modern Syria," *Middle Eastern Studies,* 29 October 1993, pp. 607–611.

White House, *The National Security Strategy of the United States of America,* Washington, DC, March 2006.

Wickham, Carrie Rosefsky, *Mobilizing Islam: Religion, Activism, and Political Challenge in Egypt,* New York: Columbia University Press, 2002.

Wiktorowicz, Quintan, "Civil Society as Social Control: State Power in Jordan," *Comparative Politics,* Vol. 33, No. 1, 2000, pp. 43–61.

Yacoubian, Mona, and Scott Lazensky, *Dealing with Damascus: Seeking a Greater Return on U.S.-Syria Relations,* New York: Council on Foreign Relations, 2008.

Yaghmaian, Behzad, *Social Change in Iran: An Eyewitness Account of Dissent, Defiance, and New Movements for Rights,* Albany: State University of New York, 2002.

Yahyanejad, Mehdi, "The Effectiveness of Internet for Informing and Mobilizing During the Post-election Events in Iran," paper presented at conference, "Liberation Technology in Authoritarian Regimes," Stanford University, Palo Alto, CA, 11–12 October 2010.

Yasin, K. N., "New Era for Iran's Private Sector," Tehran: ISN Security Watch, 26 June 2007, http://intellibriefs.blogspot.com/2007/06/new-era-for-irans-private-sector.html.

Yazdanpanah, Mohammad Reza, "Namzadi-e Mohsen Resaei Jaddi Shod," *Kargozaran* (Tehran), 12 September 2008.

Zayani, Mohamed (ed.), *The Al Jazeera Phenomenon: Critical Perspectives on New Arab Media,* London: Pluto Press, 2005.

Zisser, Eyal, *Commanding Syria: Bashar al-Asad and the First Years in Power,* New York: I. B. Tauris, 2007.

——, "Syria, the Ba'th Regime and the Islamic Movement: Stepping on a New Path?" *Muslim World,* No. 95, 2005, pp. 43–65.

Zolghadr, Tirdad, *Softcore,* London: Telegram Books, 2007.

Zubaida, Sami, "Islam, the State and Democracy: Contrasting Conceptions of Society in Egypt," *Middle East Report,* No. 179, 1992, pp. 2–10.

Zurayk, Rami, "Feeding the Arab Uprising," *Perspectives,* No. 2, May 2011, special issue, "People's Power: The Arab World in Revolt," pp. 119–125.

The Contributors

Paul Aarts is senior lecturer in international relations in the Department of Political Science, University of Amsterdam (Netherlands). His research focuses on the politics of the Arab world, with a specific focus on Gulf countries. He has published articles in numerous academic journals, including *Democracy & Society, Orient, Middle East Policy, International Spectator, Review of International Affairs,* and *Middle East Report.* He is also coauthor (with Gerd Nonnemann) of *Saudi Arabia in the Balance: Political Economy, Society, Foreign Affairs.*

Francesco Cavatorta is senior lecturer in the School of Law and Government, Dublin City University (Ireland). His research focuses on processes of democratization and authoritarian resilience in the Arab world, with a specific focus on North Africa. He has authored or coauthored articles for *Government and Opposition, Parliamentary Affairs, Mediterranean Politics, Journal of Modern African Studies, Journal of North African Studies, British Journal of Middle Eastern Studies,* and *Democratization.* He is author of *The International Dimension of the Failed Algerian Transition* and coauthor (with Vincent Durac) of *Civil Society and Democratization in the Arab World.*

Ali Fathollah-Nejad was educated in France (Sciences-Po Lille), Germany (University of Münster), and the Netherlands (University of

243

Twente). He is currently a PhD candidate in international relations in both the Department of Development Studies of the School of Oriental and African Studies, University of London, and the Institute of Sociology, University of Münster (Germany). He is author of *Der Iran-Konflikt und die Obama-Regierung: Alter Wein in neuen Schläuchen?* (The Iran conflict and the Obama administration: Old wine in new skins?).

Bassam Haddad is director of the Middle East Studies Program and teaches in the Department of Public and International Affairs at George Mason University, and is a visiting professor at Georgetown University. He is founding editor of the *Arab Studies Journal* and cofounder of the online journal *Jadaliyya Ezine* (http://www.jadaliyya .com). He is also coproducer/director of the award-winning documentary film, *About Baghdad,* and director of the critically acclaimed film series, *Arabs and Terrorism.* Recent publications include *The Political Economy of Regime Security: State-Business Networks in Syria.*

Ali Honari is master researcher in the Department of Human Behavioral and Social Sciences at the University of Groningen, the Netherlands. His areas of research include social networks in collective actions and the impact of the Internet on social movements. As a university student, he was involved in the student movement during the reform period in Iran. In 2004, he launched a group weblog, SarSar, and currently is an active blogger running his own weblog, "fromnederland."

Peyman Jafari is a PhD candidate at the University of Amsterdam and the International Institute of Social History, where he conducts research on the effects of class structure, state-society relations, and the international power structure on postrevolutionary politics in Iran. He is also a media commentator on Iranian current affairs. His publications include *Der andere Iran: Geschichte und Kultur von 1900 bis zur Gegenwart* (The other Iran: History and culture from 1900 until today).

Salam Kawakibi is director of research at the Arab Reform Initiative Centre in Paris. He was research fellow in the Department of Political Science of the University of Amsterdam. He has studied both in Syria and France and is a leading expert on Syrian affairs. He has contributed extensively to a wide range of journals in Arabic, French, and English. His most recent publications include *10 Papers for Barcelona 2010: State and Society: The Democratic Challenge* (co-edited with Esra Buklut), *Internet or Enter-Not: The Syrian Experience,* and *The Private Media in Syria.*

Line Khatib is a lecturer at the Dubai School of Government and senior research fellow at the Inter-University Consortium of Arab and Middle Eastern Studies, McGill University. She has done in-depth field research within Syria, examining how the resurgence of Islamic groups influences a number of independent variables such as secularism, policy, gender relations, and youth. She is the author of *Islamic Revivalism in Syria: The Rise and Fall of Ba'thist Secularism.*

Paola Rivetti is an IRCHSS postdoctoral fellow at the School of Law and Government, Dublin City University (Ireland). She has worked on Iranian postrevolutionary reformism, focusing, in particular, on the way it adapts to international and domestic political change. She has authored articles on Iranian politics and history, and coedited with Rosita Di Peri a volume on the rhetoric and practice of civil society in Iran, Lebanon, Morocco, and Egypt.

Mustapha Kamel Al-Sayyid is professor of political science and director of the Center for the Study of Developing Countries, Cairo University. He also teaches at the American University in Cairo. His areas of specialization include the politics of development, foreign aid, human rights, and civil society. He has published extensively on civil society, political change, and ideology, and his articles have appeared in *World Policy, Middle East Journal, Washington Quarterly,* and *Maghreb-Machrek,* among others.

Roschanack Shaery-Eisenlohr is research fellow at the Max Planck Institute for the Study of Religion and Ethnic Diversity in Göttingen, Germany. Previously, she was Syria researcher at the University of Amsterdam, where she was able to establish close contact with a variety of Syrian dissidents and activists both in Syria and abroad. She is the author of *Shi'ite Lebanon* and is currently working on a manuscript titled *Lebanese Detainees in Syria: Transnationalism, Piety, and Suffering.*

Index

About the Book

What are the dynamics of civic activism in authoritarian regimes? How do new social actors—many of them informal, "below the radar" groups—interact with these regimes? What mechanisms do the power elite employ to deal with societal dissidence? The authors of *Civil Society in Syria and Iran* explore the nature of state-society relations in two countries that are experiencing popular demands for political pluralism amid the constraints of authoritarian retrenchment.

Paul Aarts is senior lecturer in international relations at the University of Amsterdam. He developed the Zeytun Academic Exchange program with academic institutes in Syria, Yemen, Iraq, and Iran, and is coauthor of *Saudi Arabia in the Balance: Political Economy, Society, Foreign Affairs.* **Francesco Cavatorta** is senior lecturer in the School of Law and Government, Dublin City University. His publications include *Civil Society and Democratization in the Arab World* and *The International Dimension of the Failed Algerian Transition.*